Conflict, Terrorism and the Media in Asia

There are many different kinds of sub-national conflicts across Asia, that have a variety of different origins, but since September 11, 2001 many of them have been increasingly portrayed and drivers in the West as part of the global terrorist threat, to be dealt with by the 'war on terror'. This book examines a wide range of such conflicts, focusing in particular on those in Malaysia, the Philippines, Indonesia, China and India. It shows how, despite their significant differences, they share the role of the media as an interlocutor between the combatants, governments and society, and explores how the media – including the 'new media' such as the internet – exercises this role. The book raises a number of issues concerning how the media report different forms of political violence and conflict, including issues of impartiality in the media's relations with governments and insurgents, and how the focus on the 'war on terror' has led to some forms of violence – notably those employed by states for political purposes – to be overlooked. It argues that whilst the media plays a major role in sub-state conflicts, its impacts, including those of the new media, are generally limited, whilst the United States has also failed to use the media effectively to influence regional media outputs. Overall, this book is a thorough examination of the role of the media in relation to conflict and terrorism in Asia.

Benjamin Cole was awarded a PhD from Southampton University in 1998. He has published a number of articles on non-proliferation issues and British nuclear history, and co-authored *The New Face of Terrorism* (2001) with Dr Nadine Gurr.

Routledge Media, Culture and Social Change in Asia
Series Editor:
Stephanie Hemelryk Donald
Institute for International Studies, University of Technology, Sydney

Editorial Board:
Devleena Ghosh
University of Technology, Sydney

Yingjie Guo
University of Technology, Sydney

K.P. Jayasankar
Unit for Media and Communications, Tata Institute of Social Sciences, Bombay

Vera Mackie
University of Melbourne

Anjali Monteiro
Unit for Media and Communications, Tata Institute of Social Sciences, Bombay

Gary Rawnsley
University of Nottingham

Ming-yeh Rawnsley
University of Nottingham

Jing Wang
MIT

The aim of this series is to publish original, high-quality work by both new and established scholars in the West and the East, on all aspects of media, culture and social change in Asia.

Conflict, Terrorism and the Media in Asia

Edited by
Benjamin Cole

Routledge
Taylor & Francis Group

LONDON AND NEW YORK

First published 2006
by Routledge
2 Park Square, Milton Park, Abingdon, Oxon OX14 4RN

Simultaneously published in the USA and Canada
by Routledge
270 Madison Ave, New York, NY 10016

*Routledge is an imprint of the Taylor & Francis Group,
an informa business*

Transferred to Digital Printing 2009

Typeset in Times New Roman by
Newgen Imaging Systems (P) Ltd, Chennai, India

British Library Cataloguing in Publication Data
A catalogue record for this book is available from the British Library

Library of Congress Cataloging in Publication Data
Conflict, terrorism and the media in Asia / edited by Benjamin Cole.
p. cm. – (Routledge media, culture and social change in Asia)
Includes bibliographical references and index.
1. Social conflict in mass media – Asia. 2. Terrorism and mass
media – Asia. 3. Terrorism in mass media. I. Cole, Benjamin, 1967–
II. Series: Media, culture, and social change in Asia series.

P96.S632A78 2005
303.6'25095–dc22   2005028465

ISBN10: 0–415–35198–7 (hbk)
ISBN10: 0–415–54554–4 (pbk)
ISBN10: 0–203–69870–3 (ebk)

ISBN13: 978–0–415–35198–0 (hbk)
ISBN13: 978–0–415–54554–9 (pbk)
ISBN13: 978–0–203–69870–9 (ebk)

Contents

Contributors

Benjamin Cole received his PhD in International Relations from Southampton University in 1998. He is co-author of the *New Face of Terrorism*, with Nadine Gurr.

Michael Dillon is a Senior Lecturer in Modern Chinese History and was founding Director of the Centre for Contemporary Chinese Studies at the University of Durham. His publications include China's Muslims; China's Muslim Hui Community: Migrations, Settlements and Sects; Xinjiang: China's Muslim Far Northwest; Religious Minorities in China and China: a Historical and Cultural Dictionary.

Toby Miller is Professor of Cultural Studies and Cultural Policy in the Center for Latin American and Caribbean Studies, the Program in American Studies, and the Department of Cinema Studies at New York University. He is the author and editor of twenty-one books.

Prasun Sonwalkar is an Indian journalist currently teaching media studies at the School of Cultural Studies, University of the West of England and is also a Press Fellow of Wolfson College, Cambridge and a Commonwealth Scholar.

Jonathan Woodier is the Director of Regional and Corporate Affairs, Citibank Asia Pacific, and has written extensively on the media in Southeast Asia.

Acknowledgement

I would like to acknowledge all of the help and support that I received during the production of this book, particularly from Jacintha Moore for some last ditch editing and printing, and DH for giving me the time to complete the work.

Abbreviations

9/11	September 11, 2001 – shorthand for the attacks on the World Trade Centre and Pentagon on that day
ABRI	Angkatan Bersenjata Republik Indonesia – the Armed Forces of the Republic of Indonesia
AFP	Armed Forces of the Philippines
ANTARA	Indonesia's Wire Service
AR	Autonomous Region
ARMM	Autonomous Region of Muslim Mindanao
ASEAN	Association of South East Asian Nations
ASG	Abu Sayyaf Group
BBC	British Broadcasting Corporation
BIN	National Intelligence Body – Indonesia
BJP	Bharatiya Janata Party
CCP	Communist Party of China
CIA	Central Intelligence Agency
CMFR	Center for Media Freedom and Responsibility
CPP	Communist Party of the Philippines
ETIM	Eastern Turkistan Islamic Movement
ETPP	Eastern Turkistan People's Party
ETR	Eastern Turkistan Republic
GAM	Gerakan Aceh Merdeka (Free Aceh Movement)
GMI	Gerakan Mansuhkan ISA
ICG	International Crisis Group
IMF	International Monetary Fund
ISA	Internal Security Act
JI	Jemaah Islamiyah
KBP	Kapisanan ng mga Brodkaster ng Pilipinas – TV standards Authority of the Philippines
KMM	Kumpulan Militan Malaysia
MILF	Moro Islamic Liberation Front
MNLF	Moro National Liberation Front
NDF	National Democratic Front
NPA	New Peoples Army

PKI	Communist Party of Indonesia
PLA	Peoples Liberation Army
PNP	Philippines National Police
PRC	People's Republic of China
RSS	Rashtriya Swayamsevak Sangh
SEAPA	South East Asian Press Alliance
TNI	Tentara Nasional Indonesia – the Indonesian Armed Forces
TVRI	Televesi Republik Indonesia
UN	United Nations
VHP	Vishwa Hindu Parishad (World Hindu Council)
XPCC	Xinjiang Production and Construction Corps

Introduction

Benjamin Cole

Today in states across Asia, a range of different forms of violent political transaction operate through the mass media. This includes separatist movements driven by various ethnic, nationalist and religious factors; revolutionary groups seeking to subvert the state; inter-communal violence; and terrorist groups pursuing a variety of national and regional objectives. The majority of these conflicts are indigenous in nature, involving national groups seeking specific national objectives, although the interconnections between combatant groups in different countries in Asia were progressively strengthened during the 1990s, partly as a result of the expansion of the al Qaeda network (Gunaratna 2003). The nature, origins and drivers of these conflicts are often very different, but what each type of conflict has in common is the role that the media plays as an interlocutor between the government, combatants and society.

The dissemination of information by governments through the media used to be a cornerstone of nation building and political control, but unfettered access to media communications is increasingly facilitating challenges to established regimes by activist and militant groups. Acts of terrorism and political violence are acts of communication that are not just ends in themselves but part of a wider process of communicating a message and generating a desired response. The media is the principle mechanism by which those communications are disseminated, but it is more than just a passive conduit for relaying messages. The media is a political actor in its own right and is capable of playing a number of political roles, which include agent of stability, agent of restraint (through monitoring and challenging governments) and agent of change (McCargo 2003: 3–4).

For those engaged in political violence the objective is to use violence to acquire heightened attention from the public, political elites and policy making circles, as a trigger to promote debate on their objectives. Violence serves as a universal key to focus media attention and gain publicity (Nacos 2002: 99), thereby enabling non-state combatants to set the media agenda. It is through setting the media agenda and influencing political debates that combatants transform their violence into political power (Schaeffert 1992: 63).

Brigitte Nacos defines the relationship between the media and terrorists as a 'marriage of convenience' in which terrorists need the media to communicate their messages, and the media reports terrorism as a means of boosting their ratings (Nacos 2002: 9). This suggests that there is a symbiotic relationship between non-state combatants and the media, but the relationship is actually more complex. The media might seek sensationalism in order to improve its ratings, but it also has a vested interest in ensuring the survival of the state. It is rare for a mainstream media source to champion the goals of a terrorist or revolutionary group. The media also has close relationships with other powerful actors, such as political and business interests, and their owners. Therefore non-state combatants might be able to set the media agenda through using violence, but this does not necessarily give them influence over the content of media outputs.

This communication process is transactional and bi-directional, since the combatant both sends and receives communications and the receiver does likewise. Other audiences may also be involved, which may communicate with each other and also feed back independently to the combatants. The news media relays messages beyond the immediate target of the violence to wider audiences, and also feeds back the reactions of government, victims and society to the perpetrators of the violence (Tuman 2003: 17–19).

Different groups of non-state combatants can, however, have different approaches to the issue of publicity and consequently have different relationships with the media. Publicity can be directed at a variety of audiences for a number of purposes. At one level, violence can be intended to intimidate public opinion and political elites in order to elicit a response. At another level, groups need popular legitimacy in order to recruit members and build political support, which requires reporting of the groups, goals and ideology. These messages can be directed at both the combatant's domestic constituency and an international audience.

In the same way, and at the same time, governments communicate their own messages to challenge the legitimacy of the methods, ideology and objectives of their opponents and to maintain popular and political support. This is typically achieved through negative reporting of their opponent's ideology and objectives, combined with positive reporting of the political and security initiatives that the government is employing. Again, the mainstream media is the principal mechanism for communicating these messages.

The interconnections between some non-state combatants in Asia means that communications from a conflict in one state can have a direct impact on communities and national conflicts of others. The flow of these communications has been facilitated by the increased globalization of the news media. Al Qaeda has tried to exploit this in the videos, audiotapes and fax messages that it has released to the al Jazeera TV network. These messages have attempted to mobilize Muslims worldwide to fight the US and to support various Muslim communities around the world which are in conflict with their national governments. Some of these messages have made specific reference to conflicts in Indonesia, the Philippines, the Xinjiang region of China as well as the inter-communal violence in the Gujarat province of India.

Al Qaeda's use of the media in this way was considered to be such a threat that the US National Security Strategy, which was published in 2002, stated that the

US had to engage in a 'battle of ideas' with al Qaeda as part of its 'war on terror' (The White House 2002: 6). Using the media to explain and justify its actions in the 'war on terror' was one of the principal means by which the US aimed to de-legitimize al Qaeda and build an international consensus to stifle grass roots support for militant groups. A regionalized and globalized media is therefore one of the key agents for communicating messages from local conflicts to a broader regional audience and for communicating US and al Qaeda messages in the 'war on terror' to national audiences in Asia.

A key element in the communication process is how the media helps to shape public perceptions of combatants and their violence. It does this though the labels and definitions that it attaches to groups and individuals who engage in violence. Traditional labels such as 'terrorist,' 'rebel,' 'insurgent,' 'revolutionary,' or even 'bandit' which are commonly used to describe groups engaged in sub-state conflicts have no universally accepted definitions which raises a number of issues for the media when using them. Since the 1990s analysts have also labelled non-state combatants as being either 'religious' or secular' in orientation. This is reflected in the increasing use of the term 'Islamic terrorism' since 9/11, despite objections from Muslim communities.

Definitions and labels are important because they create possibilities for empowering or taking power away from individuals, groups and actions, mainly by creating an implicit contrast and comparison between what is acceptable and desirable and what is not (Tuman 2003: 33). The vagueness of the popular terminology has meant that the labels which are attached to different types of violence can be given a variety of definitions by the media. But these definitions frequently overlook the fact that extra-legal movements do not rely exclusively on violence but often pursue their goals by a variety of means including social programmes, propaganda, civil disobedience, or even participating in elections (Guelke 1998: 44–47). Different conflicts therefore need to be assessed and defined on an individual basis, which poses a challenge for the media.

In this way, the media plays a dual role between governments and combatants, or between communities in conflict. The media is not however, a neutral actor that offers passive communication conduits. Rather, it acts as a 'gatekeeper' with the power to determine what it reports, and equally as important, how it reports it. Many combatants have learnt to manipulate news media in order to ensure publication and distribution and to try and influence media outputs in their favour, yet the news media has the ability to control whether the combatants communicate their message and can manipulate how it communicates that message (Tuman 2003: 116 and 135).

This relationship between the media and non-state combatants is negatively influenced by the limitations placed upon media freedom, and states across Asia have some of the worst records of press freedom in the world. In the Reporters Without Borders 2004 *Ranking of Press Freedom*, out of 167 states the Philippines was ranked 111, Indonesia was ranked 117, India was ranked 120, Malaysia was ranked 122 and China was ranked 162 (Reporters Without Frontiers 2004). Yet press freedom does not necessarily ensure improved reporting.

Deficiencies in media practice can also negatively impact on non-state combatants, ability to access the media. These deficiencies include: partisanship, lack of professionalism, willing collusion with the state or other elites, the pursuit of sensationalism, corruption and reluctance to challenge hierarchies that pervade the societies in which they operate (McCargo 2003: 16–17).

Over the past decade the advent of new media communications in Asia, particularly the internet, has diminished the impact of censorship and added a new dimension to the role of the media in sub-state conflict. One of the principal advantages of the internet is that it offers combatants the opportunity to bypass the media 'gatekeepers', ensuring that they can communicate their message when and how they want. Consequently, it is widely believed that the new media is a critical actor in facilitating social and political change in states across Asia.

The new media offers greater opportunities for non-state combatants to communicate their message, bring people together, incite violence, and legitimize their struggle to a wider audience. Militant use of the internet has significantly increased over the past decade. Since the war in Afghanistan in 2001–2002, al Qaeda has increasingly focused on communicating through the internet, allegedly moving between some 50 different web addresses (*BBC News Online* 2004a). Al Qaeda primarily uses websites for general debate and for spreading its ideology. In some cases, messages are issued to set broad strategic objectives or target lists of places and people in the hope that independent cells, individuals and networks will act on them. There is less evidence of the internet being used to issue specific orders or for fundraising, but some sites are used for training purposes. Arguments also rage in chat rooms over the validity of different tactics and methods, and some recruitment may also take place through chat rooms (*BBC News Online* 2004b).

Despite this, the impact of the internet on conflicts in Asia remains unclear because its role in cultural transformation is both complicated and unpredictable. It can be used to extend and consolidate traditional values, as well as to challenge dominant political visions and cultural traditions (Woodier 2002: 85 and 88). A feature of news reporting on the internet is also its interactivity, with users being significantly less trusting and more questioning than the users of traditional media (Budha 2003: 79). This poses problems for groups trying to disseminate militant ideologies as well as for governments striving to maintain political and social stability.

The international dominance of the conceptual framework that the US has established for its 'war on terror', combined with the operating constraints and deficiencies of the local media, and the potential impact of the internet, raises a number of issues concerning the role and impact of the media in sub-state conflicts across Asia. This book will assess how and to what extent non-state combatants in a number of states in Asia access the media and influence its outputs; how the 'war on terror' influences media outputs on those conflicts; and the role and impact of the media on those conflicts.

1 US journalism

Servant of the nation, scourge of the truth?

Toby Miller

Introduction

The period since 11 September 2001 has seen both continuity and change in the way the US media and state have combined to produce realities for their audience and citizenry. This Chapter lays out how the mainstream US media, notably network and cable television, have worked as effective spokespeople for nationalism, in ways that coincide with the enunciation of national interest by the state. I will show it is no surprise that almost three quarters of the US public supported the invasion of Iraq (Pew Research Center for the People and the Press 2003a). It would have taken immense initiative, knowledge, and drive to think otherwise, especially given the shock of September 11 (Taylor 2003: B2) and the way that it heightened a sense of risk and hence self-protectiveness in the population of a world power capable of supreme destruction. The White House's 2002 *National Security Strategy* was correct in identifying the nation's gravest peril as located 'at the crossroads of radicalism and technology'. But was that taken to signify the logocentric interdependence of US Zionism, militarism, transportation, construction, and high-octane fuel, which, together with Middle Eastern authoritarianism, economic inequality, and Islamic hyper-masculinity and religiosity produced the conditions of possibility for September 11?

No. It was taken as the cue for a reinvigorated propaganda effort via the euphemism 'public diplomacy'. The desire to win over the 'hearts and minds' of the global south (signifying Islam) was invoked again and again. The new public diplomacy is supposed to transcend the material effects of policies and businesses and instead permit closer communication at a civil-society level, directly linking citizens across borders to 'influence opinions and mobilize foreign publics' (Council on Foreign Relations 2003: 15; also see Gilboa 1998) by, as the State Department puts it, 'engaging, informing, and influencing key international audiences' (Brown 2004). The idea is to achieve these goals in ways that work for the interests of the US government but avoid both that connotation and potential opposition from other states.

Republicans had nearly ended public diplomacy once they took control of the Congress in the mid-1990s, diminishing funding and staffing by 20–25 per cent, but quickly turned to it under George Bush minor as a way of affirming that 'misunderstanding' was responsible for the situation of the country internationally, creating the White House Office of Global Communications and a Policy Coordinating Committee on Strategic Communications. In 2002 they began Radio Free Afghanistan. That year also saw the advent of Culture Connect, which sent artists, writers, and musicians around the world to demonstrate US sophistication and decency and give young people a belief in their place in the world that was to do with something other than violence. Radio Sawa and Radio Farda began offering Arabic and Farsi language music and news. Later they developed TV links. And the venerable Voice of America extended its Indonesian and Cantonese programming (Center for Arts and Culture 2004: 8; Council on Foreign Relations 2003: 9, 27, 75; Schaefer 2004). I shall argue that, quite apart from the operation of US foreign policy, this goal is improbable given the manifest way that the US media operate as little more than a mouthpiece for official rhetoric in the discourse of terrorism and state action.

I investigate in this chapter various forces at play in the coverage of the invasions of Afghanistan and Iraq in 2001 and 2003 – notably journalistic nationalism, coverage of foreign news and the role of intellectuals – that produce a body of work about terrorism that is literally stunning in its unanimity of approach and renders laughable the duplicity of 'public diplomacy' – which if it were to work, should be based on dissent, not obedience! No conspiracy theories are needed to explain this unanimity – it derives from mundane policies to do with media economics and banal practices of nationalist ideology at a time of risk. Its impact, of course, is far from mundane or banal.

In the last ten years, the US media have gone from being controlled by 50 competing companies to 5 (Schechter 2003a). Many of these institutions are corporate conglomerates, for whom the traditions of journalism are incidental to their core businesses. News divisions have been fetishized as individual profit centres, rather than their previous function as loss-leaders that helped to give broadcast networks a character that 'endorsed' other genres (Smith 2003). So the major broadcast TV networks, still the principal sources of news for most of the US population, have closed investigative sections and foreign *bureaux* (Chester 2002: 106). Where ABC News once maintained 17 foreign *bureaux*, it now has 7 (Higham 2001). Why? The moment that tobacco and real-estate expert Lawrence Tisch bought CBS in 1987, he commenced a programme of disinvestment and disemployment. Hundreds were fired from the news service following a budget cut of millions, and *bureaux* were closed in Europe and Asia. By 2001, CBS had 1 journalist covering all of Asia, and 7 others for the rest of the world. That became the model. All in all, network TV coverage of international news fell by 70 per cent from the 1970s to the 1990s. Between May 2000 and August 2001, 22 per cent of coverage was international – ten points below, for example, British and South African equivalents, and 20 points below German. Of that US coverage, just 3 per cent addressed US foreign policy (Barkin 2003: 85; Schatz 2003: xvii). Numerous academic studies have found the networks parochial and essentially incapable of devoting attention to other countries other than as dysfunctional or as threats to the US, even when covering successful democratic elections

(Golan and Wayne 2003). It should be no surprise that a major 2002 study of US newspapers with circulations of over 100,000 found 80 per cent of editors had negative views of the TV networks' coverage of international stories (Pew International Journalism Program 2002). Of course, rather than acknowledge that this was driven by business priorities, US TV hacks turned to the putative power of the audience. In CBS anchor Dan Rather's 2002 words: 'if you lead foreign you die', because 'the public has lost interest in international reporting' (quoted in Schechter 2003b: xl). This is too easy and self-serving an explanation. A 2002 survey of 218 US-newspaper editors found two-thirds admitting that their coverage of foreign news was 'fair to poor'. It disclosed no real engagement with the multicultural and immigrant populations the papers were avowedly serving. This was in stark contrast to the satisfaction expressed over their coverage of commerce. The reason for this neglect of international news was not demand but supply – their readers were interested, but their owners sought to keep costs down, and their employees lacked the necessary skills (Pew Fellowships in International Journalism 2002; Pew International Journalism Program 2002). As usual, demand is a small part of the story – supply is the determining factor. But it would be wrong to divorce that from occupational ideology.

Journalistic nationalism

Whilst comparative studies indicate a propensity for journalists all over the world to reiterate foreign-policy *nostra* at times of national crisis, there are many honourable exceptions. But the US media stand out for their nationalism (Höijer *et al.* 2004: 14). A glance at the transcript of a discussion about US terrorism coverage by the media, held in Ljubljana in November 2002, reveals a striking contrast between hyper-parochial representatives from Fox, CNN, NBC, and CBS and contributors from all other nations (Kroll and Champagne 2002). The proliferation of US flag pins on reporters, and the repeated, embarrassingly crass use of such othering Membership Categorization Devices as 'we', is simply not permitted by major global news gatherers, whether they are regionally or nationally based or funded. British viewers were so taken aback by the partisanship of Fox, which was rebroadcast there via satellite, that they protested against it through the local regulator, the Independent Television Commission. In India, where Star TV has long been dominant in ratings, the invasion of Iraq brought viewers flooding back to the hitherto moribund public broadcaster Doordarshan, while the *Manila Standard* explained to its readers that Fox was the contemporary version of the Bible for extremist Christians in the US, and Malaysia's *Berita Harian* editorialized that the threat of terrorism has been deployed 'by Bush's accomplices to influence the [US] media not to question any government actions' (Abaya 2004; *BBC Monitoring International Reports* 2004a; Sehgal 2003; Wells 2003).

The distinguished journalist-publisher Victor Navasky (2002) has noted that 'post-September 11 journalism' took as a *donnée* that 'this was a time for rallying around the flag and that those who questioned national policy were giving aid and comfort to the enemy'. When Tom Guiting, editor-in-chief of the *Texas City*

Sun, and Dan Guthrie, of the *Daily Courier* in Oregon, wrote articles criticizing Bush minor after the attack, they were fired (Ottosen 2004: 117). Adducing connections between the attack and US foreign policy 'somehow smacked of apologetics' (Navasky 2002: xiii). After the president of ABC News, David Westin, told students at Columbia University's Graduate School of Journalism that, as a journalist, he must refrain from taking a position on whether the September 11 attack on the Pentagon was legitimate, given that it could be regarded as a military target, the reaction from the right-wing media was so intense that he retracted his position and apologized (Alterman 2003: 203). Dan Rather acknowledged (on the BBC) that US journalists 'fear that you will be "necklaced" here, you will have a flaming tire of lack of patriotism put around your neck…that keeps journalists from asking the toughest of tough questions' (quoted in Solomon and Erlich 2003: 23). In reviewing this period, the Newspaper Guild Communication Workers of America found that many of its members were expected to be 'patriots first, and journalists second' and were victimized if they failed to comply (International Federation of Journalists 2001: 23–24).

Because MSNBC's Ashleigh Banfield occasionally reported Arab perspectives during the 2003 conflict, Michael Savage, then a talk show host on her network prior to being removed for telling a caller he hoped the person would contract HIV, called her a 'slut', a 'porn star', and an 'accessory to the murder of Jewish children' on-air. NBC executives rewarded this conduct by naming him their 'showman' (quoted in Lieberman 2003). Banfield told a Kansas State University audience during the Iraq invasion that

> horrors were completely left out of this war. So was this journalism?…I was ostracized just for going on television and saying, 'Here's what the leaders of Hezbollah, a radical Moslem group, are telling me about what is needed to bring peace to Israel'.
>
> (quoted in Schechter 2003a)

She was immediately demoted and disciplined by NBC for criticizing journalistic standards. Erik Sorenson, President of MSNBC, chortled that 'one can be unabashedly patriotic and be a good journalist at the same time' (quoted in Allan and Zelizer 2004: 7). No wonder Malaysian Prime Minister Datuk Seri Dr Mahathir Mohamad accused the US of hypocrisy in its calls for a separation of media and state – '[w]hen it suits them, there is no freedom of the Press'. Similar critiques came from official Iranian sources, and the *Turkish Daily News*, when pointing to the slow, begrudging reactions of the US media and political classes to revelations about torture at Abu Ghraib prison (Aktan 2004; *BBC Monitoring International Reports* 2004b; *New Straits Times* 2003b).

When it was decided to co-opt journalists for the Iraq invasion by 'embedding' them with the military, reporters were required to sign a contract agreeing with Pentagon instructions on coverage, including no off-the-record interviews, which had been crucial in Vietnam. Magazine writer Michael Wolff questioned this practice, so Fox accused him of being unpatriotic, while talk radio's resident recreational drug-use specialist Rush Limbaugh publicized his email address, leading to thousands of messages of hatred (Keeble 2004: 50; Talara 2003; Thussu and Freedman 2003: 6).

The noted CNN foreign correspondent, Christiane Amanpour, told CNBC after the 2003 invasion of Iraq

> I think the press was muzzled, and I think the press self-muzzled... I'm sorry to say, but certainly television and, perhaps, to a certain extent, my station was intimidated by the administration and its foot soldiers at Fox News. And it did, in fact, put a climate of fear and self-censorship, in my view, in terms of the kind of broadcast work we did.

She was immediately derided by Fox's Irena Briganti as 'a spokeswoman for al Qaeda' (quoted in Allan and Zelizer 2004: 9 and Zerbisias 2003). Conversely, her frank assessment drew sighs of relief from the media elsewhere, increasingly incredulous in the face of their US counterparts' performance. The *New Straits Times* editorialized that this pointed to the need for an alternative global news network for Muslims (*New Straits Times* 2003i).

The tendencies listed by Amanpour and exemplified by Briganti were not merely reactions to September 11. Their causes went deeper. For example, after the 2000 election, CNN's Judy Woodruff had told Bush minor's chief of staff Andy Card on-air that 'we look forward to working with you' (Woodruff quoted in Solomon 2001). This remark would not be altered by a journalist in most functioning democracies, where official sources are starting-points for work, not results – and the idea of 'working with' a government is seen as 'Soviet-style' (Massing 2001). But inside the US, there is a long heritage of reliance on official sources dating from the evolution of journalistic codes and norms as tools for monopolistic owners to distract attention from their market domination by focusing on non-partisan journalism and cloaking themselves in professionalism (Clark and McChesney 2001; Herman 1999: 83, 87, 158; McChesney 2003). This quick-fix/*idée fixe* is a function of both a lengthy history, and more recent pressures from deregulation and concentration, as well as keen recruiting by the CIA, which has paid hundreds of US journalists, as approved by their seniors, but hidden from their readers (Boyd-Barrett 2004: 38–39).

The White House, the State Department, and the Pentagon are referred to as 'the Golden Triangle' for reporters (Love 2003: 246). Most US news gathering produces a feedback loop of staggeringly self-interested proportions. 'Research' is based on leaks and leads provided by the Administration, which then quotes the resulting stories as objective correlatives of its own position. That tendency reached its awful apogee in the weapons of mass destruction falsehoods perpetrated by Bush minor's *apparatchiks* and the *New York Times* in 2003 – falsehoods of a cosmic magnitude, which drew zero public self criticism for an entire year, even as the paper was purging staff over invented fact checking on human interest stories (MacArthur 2003). As dissident writer Greg Palast (a dissident in the US, but a regular in the UK for the BBC and the *Guardian*) put it, 'I can't tell you how many reporters I've said, "Where do you get this stuff?" And they say, "Well, it was in a State Department press release", as if that's an acceptable source' (Bosse and Palast 2003). Elsewhere, '[i]t's not the job of a journalist to snap to the attention of generals' (Fisk in Fisk *et al.* 2003), but that appears to be a qualification in the US.

The golden triangle focuses the US media on the state, as embodied by the party in power. A study conducted at the beginning of 2002 disclosed that CNN had covered 157 events featuring Bush operatives and just 7 that centred on Democrat politicians (Alterman 2003: 206). In the fortnight running up to the 2003 invasion, the major networks and PBS dedicated less than 1 per cent of related airtime to opponents of the war. During the war, a sample of National Public Radio's guest list on all topics over one month shows that 64 per cent were officials or corporate spokespeople (Rendall and Butterworth 2004). In justifying this state of affairs, CNN anchor Aaron Brown complained that 'there was no center to cover' in opposition to the Administration, because the Democratic Party had not opposed invasion (Goodman *et al.* 2003), while Fox News accompanied anti-war protests in Manhattan with a ticker news crawl taunting the demonstrators (Folkenflik 2003). When its own programme, *The Simpsons*, mocked this via a ticker that read 'Do Democrats cause cancer? Find out at foxnews.com', the network immediately threatened the creator with legal action (Byrne 2003b). Bush minor dismissed the anti-war movement as 'focus groups' (quoted in Grieve 2003) and Republican Party mavens referred to these 'few protestors in the streets' as akin to 'mob rule' (Boot in Goodman *et al.* 2003). All this even as Viacom, CNN, Fox, and Comedy Central were refusing to feature paid billboards and commercials against the invasion (Hastings 2003), and UN activities in the region, including weapons inspections, became the least-covered items on network news (Huff 2003).

Since 2001, there have of course been some changes, as this nationalism has developed a texture derived from the specific conjuncture of terrorism as an external threat, experienced at home, that countenances invasions elsewhere. The US media and war planners have supplied narrow frameworks for interpretation of terrorism into a starting point for escalating global violence. Consider the immediate obedience of TV news executives after Condoleeza Rice, the National Security Adviser, asked them to cease playing tapes of Osama bin Laden speaking, purportedly lest he pass on coded instructions to followers; Bush minor's Press Secretary Ari Fleischer had already said people should 'watch what they say' about terrorism and US foreign policy (quoted in Navasky 2002: xv–xvi), although this was excised from White House transcripts (Magder 2003: 36). Media martinet Rupert Murdoch promised 'We'll do whatever is our patriotic duty', later intoning that removing Saddam Hussein would reduce the price of oil: 'The greatest thing to come out of this for the world economy' (quoted in Solomon 2001 and Greenslade 2003). Each of the 175 newspapers he owned across the world endorsed the invasion (Harvey 2003: 12). But this went further than the Oedipalised son of a renowned embedded journalist from the Somme. NBC's Tom Brokaw said on air during the initial invasion 'One of the things that we don't want to do is to destroy the infrastructure of Iraq, because in a few days we're going to own that country' (quoted in *EXTRA!Update* 2004: 2). That shocking remark revealed more than he meant.

Of course, 'infrastructure' was inanimate. People could move and bleed and die – but they were not worth owning in quite the same way. Not surprisingly, the US networks' censorship of footage of Afghan civilian casualties in October 2001 was almost total (Hudson *et al.* 2002). Military manoeuvres took second place to civilian suffering in the rest of the world's media coverage of the Afghan and Iraqi crises, invasions and occupations (della Carva 2003). Al Jazeera dedicated only a third of its stories to war footage. Unlike CNN, it emphasized human distress rather than electronic effectiveness, vernacular reportage rather than patriotic euphemism (Jasperson and El-Kikhia 2003: 119, 126–127). The thousands of civilian Afghan deaths reported by south Asian, Southeast Asian, western European, and Middle Eastern news services went essentially unrecorded here, because they could not be 'verified' by US journalists or officials (Herold 2001). Several US newspapers instructed journalists to minimize coverage of Afghan civilian casualties during the invasion (Flanders 2001). Fox News Managing Editor Brit Hulme said that civilian casualties may not belong on television, as they are 'historically, by definition, a part of war'. CNN instructed presenters to mention September 11 each time Afghan suffering was mentioned, and Walter Isaacson, the network's President, worried aloud that it was 'perverse to focus too much on the casualties or hardship' (quoted in Kellner 2003: 107, 66). This perversity only applied to domestic CNN viewers – those *in* the real world were judged sturdy enough to learn *about* the real world (Williams 2003: 177). The silence was a reminder of Secretary of State Colin Powell's callous remark from 1991, when he was a military planner of the Iraq war. When asked if he knew how many Iraqis had died as a result of that conflict, he replied '[i]t's really not a number I'm terribly interested in' (quoted in Zinn 2003: x). Driven by the same attitude, in the fortnight prior to the 2003 invasion of Iraq, none of the major three networks provided any examination of the humanitarian impact of such an action. Human Rights Watch's briefing paper, and a UN Undersecretary-General's warning on the topic, lay uncovered (FAIR 2003a).

To hide and deny the carnage of its 2001 invasion, Bush's Pentagon bought exclusive rights to satellite photos of Afghanistan, shutting off scrutiny of its attacks (Solomon 2001; Magder 2003: 38). Another kind of scrutiny took its place – a carnival of exaltation over *matériel*. Thirty-eight per cent of CNN's coverage of the bombardment centred on technology, while 62 per cent focused on military activity without history or politics, as a matter of technical specifications, of instrumental rationality (Jasperson and El-Kikhia 2003: 119, 126–127). Desperate Afghan refugees in camps were filmed by the BBC, which then sold the footage on to ABC. But the soundtrack to the two broadcast versions gave them incompatible meanings:

> British media presented the camps as consisting of refugees from U. S. bombing who said that fear of the daily bombing attacks had driven them out of the city,

whereas U. S. media presented the camps as containing refugees from Taliban oppression and the dangers of civil war.

(Kellner 2003: 125)

Perhaps next time the BBC should insist on including voice-overs as part of the package.

As the invasion of Iraq loomed, Murdoch said 'there is going to be collateral damage... if you really want to be brutal about it, better we get it done now' (quoted in Pilger 2003). The Project for Excellence in Journalism's analysis of ABC, CBS, NBC, CNN, and Fox found that in the opening stanza of the Iraq invasion, 50 per cent of reports from the 1,000 journalists working embedded with the invaders depicted combat. Zero per cent depicted injuries. As the war progressed, the most we saw were deeply sanitized images of the wounded from afar, in keeping with the 50 contractual terms required of reporters in return for their 'beds' (Boyd-Barrett 2004: 30–31; Sharkey 2003). Coverage of the impact of the invaders was dismissed by PBS *News Hour* Executive Producer Lester Crystal as not 'central at the moment' (quoted in Sharkey 2003). NBC correspondent David Bloom astonishingly offered that the media were so keen to become adjuncts of the military that they were 'doing anything and everything that they can ask of us' (quoted in Carr 2003), and WABC radio's N.J. Burkett compared soldiers preparing their weapons to 'an orchestra on an opening night' (quoted in Rutenberg 2003). Marcy McGinnis, senior vice-president of news at CBS, claimed that the networks brought 'this war into the living rooms of Americans... the first time you can actually see what's happening' (quoted in Sharkey 2003) and Paul Steiger, Managing Editor of the *Wall Street Journal*, divined that US media coverage of the invasion of Iraq 'was pretty darned good' (quoted in Friedman 2003). What counted as 'happening' and 'darned good' was extraordinarily misshaped and unbalanced – in fact systematically distorted. This contrasted drastically with what other nations received.

No wonder Defence Secretary Donald Rumsfeld's thought-disordered remark about Baghdad – that 'It looks like it's a bombing of a city, but it isn't' – received much uncritical US coverage. Statements by the International Red Cross and many, many other notable non-Pentagon sources detailing Iraqi civilian casualties from the bombing-of-a-city-that-wasn't, received virtually none (FAIR 2003d; Wilkinson 2003). Nor did memorable Congressional speeches against this bloodthirsty militarism by Senators Robert Byrd and Ted Kennedy (Schlesinger 2003). First-hand accounts of an unarmed family in a car being shot by US soldiers were overridden by the desire to promote the Pentagon's strenuous insistence that the protocols for shooting an unarmed family in a car were followed (FAIR 2003e). There was no mention on any network of the US military's use of depleted uranium and virtually no consideration of the impact of cluster bombs – both major stories everywhere else and subject to serious complaints by Amnesty International and Human Rights Watch. The US claim to have dropped just 26 cluster bombs was belied by the thousands that had to be 'cleaned up', but this information was not available through domestic media outlets. The Australian and European media referred to the question of cluster bombs ten times as often as their US counterparts (FAIR 2003g; Rampton and Strauber 2003: 197, 194). Even wounded US soldiers were left unnoticed by the mainstream media, with no bedside interviews from hospitals. Journalists ran from the accusation of being unpatriotic. Fallen men and women had become the 'disappeared' (Berkowitz 2003). Friday prayers in Tehran produced a telling critique from Hashemi-Rafsanjani:

> The American newspapers are banned from printing the pictures of those killed or injured in Iraq. Aren't you really surprised? Those who exert pressure on countries like ours, as they claim, for the sake of freedom, do not allow their own newspapers, TVs, including private TV, to print or show these photos or films.
>
> (*BBC Monitoring International Reports* 2004b)

The point that much – though not all – of this censorship was self-inflicted is only partially irrelevant, so unitary were the politics and policies of the US state and media in their self-righteous denunciations.

The invasion of Afghanistan marked one of Bush minor's infrequent press conferences. On 10 November 2001, he sat alongside Pakistan's military *coup* leader, Pervez Musharraf, and described how the war on terrorism in Afghanistan would unfurl in concert with 'our friends', the Northern Alliance. In response to another question, Musharraf referred to the Alliance's record of 'atrocities', and the need to prevent it from getting near Kabul. One journalist queried Bush about the contradiction between his account of 'our friends' and Musharraf's account of their 'atrocities'. Bush refused to answer the question, on the grounds that the reporter had already posed one query. Unlike any other democracy, no journalist in the room picked up the question. And when Helen Thomas asked Fleischer during the 2003 invasion of Iraq about the propriety of televising Taliban prisoners in Guantánamo Bay, given the complaints made by the US about similar shots of US prisoners of war, she was dispatched to the back of the room for the remainder of the conflict and given no opportunity to ask questions – typical from this Administration (Hans 2001; Mokhiber and Weissman 2003a; Robbins 2003).

Meanwhile, Guantánamo prisoners remained uncharged years after their capture during the defeat of the Taliban, and without legal or media access other than via the demeaning film of them in cages, until the US Supreme Court finally queried this in mid-2004. The government argued that they were not entitled to legal counsel because they were *not* subject to the Geneva Convention; and that they could not be interviewed because they *were* subject to the Convention. The media elsewhere are appalled by this infraction of basic human rights. In the US, it was left up to *JAG*, a CBS drama written by ex-military officers, to address and sanitize the issue (Burston 2003: 168; *Center for Constitutional*

Rights 2003; *Human Rights Watch* 2003a; *Independent* 2003; *MotherJones.com* 2003; Shafer 2003). When Saddam Hussein was captured, the hypocrisy defied description, as one journalist after another lined up to display their memory loss, mendacity and ignorance as they celebrated his humiliation by the US (Naureckas 2004).

The government also sought to destabilize alternative views, in ways that were endorsed by the nationalism of domestic journalism. Al Jazeera may work assiduously to expose Arab audiences to official Israeli points of view from a secular perspective, and to focus on US suffering and reactions to September 11, but the US State Department disrupted it via pressure on Qatar's Emir Sheikh Hamid bin Khalifa al-Thaniof (el-Nawawy and Gher 2003; Hafez 2001; International Federation of Journalists 2001: 20), and the channel's Washington correspondent was 'detained' *en route* to a US-Russia summit in November 2001 (Miladi 2003: 159). The network was assaulted by US munitions in Afghanistan in 2001 (where it was the sole broadcast news outlet in Kabul) and Iraq in 2003, and subject to Rumsfeld's extraordinary remark that it was 'Iraqi propaganda' and regular slander by the Bush Administration as 'All Osama All the Time' (quoted in Getlin and Jensen 2003; Rampton and Strauber 2003: 186). This anti-democratic violence matched similarly tyrannical outbursts against it by the authoritarian governments of Bahrain, Libya, Saudi Arabia, Jordan, and Kuwait (Jasperson and El-Kikhia 2003: 130). Then it was denied access by its US-based internet provider and had to switch servers to France (Association for Progressive Communications 2003; Fine 2003).

Throughout the US occupation of Iraq, al Jazeera's workers were subject to violent assaults by US soldiers, culminating in murders (Parenti 2004; Eide 2004: 280). The attack on the network's Kabul operations was justified by Rear Admiral Craig Quigley, the US Deputy Assistant Defense Secretary for Public Affairs, who claimed that al Qaeda interests were being aided by activities going on there. Al Jazeera denied the charge. Quigley's proof was that al Jazeera was using a satellite uplink and was in contact with Taliban officials – pretty normal activities for a news service of any competence (FAIR 2003f; Gowing 2003: 234) but rendered abnormal through the work of agencies like Fox News, whose operatives described the Taliban as 'rats', 'terror goons', and 'psycho Arabs' during the 2001 conflict (quoted in Thussu 2003: 127). The 2003 US assault on al Jazeera was condemned by the Committee to Protect Journalists and Amnesty International as a violation of international humanitarian law, and that Committee, Reporters Without Borders, the International Federation of Journalists, and the International Press Institute all condemned US bombing of Iraqi state television (Lobe 2003). Meanwhile, the New York Stock Exchange expelled al Jazeera during the invasion of Iraq, following US Governmental criticisms of it for televising prisoners of war and Arab criticisms of the attack. The official explanation was that for 'security reasons', the number of broadcasters allowed at the Exchange had to be limited to those offering 'responsible business coverage'. The NASDAQ exchange refused to grant al Jazeera press credentials at the same time, for the same reason (Agovino 2003; FAIR 2003c; *Reuters* 2003). *Index on Censorship* proceeded to honour the network with its free-expression prize, and analysis indicated that the framing devices it used which exercised the Pentagon and other anti-democrats were identical to media norms everywhere – other than one country (Byrne 2003a; Fisk 2003b; Khouri 2003; Lobe 2003). The Associated Press Managing Editors sent an open letter of protest to the Pentagon, noting that 'journalists have been harassed, have had their lives endangered and have had digital camera disks, videotape and other equipment confiscated' by the US military (*Associated Press* 2003). Meanwhile, the US Government selected Grace Digital Media to run an Arabic-language satellite television news service into post-invasion Iraq. Grace is a fundamentalist Christian company that describes itself as 'dedicated to transmitting the evidence of God's presence in the world today' via 'secular news, along with aggressive proclamations that will "change the news" to reflect the Kingdom of God'. It is dedicated to Zionism (quoted in Mokhiber and Weissman 2003b).

For their part, the US media derided al Jazeera throughout the war and occupation. This churlishness reached its *nadir* in April 2004 when CNN's Daryn Kagan interviewed the network's editor-in-chief, Ahmed Al-Sheik. What might have been an opportunity to learn about the horrendous casualties in the Fallujah uprisings, or to share professional perspectives on methods and angles of coverage, turned into a bizarrely unreflective indictment of al Jazeera for bothering to report the deaths of Iraqi non-combatants at the hands of the invaders. Kagan complained that 'the story' was 'bigger than just the numbers of people who have been killed or the fact that they might have been killed by the US military' (quoted in FAIR 2004). At least this represented interaction with al Jazeera, a stark contrast with CNN refusing to appear on a Nordic TV panel with their representatives (Eide 2004: 280). And some analysts suggest that CNN's dependence on al Jazeera for direct images and reportage from the Afghanistan conflict helped to make for a semblance of balance between technocratic celebrations and humanitarian discussions of death (Jasperson and Al-Kikhia 2003: 120, 125).

The story of overseas news, the role of intellectuals

The US networks know precious little about any other part of the world by contrast with their western European, Asian, Latin American, and Middle East counterparts, as evident from several leading journalists' embarrassed admissions that US TV coverage of the invasion of Afghanistan was abysmal. In the absence of experienced crews with relevant knowledge of culture, language, and history they were shown up (Rosen 2002: 31). The *Sydney Morning Herald* called the result '[j]ingoistic, sugar-coated, superficial'. CBC's News Director found it 'depressing'. He experienced 'two different wars' in Afghanistan, one available on European television and the other in the US (quoted in Kellner 2003: 111). The Pew Charitable Trusts (2002) reported that opinion rather than the fact dominated reporting, in part through the inexperience of US journalists noted earlier, and in part because the Bush Administration imposed unprecedented restrictions on reporting. Interpretation displaced knowledge. Fox News Roger Ailes, who doubled as an adviser to Bush minor on foreign policy, describes Fox's new method of covering global stories in this helpful way: 'We basically sent hit teams overseas from out of here'. Leslie Moonves of CBS explained that entertainment dominated news: 'As you get further away from September 11, that will revert back to normal' (quoted in *New Yorker* 2001). And sure enough, the Project for Excellence in Journalism (2002) revealed that TV news coverage of national and international issues fell by 33 per cent from October 2001 to March 2002, as celebrity and lifestyle issues took over from discussion of the various parts of the world that the US directly and indirectly rules and controls.

Emad Adeeb, the Chair of *Al Alam Al Youm* and host of *On the Air!* in Egypt, summed up US foreign-correspondent techniques like this

> you come and visit us in what I call the American Express Tour – 72 hours. . . . you stay at the same hotel where the 150,000 colleagues before you have stayed. You eat at the same restaurant because you've been given its name. You have the same short list of people who have been inter-viewed . . . you buy the same presents for your wives or girlfriends or mis-tresses, because you have the same address from your friends before you. You don't do anything out of the norm, and you come writing the same story with the same slogan – a minute-and-a-half bite, or a 500-word story – and you think that you know the Middle East. . . . and then when a crisis happens, you are interviewed as an expert.
>
> (quoted in Pew Fellowships in International Journalism 2002)

Pakistan's *Friday Times* offered this guide on how to 'look like a CNN correspondent':

> 10. Pretend to be in grave danger while reporting from the roof of the Marriott, Islamabad.
> 9. Never learn how to pronounce 'Pakistan'.
> 8. Get a U. S. marine escort to help you do your groceries.
> 7. Bond with the locals by hanging out at Muddy's Café.
> 6. Carry big black cameras with CNN stickers pasted all over them.
> 5. Always wear a safari jacket (esp. when in big cities).
> 4. Wear a CNN t-shirt.
> 3. Wear a CNN hat.
> 2. Wear CNN underwear.
> 1. Hunt for the biggest lunatics to put on air.
>
> (quoted in Schechter and Dichter 2003: 49)

In editor Fuad Nahdi's (2003) words, dumping 'young, inexperienced and excitable' journalists in the Middle East who are functionally illiterate and his-torically ignorant means that the US media depends on 'clippings and weekend visits' of dubious professional integrity. No wonder that CNN's Jerusalem Bureau chief, Walter Rodgers, insensitively proclaims that

> [f]or a journalist, Israel is the best country in the world to work in... [o]n the Palestinian side, as is the case in the rest of the Arab world, there is always that deep divide between Islam and the West.
>
> (quoted in Ibrahim 2003: 96)

CNN, of course, reached its Middle Eastern *nadir*, and lost viewers to al Jazeera and others, when one of its 'reporters' stated that some nomads would be thunderstruck by seeing 'camels of steel' (cars) for the first time (MacFarquhar 2003). Not to mention the notorious exchange between two reporters on air during the Afghanistan invasion, where one suggested that an assault on an arms depot may have been part of the civil war and the other offered 'Oh, are they having one?' (quoted in Schechter 2003b: 6). Reactionaries celebrate such stories, regarding them as almost endearing in their status as instant responses to market demand and the flexible supply of new technologies (Hamilton and Jenner 2004), ignoring as they must the special responsibility for US citizens to know about the domination and destruction wrought in their name.

The *Tyndall Report* (2003) found that network-news coverage from September 2001 to December 2002 of the September 11 attacks and their aftermath basically ignored all the key topics that should have been relevant to a critical, historicized consideration of geopolitics at the time: Zionism, Afghanistan after the invasion, US foreign policy, and US business interests in the Middle East. Lest we imagine that the print media offer anything better that US television, we should note that whereas 10 per cent of newspaper coverage in 1983 addressed foreign news, this had fallen to 2 per cent by 1998. Covers of *Time* magazine dedicated to international relations dropped from 11 in 1987 to none a decade later, and that period saw its foreign reportage diminish from 24 per cent to 12 per cent. These institutions were adopting the 'just-in-time' techniques of post-Fordism to current affairs (Magder 2003: 33). This has led to an intense provincialism. In 1999, when India, Colombia, and Greece each had far more terrorist incidents than the entire Middle East combined, the US media dedicated virtually no attention to them (Love 2003: 247; also see Kern *et al.* 2003). The *New York Times*, for example, was intellectually unprepared to report on terrorism. Because terrorism mostly occurred outside the US prior to 2001, it was not rated as newsworthy. Throughout the 1970s and 1980s, reportage of overseas terror took up less than 0.5 per cent of the paper. Of the top 10 subjects covered by the nation's major news weeklies in their last issues before the World Trade Center attacks, 9 were reviews, human interest, or consumer reports (Schechter 2003b: 11). And coverage by the US media has historically eschewed explanations – both television and print have focused on othering terrorists through membershipping devices, to the almost absolute exclusion of discussing social inequality or state-based terror. A study of articles carried in *US News and World Report* indicates that in the seven months after September 11, reasons for the attacks focused entirely on al Qaeda and domestic security failings – virtually nothing on US foreign policy, minerals exploitation, and militarism. This was in keeping with the history of US news coverage of terrorism – enough with the aetiology, let's moralize (Traugott and Brader 2003: 183–184, 186–187). Lead *New York Times* reporter Richard Bernstein's embarrassing volume on September 11 (2002) eschewed anything even approximating a serious discussion of US foreign policy in its pious romanticization, while his soon-to-be-disgraced Executive Editor Howell Raines referred in the Preface to Hiroshima's decimation by the US as having arisen 'from dictatorial passions run amok' in Japan (2002: xi). All historical perspective was lost. Terrorism is regarded either as a struggle over ideas or feelings – never as an example of political violence against civilians that derives from material causes (Schlesinger *et al.* 1983: 2, 5).

When a sense of history, geography, or language is needed, who receives the call? The right-wing think tanks that dominate Washington policy on the Middle East have sought to discredit area studies across US universities, especially Middle Eastern programmes. The Washington Institute for Near East Studies is the key front organization for the Republican Party, while institutions like the American Jewish Congress, Campus Watch, and the American Council of Trustees and Alumni (run by the Vice-President's wife) warn against 'Middle Eastern Arabs' in universities, and place conservatives in vital opinion-making *fora* that feed into TV current affairs, such as the op-ed pages of the *Wall Street Journal*, the *Jerusalem Post*, the *Los Angeles Times*, the *Washington Post*, and the *New York Times* (Abrahamian 2003; Beinin 2003: 135; Brynen 2002; Davidson 2002; Merriman 2004; Whitaker 2002). There are over 300 right-wing think tanks in Washington, dealing with topics from sexuality to foreign policy. They hire ghost-writers to make their resident intellectuals' prose attractive, as part of a project that is concerned more with marketing opinion than conducting research – for each 'study' they fund is essentially the alibi for an op-ed piece. The government also establishes front organizations that select, train, and promote apparently independent figures. The State Department financed the Iraq Public Diplomacy Group, which coached Iraqis to appear on US television and speak positions prepared for them, on the grounds that they would be more effective than Yanquis. For instance, the Iraqi National Congress was the creation and creature of the CIA, via the Agency's public-relations consultant, the Rendon Group (Alterman 2003: 82–83; Rampton and Stauber 2003: 55, 43).

Progressive think tanks had a sixth share of media quotation compared to these institutions during the 1990s (Alterman 2003: 85). In 2002, conservative groups received 47 per cent of think-tank citations by the mainstream media, centrists 41 per cent, and leftists 12 per cent. The latter was the lowest proportion for progressives since 1998 (Dolny 2003). Media attention does not correlate with scholarly esteem or achievement, and the academics most likely to be interviewed are those who have worked in government (Claussen 2004: 56). Ninety per cent of news interviewees on the major networks are white men born between 1945 and 1960 (Love 2003: 246). That might expose us to the cohort that is responsible for most of our troubles, but not to disinterested critiques – or critiques from interested positions that are at variance with the tenor and word of the White House.

The supposed choice guaranteed to US citizens by competition for cable-news viewers was nothing of the sort. Having repeatedly instructed him to feature more right-wing people on his programme, MSNBC fired its liberal talk-show host Phil Donahue immediately prior to the 2003 invasion, even though he had the network's top-rating programme, because his 'anti-war agenda' would look bad when 'our competitors are waving the flag...a difficult face for NBC in a time of war'. This was a programme that showcased more pro-war than anti-war guests (quoted in FAIR 2003c and Nader 2003; also see Ellis 2003). MSNBC hired as a talk show host the improbably hypocritical Republican Joe Scarborough. As a Congressman, he had appeared on Fox during the 1999 bombing of Serbia and described the assault as 'an unmitigated disaster', specifying 'the people in Belgrade we've killed...the refugees that we've killed...the people in nursing homes...the people in hospitals'. Four years later, as the focal point of *MSNBC Reports*, he attacked 'leftist stooges for anti-American causes' whose beliefs 'could hurt American troop morale' by criticizing military actions. He ranted that such people must be held accountable for their views (quoted in Rendall 2003) – unlike Scarborough himself. Such double standards are hardly surprising, given that the network's parent is the world's biggest arms supplier, General Electric, a conflict of interest rarely discussed openly.

Consider also the extraordinary proliferation of superannuated military and government white men who are deemed to be competent media commentators on what their colleagues are doing. More than half of US TV-studio guests talking about the impending action in Iraq in 2003 were former or contemporary US military or governmental personnel (FAIR 2003b). Television news effectively diminished the available discourse on the impending struggle to one of technical efficiency or state propaganda. A study conducted through the life of the Iraq invasion reveals that US broadcast and cable news virtually excluded anti-war or internationalist points of view: 64 per cent of all pundits were pro-war, while 71 per cent of US 'experts' favoured the war. Anti-war voices were 10 per cent of all sources but just 6 per cent of non-Iraqi sources and 3 per cent of US speakers. Viewers were more than six times as likely to see a pro-war than an anti-war source, and amongst US guests, the ratio increased to 25:1 (Rendall and Broughel 2003). When the vast majority of outside experts represent official opinion, how is this different from a state-controlled media (Johnson 2003)? The *Los Angeles Times* refers to these has-beens and never-wases like this: '[p]art experts and part reporters, they're marketing tools, as well' – and of course, the retired killing-machine hacks are paid for their services, something quite shocking given the traditions of independent critique (Jensen 2003). Their virtually universal links to arms-trading are rarely divulged and never discussed as relevant. Retired Lieutenant General Barry McCaffrey, employed in this capacity by NBC News, points to the *cadre*'s 'lifetime of experience and objectivity'. In his case, this involves membership of the Committee for the Liberation of Iraq, a lobby group dedicated to influencing the media, and the boards of three munitions companies that make ordnance he proceeded to praise on MSNBC. Nine members of the US government's Defence Policy Board have links to companies with defense contracts (Roy 2004). Could these ties constitute conflicts of interest (Benaim *et al.* 2003)? Even amongst the thoroughly ideologized US public, 36 per cent believed that the media over-emphasized the opinions of these retirees (Pew Research Center for the People & the Press 2004a: 15). CNN's gleeful coverage of the invasion of Iraq was typified by one superannuated military officer who rejoiced with 'Slam, bam, bye-bye Saddam' as missiles struck Baghdad (quoted in Goldstein 2003).

Improper links were not only directly connected to killing. Clear Channel Worldwide, the dominant force in US radio and concert promotion with over 1,200 stations, had banned 150 songs after September 11, including 'Bridge over Troubled Water'. It refused permission for protest groups to disseminate literature at an Ani DiFranco concert and organized pro-war rallies and boycotts of anti-war performers, just as it was lobbying for new ownership regulations from Federal Communications Commission, Chair Michael Powell, son of the Secretary of State Colin Powell. Another concentration beneficiary, Cumulus Media, rented a 33,000-pound tractor to destroy Dixie Chicks music and memorabilia and purged the band from 262 play lists for daring to question Bush minor. Further, Clear Channel's board included a Republican activist who had paid Bush minor vast sums for his failed baseball team and handed over public money to Bush and his *apparatchiks* (Aufderheide 2004: 335; D'Entremont 2003; Grieve 2003; Jones 2003; Kellner 2003: 68; Krugman 2003). Could such arrangements constitute conflicts of interest?

In a competent media system, they would be understood as precisely that (Timms 2003), with independent intellectuals trained in area studies, military strategy, international law, and business ethics as counters. But that would depend on power to cosmopolitan working journalists, rather than hack finance executives, and serious action to provide media coverage that was both impartial and seen to be so. Instead, the paranoid form of reporting favoured by US networks militates against journalistic autonomy, other than when the information comes directly from battlefields and is a 'soldier's story' or derives from the Pentagon or the Israeli government (Fisk 2003a). The prevailing doctrines of regulation favour ownership of television stations by a small number of large entities that appeal to anti-intellectual tendencies, regardless of their niches. For example, CNN and Fox market themselves differently – the former to urban, educated viewers, the latter to rural, uneducated viewers. One functions like a broadsheet, the other like a tabloid, with CNN punditry coming mostly from outsiders and Fox punditry as much from presenters as guests. CNN costs more to produce and attracts fewer routine viewers (but many more occasional ones). It brings in much higher advertising revenue because of the composition of its audience and because of its fawning and trite business coverage addresses and because it valourizes high-profile investors and corporations in ways that Fox's down-market populism does not (Alterman 2003: 136–137; Farhi 2003). Neither has any interest in academic expertise.

Those intellectuals who do obtain access to the US media have mostly adopted the logic of global manifest destiny. For example, philosophical liberal and lapsed feminist sex symbol Michael Ignatieff (2003) has called for a new and thoroughgoing imperialism in the *New York Times* magazine, echoing *Time*, which cited Puerto Rico as an instance of the US as a benign despot. Similar sentiments are on display from think-tankers in the *Weekly Standard*, *Foreign Affairs*, the *Harvard Review*, and *Atlantic Monthly*. Robert Kaplan hails the Monroe Doctrine, the justification for two centuries of aiding fascism and mass poverty in Latin America, as a model for world hegemony by the United States, because it shows how to crush leftism (Schell 2003). And journalism professor Lance Morrow writes an essay entitled 'The Case for Rage and Retribution' in *Time* that calls for 'the nourishment of rage … purple American fury … focused brutality' (quoted in Eisman 2003: 60). The neo conservative minority has taken a term once used derisively by the left and made it a badge of honour and identification.

The reality of the US as an imperialist nation is suddenly embraced (Wade 2003). Absent access to adequate academic analysis, in Edward Said's words, 'the airwaves are filled with ex-military men, terrorism experts, and Middle Eastern policy analysts who know none of the relevant languages, may never have seen any part of the Middle East, and are too poorly educated to be expert at anything' (2003).

Conclusion

Comprehensive studies by the Program on International Policy Attitudes and Knowledge Networks (2003 and 2004; Kull *et al.* 2003–2004) found that a minority of the US population knew that clear majorities all over the world opposed the 2003 invasion, and a significant minority thought the war was supported globally. These people also believed that there were indisputable ties between Iraq and September 11 and that weapons of mass destruction had been found in Iraq. The credulity held firm a year after the invasion, and it correlated with viewers' support for the Republican Party and their consumption of commercial TV news. The truth was only known to those who watched or listened to public broadcasting.

The extent and power of this bulwark of ignorance and violence have led Robert Fisk (2002), the *Independent* newspaper's noted foreign correspondent, to the brink of despair in the face of the hysteria his reports engender here. Ex-US diplomat George Dempsey identified Fisk as partly to blame for the events of September 11 (International Federation of Journalists 2001: 13), and actor John Malkovich told the Cambridge Union that he 'would like to shoot' Fisk. The reporter's reaction was to say: 'If we want a quiet life, we will just have to toe the line, stop criticizing Israel or America. Or just stop writing altogether' (Fisk 2002).

Brave seekers after truth on CBS's *Face the Nation* almost joked with the egregious Rumsfeld about a serious matter – that, in David Martin's words, 'You've turned into a Secretary of War', to which the oily technocrat replied 'That's true' (*Washington File* 2003). Similar rejoicing could be heard from Rather on *Larry King Live* during the invasion:

> Look, I'm an American. I never tried to kid anybody that I'm some internationalist or something. And when my country is at war, I want my country to win, whatever the definition of 'win' may be. Now, I can't and don't argue that that is coverage without a prejudice. About that I am prejudiced.

The way the US state and media comport themselves has an inevitable impact on the rest of the world. A study by the International Federation of Journalists in October 2001 found blanket global coverage of the September 11 attacks, with very favourable discussion of the US and its travails – even in nations that had suffered terribly from US aggression. But with attitudes like Malkovich's, is it any surprise the giant advertising firm McCann-Erickson's evaluation of 37 states saw a huge increase in cynicism about the US media's manipulation of the events and the Pew Research Center for the People & the Press' (2002) study of 42 countries in 2002 found a dramatic fall from favour for the US since that time? Or that Pew's 2003 follow-up (Pew Research Center for the People & the Press 2003b) encountered even lower opinions of the US nation, population, and policies worldwide than the year before, with specifically diminished support for anti-terrorism, and faith in the UN essentially demolished by US unilateralism and distrust of Bush minor? Public diplomacy becomes a thin reed.

'Which country poses the greatest danger to world peace in 2003?', asked *Time* magazine of 250,000 people across Europe, offering them a choice between Iraq, North Korea, and the US. Eight per cent selected Iraq, 9 per cent chose North Korea, and…but you have already done the calculation about the most feared country of all (Pilger 2003). A BBC poll in eleven countries in mid-2003 confirmed this. It found sizeable majorities everywhere disapproving of Bush minor and the invasion of Iraq, especially over civilian casualties (*BBC News Online* 2003). When Dick Cheney immediately and repeatedly spoke of the need for war against '40 or 50 countries' after September 11, it was only right to feel anxious (quoted in Ahmad 2003: 16). This was a shift, in the words of the philosopher Leopoldo Zea (2001), from 'la Guerra fría a la sucia' (from the Cold War to the Dirty War). Two years later, after Cheney encouraged the unsubstantiated belief among the US public that Iraq was behind the World Trade Center's destruction, even Bush minor felt obliged to correct this lie immediately. There was no attempt by the mainstream media to publicize this to the 70 per cent of the population that had believed the original canard – Bush's admission was not deemed newsworthy. Of the country's twelve largest-circulation daily papers, only the *Los Angeles Times*, the *Chicago Tribune*, and the *Dallas Morning News* mentioned it on their front pages. The *New York Times* ran it on page 22, *USA Today* on page 16, the *Houston Chronicle* on page 3, the *San Francisco Chronicle* and the *New York Daily News* on page 14, the *Washington Post* on page 18, and *Newsday* on page 41. Republican-Party house organs the *New York Post* and the *Wall Street Journal* did not mention the revelation at all (Porges 2003). No wonder that the empirically-challenged US population held firm to the fantasy that the invasion of Iraq had demonstrated to the world that the US was 'trustworthy and supportive of democracy' (Pew Research Center for the People & the Press 2004b: 2). With the bellicose tone of Bush minor's second inauguration ringing across the world, the *South China Morning Post* was just one of many sources querying the absence of any critical interrogation by the US media of the government's apparent next obsession, Iranian nuclearity (Dyer 2005). This lack of insight is a direct result of the policies and proclivities of the US state and media – peas in a pod, harvested by ideologues and corporations. In the service of the nation, mainstream journalism has become a baying scourge of the truth.

2 Al Qaeda and the struggle for moderate Islam in Malaysia

Benjamin Cole

Introduction

Malaysia today remains largely free of terrorism and other forms of political violence. It has experienced sporadic terrorist violence in the past, but none posed a significant threat to the stability of the government or society. It has also experienced periodic bouts of inter-communal violence between Malays and Chinese in 1969, and Malays and Indians in 2001, but these have remained isolated incidents. Nevertheless, Malaysia is geo-strategically sandwiched between sub-state conflicts in southern Thailand, the Philippines and Indonesia, and there exists a latent threat of these conflicts spilling over into Malaysia itself.

The principal militant group operating in Malaysia is the Kumpulan Militan Malaysia (KMM). This group has been blamed for a number of violent acts including an arms robbery at a police station, the murder of a state assembly member, and the bombing of a number of churches and temples. It was also allegedly planning to target a US warship prior to 9/11. The KMM was founded in 1995, and has significant cross membership with Jemaah Islamiyah (JI), the regional arm of al Qaeda, ensuring close links between the two groups. In 2002 it was estimated that some 45 of its estimated 68 members had been trained in al Qaeda camps in Afghanistan. Between December 2001 and January 2002, 47 KMM suspects were detained by the government under the Internal Security Act (ISA) (Gunaratna 2003: 197).

Malaysia has also been identified as a focal point for al Qaeda activity across Southeast Asia. JI uses Malaysia as its operational base, or regional shura, which handles training and operational planning, and has also coordinated its support and operational activities with the KMM (Gunaratna 2003: 192–193). In 2002, when the Police arrested a militant cell, one of those arrested had played host to two of the 9/11 hijackers on different occasions, as well as to the suspected mastermind of the bombing of the USS Cole in Yemen, in 2000 (Gunaratna 2003: 196). The KMM and JI share the objective of establishing a pan-Islamic state in Southeast Asia incorporating Malaysia, Indonesia, Singapore and parts of southern Thailand and the Philippines. As a result, the US has placed both the KMM and JI on its list of foreign terrorist organizations, drawing them into the 'war on terror'.

The nature of the Malaysian media has a profound effect on the nature of the information flows between these militants, the government, and society. Malaysia has a well developed national media network (CIA 2005) but also has some of the toughest censorship laws in the world. The Paris-based Reporters Without Borders rated Malaysia number 122 out of 167 states in its 2004 worldwide index of press freedom (Reporters Without Borders 2004). Under the Printing Presses and Publications Act, the Home Ministry is responsible for licensing newspapers. This enables the home minister to impose restrictions on the media such as suspending or revoking publishing permits, in the name of national security. As a result, the mainstream media largely functions as an agent of stability in Malaysia.

Government controls are evident both in the frequency with which government press releases and speeches are reported, the high prominence that they are accorded, and also in the restrictions which are imposed on the opposition media. One of the most high profile targets has been *Harakah Daily*, the newspaper of the mainstream Islamist political party, Parti Islam si Malaysia (PAS), which is the only major Malay and English language media forum for opposition views, and which had a circulation rivalling that of mainstream newspapers. It has been warned by senior government leaders not to print 'slanderous' remarks and to limit its distribution to PAS party members only. As a result, the newspaper is generally no longer sold openly. In March 2000, the government went even further by stipulating that *Harakah Daily* could publish only twice a month instead of twice a week (United States Embassy Stockholm 2002). *Harakah Daily* was fortunate in many respects, because some other publications have not had their licenses renewed at all. This government control is so pervasive that it encourages a high level of self censorship among the mainstream media.

The printed media that is most critical of the government are illegal publications, including newsletters and magazines which lack publishing permits. There are also several other opposition newsletters which are published and distributed without government permission (United States Embassy Stockholm 2002). However the circulation of these products must be fairly limited given that they cannot be sold openly.

National media sources are also available online, and it is on the internet that the most independent reporting is to be found. In addition, internet access to international media sources gives Malaysians access to a wider range of perspectives. As well as these mainstream sources there are also websites supporting a range of different ideologies and causes. Websites supporting the Palestinian and Chechen causes are easily accessible and often have links to Malaysian media sites. This gives Malaysians access to more varied, if one-sided, reporting, although such sites are largely only available in English or Arabic.

The government had previously promised not to censor the Internet, but Internet Service Providers (ISPs) still require a licence from the Public Communications and Multimedia Commission, which can be used as a control mechanism. This greater freedom to report on the internet has prompted increasing government concern, resulting in increased restrictions on internet reporting. The offices of the online newspaper *Malaysiakini* have previously been raided by the police, and the Government has monitored 'every article' it published in order to ensure that its writings did not 'upset public order' (United States Embassy Stockholm 2002). *Harakah Daily*'s internet edition has also been restricted to the same twice monthly frequency of publication as the printed version (*Asia Times Online* 2000).

Despite its attempts to control internet media sources, it was not until 2004 that the government acted to shut down radical Islamist websites being hosted on Malaysian ISPs. The catalyst was the discovery of a site containing video footage of a US citizen being de-capitated in Iraq. It was subsequently discovered that the Malaysian web hosting company also provided space for other sites linked to al Qaeda, Hamas and the Chechen independence movement. The government now claims that it will not allow any web page or company that operates on behalf of terrorists. Malaysia's cyber laws state that they are not designed to censor but do allow for action against sites that are indecent, obscene, and incite hatred or launch personal attacks against individuals (*BBC News Online* 2004d).

The effects of these media controls are compounded by deficiencies in media practice. In particular, there is lack of analysis when reporting on official state-ments about the extent of the terror network in Southeast Asia. The mainstream media seem content to accept at face value what the authorities, or those claiming to be terrorism experts, tell them, when there is little hard evidence to back up those claims (*Asia Times Online* 2002b).

The KMM–Media relationship

The relationship between the KMM and the Malaysian media does not reflect a typical media terrorist relationship. To start with, the mainstream media typically labels the KMM as a 'militant' or an 'extremist' group, rather than a 'terrorist' group. These labels are not defined, but the media implicitly links the KMM with terrorism in numerous articles that highlight it's links with JI and al Qaeda, which are defined as terrorist groups.

The KMM is also not currently engaged in a campaign of violence within Malaysia and so is not using violence as a means of gaining access to the media. Neither does it release communiques through the media as bin Laden has done through al Jazeera. Neither is there any indication that the KMM operates a web-site. The overall result is that the KMM is failing to use the media to publicize its militant Islamist ideology and objectives.

There are occasional reports in the media warning of possible KMM and JI attacks within Malaysia (*Malay Mail* 2003b) and even a report that some members of the KMM were willing to become suicide bombers (*Malay Mail* 2002e). And there have also been reports linking the KMM to a number of crimes over the years, even though KMM complicity in these crimes remains unproven. In 2004 a *New Straits Times* article linked the KMM to a number of murders and robberies and claimed that KMM members had became an 'anonymous conveyor belt of violence against non-believers'. In response, *Harakah Daily* published a rebuttal by Gerakan Mansuhkan ISA (GMI), a movement that is working to abolish the ISA, which reminded readers that the KMM had not been proven to be responsible for any of the mentioned crimes (*Harakah Daily* 2004b). The emphasis in this reporting is also that this violence, and potential violence, is directed at overthrowing the Malaysian government, thereby distancing it from bin Laden's war against the US. This report-ing helps to maintain the public perception that the KMM is committed to violence, and remains a potential threat, although the level of this reporting is not so great as to intimidate public opinion or to give the impression that the government does not have the situation under control. It also works to distance militant activity within Malaysia from the wider 'war on terror', contrary to US perceptions.

The government is able to manage the majority of the communication flows through the mainstream media, and the KMM is not being proactive in trying to set the media agenda or its media outputs. It is possible that the KMM has been so damaged by the arrest of many of its members that it chooses not to communicate through the mainstream media at this time, and it certainly has no leader with a public profile, or a political wing, to speak for it. It seems to be avoiding public attention in order to be left in the shadows to rebuild its strength – which would be hindered by a high media profile and the likely government backlash that it would provoke.

When the media reports on the KMM it is predominantly to report police manhunts or the arrest and detention of KMM members. In the *Malay Mail* this reporting is primarily factual in nature, with little analysis. There is some mention of the KMM objective to create an Islamic nation called 'Darul Islam' in Southeast Asia through a holy war, but such reports are rare, or tend to downplay the issue. One article in *Malaysiakini* for instance, argued that the pan Islamist vision for Southeast Asia has crumbled during the course of the 'war on terror' (*Malaysiakini* 2003c).

There is little reporting of why the KMM exists or why some Malaysians have joined militant groups. The few stories that have reported the motivations of individual militants, identify international issues rather than domestic issues. In 2002 it was reported that two KMM members, who had been arrested, had undergone military training in Afghanistan because they wanted to help their Muslim comrades in Ambon (a region of Indonesia) and the Philippines (*New Straits Times* 2002d). Similarly, a Colonel in the Malaysian Airforce became involved with JI because of his experiences in Bosnia (*Malay Mail* 2003c). It was also reported that three Indonesian preachers had been identified as being responsible for religious and militant indoctrination within the KMM (*Harakah Daily* 2004a). This fits with the general government line, as publicized by the mainstream media, that the KMM originated from 'influences brought into the country by foreigners' (*New Straits Times* 2002c). Overall, the KMM receives a significant amount of media exposure, but it shows the KMM to be weak and on the defensive (*Malay Mail* 2002a, 2003a,f).

Rather than generating their own communications through the media, the KMM relies instead on the communication flows from conflicts in other states to achieve its purposes. The majority of the reporting of sub-state violence is of conflicts in other countries, particularly Indonesia and the Philippines. Events such as 9/11, and JI bombings in Indonesia are widely reported, but the coverage is largely factual with little analysis.

The role of Malaysian citizens within JI is widely reported by the media, and statements made by JI suspects in Indonesian custody justifying militant and terrorist activities are reported. This has included a number of statements made by Abu Bakar Ba'asyir, the alleged spiritual head of JI, which have included comments that the Bali bombers were misguided but praiseworthy, that attacking US government targets in Indonesia was acceptable, and accusing the US, Christians and Jews of destroying Islam (*Malay Mail* 2003i,e). Similarly, all of Osama bin

Laden's messages that are released through al Jazeera are reported at length in the mainstream Malaysian media. In highlighting the links between the KMM, JI and al Qaeda (*Malay Mail* 2002c,d,f), the media explicitly identifies Malaysians as a target audience for bin Laden's and Ba'asyir's messages. Despite this, there is little analysis of what threat this might pose to Malaysian security.

The most extensive report of the role of Malaysians in JI came in 2004 when TV-3 broadcast an interview with four Malaysian JI members who were being held in Indonesian custody. The interview was also widely reported throughout the mainstream print media. The four explained that killing Americans, robbing financial institutions, and creating an Islamic nation through violence were objectives of JI. They cited a 'fatwa' issued by bin Laden, which stated that all Muslims should take revenge on Americans:

> This is because the Americans have victimised or have killed civilians everywhere, and so we can reciprocate by killing American civilians anywhere, irrespective of whether or not they are armed, whether they are soldiers or civilians, women, men or children.

The impact of publicizing this message was negated by the fact that all four expressed remorse and asked forgiveness from society for their involvement in JI. They stated that JI had deviated from true Islamic teachings and called on their colleagues to leave the group and return to the true path (*Bernama* 2004). It is an interesting question as to whether this interview would have been broadcast if the four had not recanted in this way.

Some elements of the media however, have tried to play down the links between JI and al Qaeda. Of the four Malaysian members of JI who were interviewed by TV-3 in April 2004 the *New Straits Times* indicated that only one of them had been an Afghan war veteran and that the others had no direct affiliation or contact with al Qaeda but rather had been influenced by bin Laden's messages (*New Straits Times* 2004).

The direct significance of the media for recruitment to the KMM and JI is probably quite limited. For militant groups that operate within Muslim communities, religious schools and Mosques are traditional places for recruiting and indoctrinating militants. Much of the networks of Indonesian terrorists are linked to pesantren (religious schools), which indoctrinate their students in militancy. The pesantren are akin to Malaysia's sekolah pondok, which are communal settlements where students live together and pursue religious education. Abu Bakar Ba'asyir, the alleged spiritual leader of JI, and Hambali, the alleged former operations chief of JI, are both known to have participated in the union between pesantren and sekolah pondok (*New Straits Times* 2003c).

The role of educational establishments was confirmed by the TV-3 interview in 2004, in which the four suspects indicated that recruitment was made directly through Madrassas and Universities. The government has now shut down the al-Tarbiyyah al-Islamiyaah Luqmanul Hakiem madrassa in Johor, which was identified as being run by JI and the KMM, and several of the teachers were detained. Similarly, the KMM presence at various universities was severely damaged by a police clamp down in 2002 (*Malay Mail* 2002b, 2003d).

Organizations affiliated to al Qaeda are also known for recruiting relatives of existing members, and the KMM/JI are no exception. In 2003 thirteen Malaysian students who had been studying at madrassas in Pakistan were arrested and accused of being groomed to be future militant leaders. All of them had been students at the al-Tarbiyyah al-Islamiyaah Luqmanul Hakiem madrassa in Johor, and the fathers of four of them were already in detention in Malaysia (*New Straits Times* 2003g).

Overall, the direct role of the media in facilitating communication between the KMM, its constituency and Malaysian society is questionable. In a sense though, it does not matter what the media reports since the KMM and JI are not mass movements but rather small, close knit clandestine organizations that can survive with a very small support base. Instead, the media is possibly more significant through its potential ability to infect the wider population with militant ideologies or militant perspectives on specific issues, which KMM or JI recruiters can potentially exploit.

Reporting the underlying causes of militant violence

At one level the mainstream media can potentially infect public opinion with militant attitudes through its reporting of the domestic and international causes that militant groups such as al Qaeda and JI champion. This makes Malaysian public opinion one of the target audiences of both the communication flows that have been established by Muslim non-state combatants and the media in other countries, and also for US messages in its 'war on terror'.

This reporting largely falls into two broad categories: stories about the 'war on terror' and stories about the 'oppression' of Muslims by non-Muslims in other states. The plight of Muslim civilians in countries such as Afghanistan, Iraq, the occupied Palestinian territories and Chechnya acts as a catalyst for small numbers of Muslims from all over the world to join or support militant groups. It enables militant recruiters to exploit the sympathies generated by news coverage of these issues in the mainstream media to encourage Muslims to join militant groups.

The reporting of these conflicts in the Malaysian media is extensive and has a heavy anti-US and anti-western bias. There is considerable negative reporting of the motives and policies of the west, Russia, Israel and Australia in the 'war on terror'. Prominent attention is given to the civilian casualties of these conflicts. There is widespread popular support for the Muslim populations of those countries within Malaysia, and the risk is that this reporting might encourage some Malaysians to join militant groups and become directly involved in those conflicts.

A key element of this reporting is the suggestion of a causal link between US policy and terrorism, The *New Straits Times* has argued that

> Yet some suggest that acts of terror against the US, its allies and their interests are to retaliate for what Washington has done to Muslims, especially in the Middle East. Western forces have not dealt with terrorism any better than the terrorists they hunt. The war on Iraq was justified with lies and embellishments,

causing those who feared terrorism to wonder if Washington and London were actually perpetuating terrorism. At the same time, quite a number of Malaysian Muslims sympathise with Islamist movements as they feel that their Muslim brothers have been suppressed and victimised by their Governments. To make matters worse, while some freedom fighters and separatists are true to their ideals and struggles, there exists in their movements those who believe that terror is the way to achieve their objectives. Then, there are the infiltrators who use these groups as vehicles for terrorism. Sympathy for the JI abounds. Some believe that JI, like other Islamic-based movements, is a victim of a conspiracy by the US and other foreign nations to wipe out believers of the faith. Washington's behaviour and manner in its war against terror, has convinced most of these Muslims of their suspicions of a conspiracy. This has created a siege mentality in Muslims throughout the world, Malaysians included. For as long as Muslims feel they are under siege, the birth of individuals who resort to terror will prevail.

(*New Straits Times* 2003b)

The suggestion of a causal relationship between terrorism and the actions of governments is also examined by the internet journalist M.G.G. Pillai who writes columns for *Harakah Daily* and *Malaysiakini*. He suggests that, 'For when the United States has no compunction to killing innocent men, women and children in its military adventures; so why should terrorists and others fighting back bother killing Western men, women and children?' (Pillai 2002b). Whilst not necessarily condoning terrorism itself, this reporting is essentially condoning its justifications.

The Malaysian government is in a difficult position because it opposed the extension of the 'war on terror' into Iraq and supports the Palestinian and Chechen causes, yet it needs to keep radical attitudes within the population in check. Consequently the government communicates its support for these causes through the media and in doing so puts itself forward as a champion of oppressed Muslim communities.

A recurrent theme in government speeches is that Islam is being attacked and is on the defensive. In a speech in Damascus in 2003, former Prime Minister, Mahatir argued that

In the wake of the Sept 11 attacks on the US, Islam is perceived as a religion that promotes acts of terror. The Muslims are weak and divided and are being discriminated against in the West. Islamic countries were invaded on the pretext of either harbouring terrorists, or on mere suspicion of possessing weapons of mass destruction. Several more Islamic countries are now being threatened or targeted for regime change. It is unfortunate that in the unipolar world we live in today, there exists a trend for the law of the jungle, where might is right, to be applied in resolving international disputes. Weak and least developed nations, many of them Islamic nations, are vulnerable and could become easy prey for invasion and colonisation. The events of Sept 11, which triggered the war on terrorism followed by the invasion of Afghanistan and Iraq, should serve as a loud wake-up call for us Muslims.

(*New Straits Times* 2003d)

ᴊᵢₘilar messages can also be found throughout the independent and opposition media, where they are frequently given an anti-government spin. Among the mainstream media *Harakah Daily* is the most outspoken. Taking one example from 2004, in reporting the killing of Muslim separatists in Southern Thailand, it argued that:

> The Malaysian Government equally stand condemned for turning a blind eye, indeed for endorsing the licence for the Thai Government to conduct the massacre against the Muslims in southern Thailand. Such a stand from a brother Muslim nation is nothing short of blasphemy. The problems surrounding the Muslim populations in southern Thailand suffering from ill treatment, mistreatment and neglect by the Thai Government is a longstanding one.
>
> (*Harakah Daily* 2004c)

Since 11 September 2001, M.G.G. Pillai has produced a string of articles about the 'war on terror' which challenge both the war itself and Malaysia's role within it. Some of the core themes in his articles are that the war is a Christian crusade, that it is a war against Islam, and that thousands of Muslims are being killed as a result of it (*Harakah Daily* 2001, 2002, Pillai 2001a,b, 2002a,c,d, 2003). Pillai questions even the most fundamental elements of the war by denying that it was Muslims who were responsible for 9/11 (Pillai 2002b). In a similar vein, he suggests a number of alternative culprits for the Bali bombing, including the CIA, Indonesian nationalists, the Indonesian armed forces or the combatants engaged in religious conflicts inside Indonesia (Pillai 2002b). These arguments tie into Pillai's central allegation that Islam is the target of the 'war on terror', having replaced communism as the target of the day (Pillai 2002c).

In some respects the nature and tone of some of this reporting resonates with the rhetoric of al Qaeda and JI. The risk is that it will contribute to a radicalization of Malaysian society, by highlighting the links between the actions of al Qaeda and these causes. But despite reporting the linkages between the KMM, JI and al Qaeda, the Malaysian media does not explicitly link JI and the KMM, or events in Malaysia, to the 'war on terror'. In fact, the media displays a certain sensitivity about Malaysia being linked to the 'war'. When links were uncovered between Malaysian citizens, the 9/11 hijackers and the letters containing anthrax which were posted in the US following 9/11, one headline in the *News Straits Times* proclaimed, 'Is Malaysia Being Blamed for the Sept 11 Attack?', even though it patently was not.

The implicit message in the media is that militancy within Malaysia is a national and regional problem, not a global one. As a result, US messages in the 'war on terror' are not considered to be relevant to defeating militancy within Malaysia. Consequently, US messages justifying and explaining the policies of the 'war on terror' are not reported. There is some reporting of statements made by President Bush, but they are generally qualified. Following the Bali bombing in 2002, comments made by Bush in Indonesia that 'Islamic terrorists' defiled one of the world's great faiths were reported, but their impact was immediately undermined by additional reporting of how Bush had alienated leading moderate Indonesian clerics (*Malay Mail* 2003g). As a result, the US has failed to win the 'battle of ideas' in the Malaysian media, but considering the extent to which the 'war on terror' has been discredited within Malaysia, it would be positively detrimental for Malaysian counter-terrorism efforts to be linked to the 'war'.

Debating Islamist Ideology

There is also the risk that the media might infect increasing numbers of the Malaysian population with militant ideologies. But despite reporting al Qaeda and JI messages, there is little reporting of the underlying Islamist ideology of JI and the KMM in the mainstream media. However the media does report on PAS, the non-violent mainstream Islamist political party. In general terms, the stricter more traditional interpretation of Islam that is typically defined as 'Islamism' is closer to the ideology of militant Islamic groups than the modern, more relaxed interpretation of Islam that underpins government policy in Malaysia. PAS, though, has gone to great lengths to try and distance itself from the image of religious extremism.

PAS achieved considerable success in the 1999 election when it won approximately 60 per cent of Malay Muslim votes, together with political control of the two northern states of Kelantan and Terengganu. There are no formal institutional links between PAS and the KMM or JI, although some members of PAS have been detained for allegedly being members of the KMM. The central policy of the PAS political agenda is the creation of an 'Islamic' state, a form of which is also an objective of the KMM and JI. Since PAS is part of the democratic political opposition, debate on a form of Islamism is part of the mainstream political discourse in the Malaysian media.

PAS argues that western-style democracy has led to 'endemic social decadences and rampant injustices' and that the common law system is un-Islamic. The 'Islamic State Document' which was produced by PAS in 2003 stated that it would implement Sharia law to achieve the five imperatives of the Sharia: to protect a Muslim's beliefs, life, intellect, dignity and property. In seeking to fulfil these five imperatives, the document stated that 'all vices and crimes that pertain to the above stated aspects would be controlled. Man-made laws have been [proved] a failure in securing the security and dignity of the human race'. Such a move would put the clerics in a powerful position in the judicial system as the sole interpreters of the Koran (*Far Eastern Economic Review* 2003).

PAS was only prevented from introducing Sharia law in Kelantan and Terenganu by the intervention of the central government. Measures which it did introduce, however, were the banning of gambling, dancing and public consumption of alcohol by non-Muslims, whilst men and women had to use separate checkouts at supermarkets (*BBC News Online* 2003e).

The potential synergies between political Islamism and the Islamist ideology of militant groups means that the political dimension of Malaysia's counter-terrorism strategy blends with the government's broader political strategy to undermine popular support for PAS. As part of this struggle, the government has used the media to publicize government initiatives in a positive light and to engage in a battle of ideas with the Islamists.

The central thrust of government policy is to co-opt Islam and 'out-Islam' PAS. It has built mosques, social and educational facilities, and other infrastructure, especially in rural areas, and has initiated a host of initiatives including financial support for pilgrimages to Mecca, as well as setting up an Islamic bank and an International Islamic university. Former Prime Minister Mahatir also led Malaysia to play a leading role in the Organization of Islamic Co-operation. This approach to fighting PAS also forms the foundation for the political dimension of the fight against the KMM.

The government also uses the media to control the theological debate by claiming that the use of Islam for political ends often results in the deliberate misinterpretation of Islam to support political agendas. It attempts to educate the population about what it argues are the 'true values' of Islam. Its basic message is to emphasize the Islamic credentials of the government by arguing that the government is following a fundamentalist form of Islam and is leading a return to the true teachings of Islam. This definition of Islamic fundamentalism is opposed to militancy and the Islamists' rejection of modernization (*New Straits Times* 2003b).

The government has also highlighted cases of militancy in the hope of frightening voters away from PAS (Abdoolcarim and Mitton 2001). The media has at times aided this process by attempting to link PAS to militant violence. In 2003, television stations ran footage of a bloody clash between police and villagers in the late 1980s in an attempt to portray PAS as being prone to extremist tendencies (*Asia Times Online* 2002a), and stories also circulated that the leader of PAS had attended a meeting with militant leaders in Indonesia in 2000 (*New Straits Times* 2003c).

Government control of the media means that it has a significant advantage in publicizing these messages but its control is not all pervasive. Opposition and independent media sources do challenge the Islamic and fundamentalist credentials of the government. However, government controls mean that these stories are outnumbered by pro-government stories.

Analysis of media coverage proves that the government receives significantly more coverage than the opposition, the majority of which is positive in nature. Yet the impact is perhaps not as great as it could be because the mainstream media has a declining level of credibility with the public. Analysis has shown that in 2000 Malays believed less in the mainstream media than they did in 1990 (Oorjitham 2000), and in March 2004, a survey found that only 56 per cent of Malaysians believed news obtained from the media (*The Straits Times Interactive* 2004).

The other risk factor for infecting popular opinion with militant ideologies is the internet. Militant websites offer Malaysians direct access to these ideologies together with opportunities for communicating with individuals who share similar views. As noted previously, Malaysian ISPs are known to have hosted militant websites. The numbers of such sites is unknown, but it is in any case possible to access a whole variety of international militant sites, assuming that language barriers can be overcome.

The impact of the internet should not be overstated, however, since cyberspace is more than just a forum for militants to propagate their messages. Ordinary Malaysians also post messages on websites and message boards expressing concern about what life in an Islamist state would be like, rejecting radical Islamism and stressing the non-violent aspects of Islam (*Malaysiakini* 2003a). A survey in

2004 found that 85 per cent of respondents did not rely on the Internet for political news and 87 per cent did not believe information obtained from the Internet (*The Straits Times Interactive* 2004).

In the 2004 elections PAS was soundly defeated by the government, losing 20 of its 27 seats in parliament, as well as power in the state of Terengannu. The reasons lay primarily in a shift of popular support in favour of the government's progressive approach to creating a Muslim state. Many women and young people in particular, voted against PAS edicts banning rock concerts, encouraging modest dress and separating the sexes in supermarkets and on beaches. The efforts of the new Prime Minister Abdullah Badawi to distance the government from the excesses of the Mahatir years also undercut the PAS claim to be the anti-corruption party. But underlying the result were accusations of electoral malpractice and a system that is biased against the opposition (*The Economist* 2004: 72).

The political debate on Islamism provides a democratic outlet for popular discontent and potential radicalism. PAS, itself, has also been careful not to whip up extremist sentiments in its criticisms of the government and the 'war on terror'. The danger, however, is that the inherent bias in the institutions of the state could encourage the growth of militancy if it is believed that PAS is being prevented from gaining power by democratic means. Such a development, however, seems unlikely. The results of the 2004 elections indicate that the population at large has not been increasingly radicalized. What is less clear, however, is the extent to which PAS' rump support has been radicalized or could be in the future.

Defining militancy

An important feature of the government's strategy for de-legitimizing militant groups is its use of the media to label and define 'terrorism'. The central tenet of this definition is that killing of innocent civilians is an act of terror but in some cases there are mitigating circumstances. Working together, the government and the media publicize this definition to create stereotypes and images which frame the public consciousness and debate.

Former Prime Minister Mahatir made a keynote speech on this subject in Damascus in August 2003, which was reported in full by the *New Straits Times*. He stated that:

> We are angry and very frustrated now, people are oppressing us but we cannot do anything against them. But to kill people who are innocent because of our anger is not right. At least to me, I don't think it is right. To kill people, not even the person who hit us, is wrong. We must admit that it is wrong. And we should avoid it if we can. If we have other means, we should resort to other means.
>
> (*New Straits Times* 2003f)

Yet Mahatir did not use the term 'terrorist' in absolutist terms. He argued that in some instances, such as communities fighting for independence, there are mitigating circumstances for the use of violence if those people have no other choice. This links the definition of terrorism, and, therefore the legitimacy of using violence, to the perceived validity of the causes that the combatants are fighting for, which is an inherently subjective judgement. He argued that

> We do not want the independence fighters to be called terrorists. But we have to accept the fact that certain acts like killing civilians who have nothing to do with their fight, are acts of terror but there are mitigating circumstances. The Israeli Government can avoid committing acts of terror because they have the means, they don't have to carry out acts of terror. The Palestinians, they have no aeroplanes, no tanks, no nothing; the only way they can fight back is the way they fight back. They may carry out suicide bombings. If they act against civilians and not soldiers, it is still acts of terror but it is mitigated; it is because they have no choice. If they have a choice, I'm sure they would not do this.
>
> (*New Straits Times* 2003f)

In this way the government and the media attempt to control the use of the terminology by determining what is a legitimate cause and selectively using the label 'terrorist' to try to de-legitimise some conflicts, whilst preserving the legitimacy of others. Significantly, the concept of 'terrorism' is also broadened out to include state terrorism. Mahatir argued that

> The Israeli government, however, has no excuse as they have other means to defend themselves and need not carry out acts of terror. The Israeli government has a choice, the Americans have a choice not to terrorise people by bombing civilians, hospitals etc. But they do that, so that is an act of terror that cannot be excused.
>
> (*New Straits Times* 2003f)

The labelling of the actions of states – particularly Israeli military operations in the occupied territories and US operations in the 'war on terror', as terrorism, is a recurrent theme in government speeches that are reported in the media.

The dominance of these definitions was confirmed in September 2003, when Abdul Hadi Awang, the leader of PAS condemned JI bombings in Indonesia. Yet he went on to declare that they support Hamas, on the grounds that they are being oppressed, and described Israel as being 'terrorist and criminal'. He also hailed Palestinian suicide bombers as Martyrs (*BBC News Online* 2003c).

Broadly speaking the KMM, JI and al Qaeda are not defined as 'Islamic' or 'Islamist' terrorists. Islam does not permit terrorism, so terrorism perpetrated by Muslims is not of its nature, Islamic. Since 9/11 the majority of mainstream media articles specifically de-link Islam from terrorist acts (*Malaysiakini* 2003b). As a consequence there is no differentiation between 'religious' and 'secular' terrorism. Instead, all terrorism is implicitly identified as being political in nature, because its objectives are to achieve political goals such as overthrowing existing governments.

Yet the Malaysian media is not wholly consistent in the use of terminology; articles in the *Malay Mail* for instance, have on occasion used the term 'Islamic terrorist'. More commonly used labels for the KMM and JI are 'Islamic militant' or 'Islamic extremist' or 'Islamic radical'. These labels implicitly suggest that the activities of the KMM and JI have a theological basis but are not terrorist activities.

This lack of consistency within the media conveys conflicting messages. The de-linking of Islam and terrorism is important as a key element in denying the militants theological legitimacy. To explicitly confirm that terrorist acts have a theological underpinning would confer some form of theological legitimacy, which could undermine one of the cornerstones of the government's counter-terrorism policy. Yet the linking of Islam with militant activity in some of the other terminology specifically confirms that militant activity has a theological underpinning. Therefore the various labels attached to the KMM and JI can be argued to both legitimize and de-legitimize the two groups.

Reporting the government message

In order to counteract the potential negative effects of publicizing the causes which militants groups champion, the government uses the mainstream media to communicate its counter-terror messages to both public opinion and the militants. Its counter-terrorism policy focuses on addressing the root causes of violence in order to win the hearts and minds of the militants and their potential supporters (Mahathir 2002). To achieve this, the government uses the media to publicize four key policies that are designed to prevent the radicalization of the population.

The first is to challenge the objectives of the militants. Just as there is not much reporting of militant objectives, neither is there a significant amount of overt government rejection of them, but it is nevertheless an aspect of the government media strategy. Taking one example from 2002, *Bernama* reported a speech by Mahatir in which he argued that people resorting to terrorism to create an Islamic state in Malaysia did not understand the meaning of Islamic nationhood, since Malaysia is already being administered by people of their own race and religion. Instead, he urged would-be terrorists to go and fight in those countries where Muslims were being oppressed. He concluded that using terrorism to gain power would weaken the country and pave the way for Malaysia to be controlled by foreigners (*Bernama* 2002b).

The second policy involves the government portraying itself as a champion of oppressed Muslims across the world in order co-opt those causes from the militant agenda. This was reflected in government opposition to the war in Iraq and support for the Palestinians. In 2003 Deputy Prime Minister Abdullah warned the international community of the adverse consequences if they failed to tackle three main areas of Muslim concern: the Iraq issue, the Palestinian–Israeli conflict and terrorism (*Asia Times Online* 2003).

This helps to establish the legitimacy of the government as a protector of Muslim rights and undercuts the support which militant groups might receive on these issues. Mahatir argued that

> The situation in the Middle East remains of great concern to all of us. At the root of this is the Palestinian-Israeli conflict. Venting our anger by simply killing people as is done by both sides will solve nothing. We need to know our strengths and strategise so that every sacrifice will contribute towards our ultimate success. The US-engineered road map for solving the Palestinian problem would have had a better chance of success if Iraq had not been invaded. As it is, there is now an Iraqi insurgency in addition to the Palestinian problem. And terrorism still threatens the world.
>
> (*New Straits Times* 2003d)

The third policy is the rejection of violence as a means of redressing the problems facing Islam. This is pursued at a theological level by publicizing the peaceful aspects of Islam and the damage that is being done by its violent image in the wider world. The following statements give a flavour of the sort of messages that are regularly repeated: 'The fundamental of Islamic teaching is peace, moderation, honesty, integrity and being friendly to others' (*Bernama* 2003a); 'there are groups of Muslims who have hijacked Islam and its teachings to support terrorism activities'; and 'We cannot accept Islamic extremism even if it is based on Islam because it is not the teachings of Islam' (*Bernama* 2003b).

The fourth and final element of the strategy is the presentation of an alternative vision for confronting the perceived threats to Islam that focuses on modernization and unity within the Muslim world and Malaysia itself. In presenting this vision the government co-opts the rhetoric of the Islamists – for example in terms of 'defending the faith', 'restoring honour and respect for Islam', and restoring 'the past glory of the Islamic civilisation' (*Bernama* 2003a,b). Mahatir made this one of the driving forces of Malaysian foreign policy. He argued that

> We can no longer stay disunited if we do not want to fall one by one. Muslims must acquire information, knowledge and technology and keep abreast with developments in the Western world. Malaysia strongly believes that with financial wealth and natural resources at our disposal, Muslim countries can become strong if we manage our internal affairs well.
>
> (*New Straits Times* 2003d)

The government's vision for a peaceful and prosperous future is also heavily based on maintaining national unity within Malaysia itself (*Bernama* 2002a). Developments which threaten this harmony are strongly criticized. For example, the letters section of *The Sun*, which is the largest Chinese daily newspaper, carried a letter which argued strongly against voting for PAS during the 2004 elections because of the perceived threat which the introduction of Sharia law posed to national harmony (*The Sun* 2004). Whilst the Chinese and Indian communities readily buy into this vision, the problem for the government lies with impoverished Muslims in rural communities who have not shared in the prosperity of the rest of the country.

These messages are regularly repeated in speeches by government ministers, which are reported through the national news agency *Bernama* and subsequently covered in the mainstream media with little or no direct criticism or analysis. For instance, the Daily Express prints the verbatim text of *Bernama* reports on terrorism related issues.

Reporting counter-terrorism policy

A further element of the propaganda battle between the KMM and the government is the reporting of the government's security policies. The media is full of positive stories about the success of the Malaysian security forces in arresting suspected militants and Malaysia's cooperation with other Southeast Asian states on counter-terrorism. Again, this serves to create the impression of a government that is in control of events and of a militant movement that is weak and on the defensive. Yet this reporting does not paint all government counter-terrorism policies in such a positive light.

The main issue is the government's use of the ISA to detain militant suspects indefinitely without trial. Some detainees have links to militant groups but others are prominent members of the political opposition (*The Economist* 2002). As a result, it is believed in some quarters that the ISA has been used as an instrument of political repression (Abdoolcarim and Mitton 2001). The most prominent detainee is Nik Adili Nik Aziz, the son of the PAS leader Nik Aziz Nik Mat, who was detained in 2001 after being identified as the leader of the KMM (Suh 2001; Gunaratna 2003: 196).

The independent and opposition media constantly criticizes the government for alleged abuses in its counter-terrorism policy, particularly that it is using the 'war on terror' to isolate what it defines as Islamic fundamentalists in order to stifle political debate and dissent. However, the government and the majority of the media deliberately avoid linking detentions under the ISA with the 'war on terror'. Reporting typically stresses that detentions are made to combat threats to the stability of Malaysia, which is strengthened by the fact that the media does not link militancy within Malaysia to the 'war on terror'. For public opinion, this helps to maintain the legitimacy of the government's use of the ISA. Nevertheless, on this issue, at least some sections of the media can be seen to be acting as an agent of restraint.

The alleged abuse of the ISA is fairly widely debated across the mainstream media. Even *Bernama* has reported PAS opposition to the ISA, including a statement issued by Nik Abdul Aziz Nik Mat that 'The ISA is not correct, from the religious aspect we are not respecting mankind, from the democratic aspect also we are violating basic human rights' (*Bernama* 2003d).

Opposition to the ISA is strongest amongst internet sources which publicize human rights abuses. The Malaysian human rights organization Aliran has documented alleged cases of torture and mistreatment in detention centres, as have other independent media sources. This de-legitmizes the use of the ISA in the eyes of the public and risks generating support for those in custody. These reports however, largely focus on individuals who are not readily identifiable as members of the KMM or JI, and many detainees specifically deny membership of militant groups.

One article published on the Aliran website suggested that

> There is another reason why they don't deny the routine abuses of power under ISA. They want the maltreatment of detainees to deter other people from standing up for their rights as citizens and from being counted among those who openly criticise wrong doings in public and high places. Consequently, the threat of ISA underlies the pervasive culture of fear we all live with. That's how ISA creates Barisan National's 'silenced majority'! The culture of fear is never more obvious than when the ruling politicians feel threatened.
>
> (Ramakrishnan 2001)

These debates tie in to wider public concern about the judiciary, which is widely considered not to be independent. The most high profile example of government control of the judiciary was the gaoling of the former Deputy Prime Minister Anwar Ibrahim in 1998 in what was widely considered to have been a politically motivated trial. Judicial inability to redress perceived abuses is another key aspect in eroding the legitimacy of the existing system of government.

Unsurprisingly, the government uses the media to rebut these allegations. It argues that terrorism is a threat and therefore harsh measures are required to deal with it. Mahatir used *Bernama* to argue that 'those in detention are people not known before as important figures in the opposition party.'. . . 'They do have links to the opposition party. Opposition parties are governed by the law and there is no special privilege for them. We apply the same law on members of government parties also' (*Bernama* 2002b). The justifications for using the ISA are supported by occasional reporting of the release of ISA detainees (*Bernama* 2003c), which reinforces the claim that the ISA is only used to detain genuine militants.

In addition, signs of renewed judicial activism in the twenty-first century, including demands for a review of the ISA, has also helped to mitigate the potentially damaging impact of using the ISA. That the institutions of the state are seen to challenge the perceived abuses of the government is an important element in maintaining popular support for the existing political system. This was undoubtedly aided by the release of Anwar in 2004.

The media debate on the ISA communicates mixed messages to militant groups and their supporters. On the one hand it illustrates that the government will not be intimidated and that it is prepared to suppress militancy, but, on the other hand, it shows that there is some popular opposition to government counter-terror policies that militant groups could try to exploit. Yet despite this, the public generally supports the way the government has dealt with the perceived terror threat.

Conclusion: media impacts

This analysis indicates that the Malaysian people are subject to numerous cross cutting information flows from militants and governments through the mainstream and new media. The impact on community action and the growth of militancy within Malaysia is difficult to assess, but it is important to bear in mind that Malaysia is not a fertile recruiting ground for militant groups because the majority of Malaysian Muslims follow a moderate view of Islam.

There are a number of issues within Malaysia which could potentially contribute to the growth of militancy within Malaysia. This includes government corruption, its control of the media and the judiciary, its unwillingness to let PAS implement sharia law in Kelantan, its use of the ISA, and its alleged abuses of human rights, which are all reported in the mainstream media. Yet these issues are not fostering a growth in militancy.

Instead, it is the reporting of the international causes which JI and al Qaeda champion, which probably has the most potential to promote increased sympathy for militant groups. One of the reasons for the durability of JI is its ability to tap into a general feeling that Southeast Asian Muslims are victims of a larger, anti-Islamic conspiracy led by the US and supported by the UK and Australia (*BBC News Online* 2004c). This perception can only be fuelled by the nature of much of the reporting of the 'war on terror' in the mainstream Malaysian media. Widespread acceptance of such views creates a favourable climate within which militant messages can be propagated.

The impact of the new media is equally uncertain. There is little evidence that access to militant websites (in conjunction with messages in mainstream media) translates into domestic militancy. The mainstream media makes little reference to the role of the new media in promoting militancy. Instead, it focuses on the role of educational establishments, both inside and outside Malaysia, in spreading militant ideologies. The government's clamp down on militant websites in 2004 was driven by the US reaction to Malaysian ISPs hosting militant websites showing a video of a US citizen being beheaded and not for domestic Malaysian reasons. This reflects a lack of official concern about the role of the internet.

The potential threat from the new media could be argued to lie in the risk of it 'infecting' people with sympathy for militant causes and ideologies which militant recruiters can then exploit. Yet there is a strong case to argue that it is the widespread reporting of statements by bin Laden and Abu Bakar Ba'asyir within the mainstream media, which poses more of a risk in terms of infecting people with militant ideas. It is those messages that people encounter in their day to day lives, and they are easily identified with mainstream media reporting of events in Iraq, Chechnya and the occupied Palestinian territories. This suggests that the role of the internet is more as an adjunct to reporting in the mainstream media. The new media enables militants to communicate directly with public opinion, but if they find a receptive audience it is because of the groundwork that has already been done by the mainstream media.

There are number of possible indicators that could be argued to indicate increased levels of sympathy for militant ideologies, including public demonstrations, support for PAS, unstructured political violence, or recruitment to the KMM and JI. Yet there is no discernable upward trend in any of these indicators.

The size of the KMM remains unknown, although a report from 2002 suggested that the police were looking for 200 people who were linked to the group (*New Straits Times* 2002b). Even more uncertain is the extent of the passive and active support that it receives. Small numbers of Malaysians do figure prominently amongst the ranks of JI, and there is occasional reporting of continued recruitment. Yet support for PAS has declined, which indicates that the majority of Malaysians are still adhering to a moderate view of Islam. As in other countries, therefore, there remains a disjunction between popular support for the causes which Islamists fight for and active engagement in militant activity. This indicates that the vast majority of Malaysians are not accepting violent militant ideologies.

Another reason why it is so difficult to assess media impacts on community action is because there are limited opportunities for direct political action in Malaysia. Political gatherings require a police permit which are rarely given to opposition groups, and the police regularly used force to break up demonstrations. In 2003 Prime Minister Badawi committed himself to allowing a wider range of views to be expressed but has been evasive about allowing political meetings and demonstrations (*BBC News Online* 2004a). There is some limited evidence of a link between media reporting and direct action. This included a demonstration organized by PAS outside the US embassy in Kuala Lumpur in October 2001, following media coverage of the US bombing in Afghanistan. Despite concern that the media coverage would radicalize Muslim opinion the demonstration was relatively small. Moderate Muslims continued to reject radicalization and PAS lost support as a result, prompting it to step back slightly from its anti-US position (Abdoolcarim and Mitton 2001).

This suggests that both the old and the new media are having a limited impact in infecting the Malaysian population with militant ideologies. The mainstream media acts as an agent of stability by reflecting and re-enforcing the views of both the government and mainstream public opinion. The media is not, however, totally an instrument of the government, and sections of the media do attempt to perform a limited role as an agent of restraint in challenging the government, although there is little evidence of it having any impact. Instead, this limited criticism of the government coupled with government messages serves to reassure public opinion that its concerns about oppressed Muslims and the US 'war on terror' are being addressed. At a more general level, some militant causes and objectives have been assimilated into the mainstream political debate. Whilst this generates broad sympathy throughout Malaysian society it has not fostered a causal link to militancy.

3 Perning in the Gyre

Indonesia, the globalised media and the 'war on terror'

Jonathan Woodier

Introduction

The chaos of competing interests left by the collapse of the Suharto regime has made Indonesia the most democratic country in Asia, accompanied by the '... blossoming of a free and aggressive local media after decades of suppression under Mr Suharto ... aiding civic activism, such as the fight against corruption' (Mapes 2004: A1). However, efforts to influence, bully and control the mass communication media continue, as powerful local figures refuse to recognise the emergence of a plural industry, and political elites, accustomed to unquestioned power, find it hard to convey their messages in an increasingly complex media environment.

Most recently, the sentencing of Bambang Harymurti, the editor of Tempo, the country's most influential newsmagazine to one year in prison in a libel case has raised serious concerns about press freedom in Southeast Asia's largest nation (Hudiono 2004; *The Jakarta Post* 2004a). Harymurti was found guilty of libelling businessman Tomy Winata in a story that suggested Winata, who has strong ties to the military and the Suharto family, stood to benefit from a mysterious fire that destroyed a Jakarta textile market in 2003. Not only did supporters of Winata attack Tempo's offices, but his lawyers also filed a series of civil and criminal complaints against the magazine. It is 'the vigour' with which government prosecutors have pursued Winata's complaints that has worried those keen to encourage democratic pluralism in the country (Mapes and Hindryati 2004: A2).

The court's decision had a 'chilling effect on freedom of expression in Indonesia' (*The Jakarta Post* 2004a). The use of libel and defamation laws to silence criticism has become increasingly commonplace, as the country's elites have moved to silence the media genie and place it firmly back in its traditional containment, perceiving court trials as a legitimate weapon to curb press freedom rather than merely refusing to comment or denying inaccurate reporting (*Asian Media and Communication Bulletin* 2004: 12).

The growing number of libel cases are, however, only the latest in a list of strategies, including ownership, influence and violence, by which politicians, local strongmen, religious groups and sectors within the police and armed forces have reasserted control of the media. These attempts to stem the free flow of information in the country come amidst renewed efforts by governments across the region to control the flow of news and entertainment products in the face of the growing impact of cross-border, mass communication media in the Asian region and beyond.

Following Douglas Kellner's hegemony model, this Chapter will examine how Indonesia's political elites are forcing the media to further their perceived interests and attempt to restore their gate keeping role over the flow of news and information within their borders by forging their own alliances among 'transnational corporations, the capitalist state, and communications technologies in the era of technocapitalism' (Kellner 1990: 90). Local elites are aware of the centrality of the media to people's lives in Southeast Asia, and that they have a battle on their hands when it comes to controlling the flow of information, facilitated by the globalisation of the media industry, across and within their borders and, perhaps, as a consequence maintaining their grip on power.

Across the Asia Pacific region, governments are using the pretext of the 'war on terror' to curb basic freedoms or crack down on their domestic opponents. This has led to what critics describe as an 'unprecedented abuse' of individual rights and freedoms (Reporters without Borders 2002). In Indonesia, this trend could strengthen even further, supported by a conservative backlash among a middle class that is troubled by fears for stability as terrorists seem able to attack the heart of the country's business district with impunity and also impatient with the years of economic pain that have followed the fall of Suharto and the onset of the Asian financial crisis in 1997.

The landslide success of former Security Minister Susilo Bambang Yudhoyono, in the presidential elections of September 2004, could be interpreted as a sign that Indonesians, concerned about unemployment, rising costs and corruption, and restive after the bomb attacks in Bali and Jakarta, are only too happy for a military strongman to restore law and order, even if it is to the detriment of some of their hard won democratic freedoms, including a plural media. There is, after all, little in the country's political culture and in the history of the development of the media in Indonesia to suggest an instinctive support for democratic pluralism, and even the market looks set to conspire with traditional pressures to limit titles and reduce diversity.

Indonesia, however, is no Singapore, where natural logistics allow for an easy grip on the media. Given the country's disparate geography and cultural make-up, and its competing political interests, it will not be simple to nail the lid back on the Pandora's Box of Indonesia's mass communication media. Indeed, as the blasts from the bombs in Bali and Jakarta continue to echo around the region, governments seem unable to contain internal unrest amidst deepening economic troubles and a turbulent sea of social change, raising the question as to whether or not Indonesia's political elite can adapt to a world of globalised media culture.

This chapter, then, will examine the implications of the fast information age and its attendant communications technology on Indonesia. It will look at the sea change in mass media and communications, whereby the media no longer functions as a mere tool of national government, but is now increasingly accessible to the ordinary citizen, with dramatic consequences for the political and social fabric of Indonesia and Southeast Asia as a whole. Political activists are increasingly harnessing the power of information and networks. And, despite the unequal distribution, falling costs mean that communications technology is more generally accessible and now being used to challenge established structures of authority. It is undermining some communities as it creates new ones, particularly where it articulates dissent.

A media explosion

On 13 September 1999, in the last days of the 17-month Habibie administration, the Indonesian House of Representatives passed the 21-article 1999 Press Law, annulling the 1966 and 1982 Press Laws made under long-time President Suharto and ushering in an unprecedented period of press freedom in Indonesia. The shackles were further dislodged when the new President, Abdurrahman Wahid – or Gus Dur, as he is more popularly known – abolished the feared Information Ministry, the state agency that had censored and controlled the communication media under the Suharto regime.

The resulting media environment may be likened to that which briefly emerged in Thailand in 1973, after the toppling of the military dictatorship of Field Marshal Thanom Kittikachorn. As in Thailand, Indonesia experienced a media explosion. There were new print titles, new radio stations and dozens of local television stations, including 4 new nationwide broadcasters, which joined the existing 7. The world's fourth largest population, 'fascinated by the sudden free flow of information, read, watched and listened in droves, fuelling a media boom when most of the economy was bust' (*The Economist* 2003: 56).

According to the South East Asian Press Alliance (SEAPA), by the end of 1999, there were some 299 newspapers, 886 tabloids, 491 magazines, 11 bulletins, 12 TV stations and 1,110 radio stations, as well as an unknown number of media-related websites (Goodman 2000). And yet, despite the apparent health of the media industry, there are concerns about interference. When Reporters Without Borders published its 2004 annual worldwide press freedom index, Indonesia sank to 117 out of 167 countries – slipping 7 places from the previous year, and 60 places from the first report in 2002, alongside a warning that press freedom in Indonesia 'remains under serious threat due to the existence of outdated laws, and killings and physical attacks targeting journalists' (Saraswati 2004).

Indonesia's elites are clearly uncomfortable with what they see as an unfettered industry. Major General Sudrajat, media advisor to then President Megawati, speaking at Newsworld Asia in July 2002, expressed his concern over media freedom. Sudrajat explained that technological change was making the media increasingly difficult to control. He maintained that its lack of maturity impacted unfavourably on the reputation of the country, yet the media was the single institution in Indonesia that could not, he contended, be criticised. 'The media needs to be more professional', he told the conference. 'The lack of control costs Indonesia in its bilateral relationships, for example with Singapore. Indonesian media flows across the border are disturbing relations. Internally, the media, both local and international, has ramifications for stability, for example the problems in Timor' (interview recorded by author 2002).

Sudrajat clearly reflected his President's unease with the media. During her time in office, Megawati Sukanoputri had a troubled relationship with the press. She reacted to criticism with the rejoinder that journalists were lacking in professionalism and were 'biased and irresponsible' and that the responsibility of the national press 'rests in its ability to protect and promote national unity' (Reporters without Borders 2004). In November 2003, the editor of the daily newspaper, *Rakyat Merdeka*, which was particularly critical of the President, was sentenced to six months in prison for libelling the president (Hantoro and Nurhayati 2003). This was the first time since the fall of Suharto in 1998, that a journalist had been convicted of insulting the President.

As the pressure on the media to toe the Megawati government's line increased, a new broadcast law went before the Indonesian parliament in November 2002. The law was aimed at increasing regional programming and diversifying ownership beyond Jakarta's business elite and the Suharto siblings. It attempted to break their influence by revoking national licences and restricting licences to a single province (of which Indonesia has 32), forbidding cross ownership of newspapers and TV stations, and limiting the stake allowed to foreign investors in local media to 10 per cent.

Outside commentators were sceptical: 'in a country where capitalists were all cronies, business and politics are not so easy to disentangle' (*The Economist* 2003: 56). But what was of greater concern for journalists was the fact that the law also proposed the limitation of foreign programmes and allowed for the establishment of a new censorship board. According to those writing it, the new legislation was aimed at tackling biased reporting of Indonesia and the promotion of Western viewpoints, at the heart of which was Indonesia's image in the international media as a haven for Islamic militants and terrorists. For many in the industry both inside and outside Indonesia, alongside the growing number of libel and defamation cases, it marked another move to regain control over the media, and mirrored similar efforts by governments across the region to stem the flow of controversial news and entertainment products.

Security in the age of a globalised media

Like its neighbours, Indonesia has been swept up by global forces both economic and political. New technologies and transnational corporations are 'colluding to make all national boundaries culturally permeable' (Sen and Hill 2000: 2). The fingers of the globalised media industry have even reached into the farthest islands of this dispersed archipelago, with consequences for national security in the post 9/11 world.

Indonesia is an imagined state, cobbled together for reasons of geographic proximity and colonial history. The Suharto government, keen to maintain its hold on power and hold this disparate nation together, kept a tight grip on local media content, forcing broadcasters, in particular, to turn to foreign providers to fill their air time. As a result, more than half of the programming on Indonesian television was imported from the US, Japan, Hong Kong and India, and a similar influence was apparent in cinema, music, magazines and literature such that it is impossible to draw a picture of the Indonesian media without reflecting on the world beyond its national borders and on theories about globalisation which attempt to understand the 'increasing interconnections between nations and media' (Sen and Hill 2000: 13).

It was a feature common to many of the states in Southeast Asia: transparent national borders became increasingly permeable in the 1980s, as governments sought to be part of the global economy, keen on securing its spoils despite the political and policy contradictions (Atkins 1999: 1). The development of the information superhighway further compounded the effect, sending a cultural wrecking crew to lay its path into the hearts of these new economies, just as it marked an upping of the ante in the competition to be a winner in this global economy (Langdale 1997: 117).

Indonesia was not alone among the nations of the Association of South East Asian Nations (ASEAN) to perceive an increase in insecurity over their lack of autonomy. Elites preoccupied with trying to counter these external pressures, however, created certain security dilemmas, particularly when regime legitimacy was linked to national security and prosperity. The pursuit of economic development creates further instability: cross border information flows must be weighed against information control, global advertising and consumerism against national financial needs, foreign ideas and values against traditional mores and beliefs. The porosity of the state increases, further diminishing its autonomy, as it becomes a part of the global economy.

Security is an overriding concern for Southeast Asia's elites and a key consideration when explaining their behaviour. These are relatively new states, many of which only became independent in the 1950s and 1960s. State building is still an ongoing process and internal security is an obsession, and there is a blurring of the lines between state and regime security, and a 'predisposition to conceive of national security as regime security' (Samudaranija and Paribata 1987: 12). A colonial inheritance of 'discontinuities and distortions' (Job 1992: 69) has often resulted in low regime legitimacy as well as deep fissures in the social fabric of the new states, causing 'domestic insecurity' (Ayoob 1995: 190). These fissures can be ethnic, religious, or economic, and they often coincide, further weakening national foundations. In Indonesia they include various separatist movements in Aceh and West Papua, as well as Muslim–Christian inter-communal violence in regions like the Molukus, Ambon and Sulawesi.

These new states are also vulnerable to external pressures due to their relatively weak position on the global stage. Interference from institutions like the International Monetary Fund (IMF) and the World Bank (both dominated by the major industrial powers), as well as from the advanced industrialised states and multinational corporations, adds to the destabilising effects of the ideas and values bound up in the process of modernisation (Ayoob 1995: 37).

Just as global economic development is uneven, so different groups within the state prove more able and more prepared to embrace the changes this development entails. The social transformation results in challenges for the regime, from the emergence of new interest groups, internal migration, and a younger, more demanding, literate, educated and increasingly urban population. Many also feel dislocated and disenfranchised by the changes around them: uncomfortable and unsuccessful in the new and the modern, they turn back to traditional value systems, causing further conflict (Samudaranija and Paribata 1987: 6–9).

The Bali tragedy and the bombings in Jakarta placed the 'war on terror' firmly on the doorstep of Southeast Asia's governments, and, all the while, the media, in particular the new media, is seen as carrying change to the heart of these societies, with ambiguous and unpredictable consequences. The new technologies, moreover, have ambiguous predictable consequences. They support both a concentration and a dispersion of power. New media allow those on the periphery to develop and consolidate power and ultimately to challenge the authority of the centre. In this high-tech mobilisation of radical constituencies, the voices often speak in opposition to globalisation, fed by 'its major discontents, nationalism, regionalism, localism and revivalism' (Majod 1999: 81), challenging the authority of the centre and eliciting a response at an elite level.

In Southeast Asia, as regimes toppled in Thailand and Indonesia in the 1990s, the global communication media was increasingly identified as an important cause of regional political upheaval (Atkins 1999: 420). Governments identified the burgeoning media industry as a key variable driving political upheaval and are keen to quarantine what many see as the source of a contagion of internal instability (Ayoob 1995: 196). There are powerful forces arranged against the free media in Indonesia, which will be considered later. These are reinforced by deeper, historical and cultural understandings that reject the right to an existence for a plural media.

Politics, political culture and the Asian media: strictly one-way traffic

The world's largest archipelago, Indonesia achieved independence from the Netherlands in 1949. Today, Indonesia's population of 238,452,952 (July 2004 estimate), makes it the world's fourth-most populous nation and the largest Muslim nation. A vast polyglot nation, Indonesia's population is spread over an area comprising 17,508 islands and islets, of which 6,000 are inhabited, and stretching 5,000 kilometre east to west and 1,750 north to south, with 100 ethnic groups. Despite this, 87 per cent of Indonesians are Muslims, and the island of Java (home to Indonesia's largest ethnic group, the Javanese) is one of the most densely populated areas in the world, with more than 107 million people living in an area the size of New York State.

Indonesia has struggled to recover from the 1997 Asian Financial Crisis: estimates from 2003 indicated that its GDP based on purchasing power parity comes out at $US758.8 billion or $3,200 per capita, compared to Malaysia at $207.8 billion, approximately $9,000 pre capita, and Singapore at $109.4 billion, or $23,700 per capita (CIA 2004). Indeed, of all the Asian economies, 'Indonesia's experience in the wake of the economic crisis of 1997, has to be the most intense and destructive' (Robison 2001: 104). In its latest report, the World Bank insisted Indonesia move quickly to reinforce the country's improving economic growth, pass fresh laws to boost investor confidence and cut the country's soaring fuel subsidies (*The Jakarta Post* 2004b).

The political system is a modern construct and the political culture has a modern veneer laid by early nationalist movements in the 1920s but only really gaining roots after the Second World War and the creation of the modern independent state (Steinberg 1987). Naturally, the modern political culture has a mo traditional context, for example Kingsbury uses Wittfogel's idea of hydraulic cultures (Wittfogel 1957) to explain Indonesia's inward looking and politically autocratic nature, as well as the domination by a military elite (Kingsbury and Aveling 2003: 114). The impact of structural considerations – social and physical factors: geography, economic and sociological structure provide the institutional basis for the development of Indonesia's mass media of communication and the other objective elements that are seen as having inhibited political participation, including cultural variables such as the traditional Javanese concept of self, ideal social behaviour, patronship and power (Jackson 1978: 23).

Further, the combination of traditional, Islamic and modern culture combine with the state ideology instituted at the time of independence – *pancasila*. In its preamble, the 1945 constitution sets forth the *pancasila* as the embodiment of the basic principles of an independent Indonesian state. In brief, and in the order given in the constitution, the *pancasila* principles comprise: a belief in one supreme God, humanitarianism, nationalism expressed in the unity of Indonesia, consultative democracy, and social justice. Designed by modern Indonesia's founding father Sukarno, *pancasila* sought to meet the ideological needs of the new nation, and, as with the adoption of Bahasa as the national language, represented part of the effort to build a new nation.

These elements exist in an 'incongruous harmony' (Lubis 1983: 7): a syncretic melange imposed on society where power is still informed by a feudal past where the King's power was an extension of the power of the Gods, at the centre of society, like the head of the family. Criticism of those in power was not tolerated, and the ruling elite traditionally had very little communication with the common people – where they did, 'communication is always from the top downward, never the other way around. The traffic is strictly one-way' (Lubis 1983: 23).

But, even the strong hand of Sukarno's successor Suharto could not prevent divisions emerging across the country, even within Angkatan Bersenjata Republik Indonesia (ABRI) – the Armed Forces of the Republic of Indonesia, which is the protector of the *pancasila* faith.[1] Many were based around more localised national identities, in Banda Aceh, Timor and Papua, but recently the modern veneer has seen religious concerns push through the uneven surface, with evidence of a shift in the past decade towards greater public and private practice of the Islamic faith.

The increased religious identification, in turn, reflects wider trends in the region, the growing awareness of Islam's global identity, and the increasingly coherent emergence of its militant expression. As Marxism once was, Islam has become a change agent, 'transforming the culture and institutions of modern Southeast Asia, sometimes buttressing them against the advance of global capitalism and Western popular culture, at other times accommodating notions of democracy and universal human rights' (Raymer 2002).

But, Southeast Asian Muslims, like Muslims worldwide, face competing interpretations of Islam and themselves adopt and utilise the identity in varying ways. While rural Indonesia often reflects the mix of faiths, that is the country's inheritance, urban Indonesians have become, on the whole, modern. Moderate

:, still dominate Indonesian Islam. But, an unwillingness to
ɔre doctrinaire views of religious extremists has allowed them to
debate in Indonesia, and this has been reflected in the media, and
:ular focus for the foreign media. While in the streets, where lad's
magazine FHM and Cosmopolitan rub shoulders with religious tracts, 'the cultural
battle for the soul of Indonesia can look like a tropical rumble between the Jihadis
and the sex columnists' (Donnan 2005: W3).

Action by the US in Afghanistan and Iraq has continued to unite Indonesians
in opposition to Washington making Abu Bakar Ba'asyir (the alleged spiritual
leader of the Jemmah Islamiah terror network) a hero to many for standing up to
the US. While the more secular media like Kompass covered his trial in a way that
was fitting with the liberal intention that media be the history of first record,
coverage by Republika was seen as more pro- Ba'asyir. The new President,
Yudhoyono, even maintains that Jemmah Islamiah's existence in Indonesia is still
unproven, which 'does not bode well for Washington and its allies hope that the
organisation will be banned' (Donnan 2004: 2).

Despite the initial flurry of activity after the Bali bombings, attempts to eradicate
the cells of radical Islamic terrorists in Indonesia looked flimsy, as political ambitions
meant the elite in Jakarta were 'tracking the responses of the major Muslim leaders'
(Desker 2002). The election of Yudhoyono suggests, however, public support for those
who will seek to control militant Islam. A greater focus on security means that the
military, momentarily pushed aside by the initial surge of popular democratic fervour
in the wake of Suharto's fall, are stepping up to retake their place as a dominant force
in the country and its political culture, restored to their dual function, as both
defenders of the nation and as a social–political force in national development. This
could have an important impact on the environment in which the media operates.

The military and the media

Any consideration of the media environment in Indonesia must take into account
the military and their place in the political culture of the country. The military has
played a central role in the recent independent existence of Indonesia. Given that
the military by its very nature is neither an open nor a liberal institution, it is
likely that it can only serve as a constraint upon the development of a free press.

The Indonesian military had an active part in the development of the independent
Indonesian nation state. The army, which fought both the Dutch and the British to
secure independence after the Second World War, watched from the sidelines as
Indonesia's first president, Sukarno, courted the PKI (communist party), seizing
power with Suharto at its head in 1965, when it decided things had gone too far. For
much of Suharto's 'New Order', politics was 'centred on the officer class of the
Indonesian armed forces' (Steinberg 1987: 425). The military was given its *dwi
fungsi*, or dual function as both a military and political force in Indonesian life, with
its brief to maintain national integrity and uphold the state ideology of *pancasila*.

Today, although the Indonesian military's reputation has foundered on the
rocks of East Timor and other trouble spots in the Indonesian archipelago, and it

has surrendered its appointed positions in the Indonesian parliament, it remains politically influential. With mounting international concern over Islamic radicals in the country, and the need of politicians to quieten secessionist movements, the Indonesian military is moving back into the centre of political life.

The military is, however, an institution obsessed by security and secrecy, as two of the key elements to waging effective war (Kasper 2001). There are also special characteristics of the military as a profession, with its emphasis on discipline and hierarchy and its belief in the magnitude of the potential dangers facing the community over which it stands guard (Blondel 1969). These are not characteristics that encourage debate nor make the military conducive to an open, liberal environment. In Indonesia, then, the ongoing influence of the military remains a concern.

Moreover, as political power has moved away from the centre post Suharto, local politics have increased in importance and provincial administrations are becoming increasingly reliant on the military to underpin their authority, leading to 'new alliances between regional commanders and regional power-holders' (McBeth 2002a: 23). Nor is this a military that can be relied upon to act in a professional manner. When the IMF and the World Bank forced the military to open its books 'a crack', they saw an organisation running low on funding and relying on its own resources for half its annual spending. While the military has legal enterprises, many of these are struggling, forcing it to turn increasingly to illegal activities to finance its operations: 'it's a political lobbying group and a business conglomerate with links to organised crime. Don't look at it as an institution, but as a lobby group of individuals seeking tribute and money' (McBeth 2002b: 14).

Megawati and the military

While the fall of Suharto and the loss of East Timor marked a decline in the military's reputation and status, it was President Megawati who marked its return to favour as she looked for support as her popularity waned. As a result, Indonesia's press freedom does not extend to its conflict areas. The media has been unable to cover the conflicts from Maluku to Aceh, impartially. Threats to the safety of journalists from the parties to the conflicts were the main deterrent, and physical attacks on journalists generally went unpunished (*Asian Media and Communication Bulletin* 2002: 12).

The Indonesian authorities have tried to block the media's access to areas of civil conflict, and anti-government rebels also put pressure on journalists to get their side of the story out. Megawati gave the military hardliners a free hand in Aceh (something her successor does not seem inclined to reverse). The declaration of martial law there in May 2003 allowed the military to impose harsh restrictions on the press and effectively silence journalists trying to cover the war against the rebels of the Free Aceh Movement (Gerakan Aceh Merdeka – GAM). The Indonesian army did everything possible to keep the news media away from Aceh, where it resumed the war against the separatists. Human Rights Watch documented dozens of arrests, physical attacks and threats against journalists (Human Rights Watch 2003). Two reporters were killed in the rebel zone and dozens of others were physically attacked or threatened.

Criticism of the 'dirty war' in Aceh in respected publications such as Kompas and Tempo met with disapproval from both the authorities and other media, especially the broadcast media, which took a position of support for the war against the GAM 'terrorists'. The central government in Jakarta cautioned the media against any lack of nationalism and failure to support the security forces. By June 2003, the military had achieved a virtual lock down of Aceh, and the army announced that the foreign ministry had given orders for all foreign and national journalists working for international news media to leave the province (Reporters Without Borders 2004). This influence spread to the newsrooms of Indonesia's media: Dandhy Dwi Laksono of the independent television channel SCTV was fired in June 2003 as a result of pressure from the army, which objected to a report on torture in Aceh during the 1990s. Laksono told Human Rights Watch that his editors had made no attempt to resist the army's pressure and had described him as an 'anti-military journalist' (Human Rights Watch 2003).

The media has not played the Aceh conflict as a part of the war on terror nor has it been sympathetic to GAM's arguments – a fact that is reflected in attempts by GAM to pressure reporters covering the conflict. Media criticism of the government purely focused on the abuses perpetrated by the military in its conduct of the war and has not given wider support for the GAM cause (*Jakarta Post.com* 2005). The Aceh conflict has always been portrayed as a separatist movement, and this works better in a nationalistic Indonesia, and GAM frustration with this has been marked by violence against journalists and local media organisations.

However, it should be noted that since the 'war on 'terror', the West has already shown itself eager to support Jakarta's efforts to quell legally separatist movements, and three Achenese leaders in Sweden were arrested on suspicion of violating international laws. Indonesia, which supplied information to Sweden, claimed to have intercepted email and satellite-phone traffic ordering acts of terrorism from forces in Aceh. The three were at the forefront of peace talks that broke down in April 2003, unleashing a year-long military campaign against GAM fighters in Aceh (McBeth and Lintner 2004: 21).

Thus, although the army lost its 38 non-elected seats in the People's Consultative Assembly in 2004, the military is still understood to be the most important institution in the country, and it is still the army that intervenes in religious and ethnic conflicts. With separatist rebellions and the outbreaks of social unrest which have become commonplace since the end of authoritarian rule, there is a new obsession with preserving the unitary state that made bedfellows of the nationalist-minded President Megawati Sukarnoputri and military conservatives like army chief General Ryamizard Ryacadu and Army Strategic Reserve commander Lt General Bibit Walayu, who want to retain influence over Indonesia's thirty-two provinces (McBeth 2002a: 23).

The new president, with similar internal concerns as well as a desire to please Western allies by silencing radical Islamic opposition, could further reinforce the military's central role in Indonesian society. Yudhoyono is equally aware of the importance of the Indonesian military, the TNI. On his election as president, he replaced TNI chief General Endriartono Sutarto, who had been appointed by Megawatti, with Army chief General Ryamizard Ryacudu, after Endriartono had announced his resignation. Yudhoyono wants Endriartono to stay at the TNI's helm for the meantime (Kurniawan 2004). While this looks like Yudhoyono is attempting to limit the conservative element, it will do little to lessen the scrutiny of Indonesia's media, given the central determination of the development of the industry in the country and the importance of image in the 'war on terror'.

Imagining a nation: the media and the creation of the Indonesian State

The history of the development of the mass communication media in Indonesia is a story of the ongoing efforts by the authorities to use the media as an instrument of state development and rein in the press each time it reflected or articulated popular dissent. As with the rest of Southeast Asia, the idea of mass media was a 'tool, born, bred and developed in the West, transplanted to Indonesia' (Makarim 1978: 261). Similar to the experience of its neighbours on the Malay Peninsula, the introduction of the printing press and the creation of newspapers was a radical departure from traditional rule, expanding the public sphere, 'providing the space in which social identity or political policy might be debated' (Milner 1995: 292). The newspaper, like the novel, provided the 'technical means for representing the kind of imagined community that is the nation' (Anderson 2000: 414–434).

Radio, in the early days of its development, was a government information service, and was used to 'prepare the hearts and minds of the people' for independence (Sued 1989: 41–56). The birth of television in Southeast Asia coincided with the creation of the new post-colonial political state, and it quickly shouldered radio's mantle, becoming a vital part of government efforts to forge national unity. The widely held view that the media was influential meant it became caught between different and competing interests, religious, political, ethnic, reflecting the complex structure of Indonesian society, the multi-layered nature of Indonesian identity, and an 'overvalued' medium (Makarim 1978: 265).

But, the close connection between the media and the birth of nationalism – both modern ideas, transplanted from the West – created a tradition of Indonesian freedom fighters who were also writers who understood the power of media to spread the message of independence. These thorns in the side of the Dutch administration soon began to prick their post-colonial successors, with journalists like Mochtar Lubis and Pramoedya Ananta Toer banned and imprisoned by the post-independence regimes. The post-colonial authorities were equipped with the tools of control set out by the Dutch, in particular a 1931 law (*pressbreidel ordonantie*) allowing the Governor General to ban a publication for up to thirty-eight days for 'disrupting public order', and the 'notorious' hate sowing articles (*haatzaai artikelen*) of the Dutch Criminal Code which were regularly used to silence journalists. Sukarno and Suharto made some modifications in the language, but in effect they were the same laws used widely particularly by Suharto (Harsono 2000: 79–80).

Thus, control by the central government was a characteristic even of the early days of the development of the press in Indonesia. While the first printed news in Indonesia, what was then known as the Dutch East Indies, was a bulletin for employees of Dutch East India Company, 'Memorie Dex Nouvelles', published in 1615, the first newspaper of general interest was the Bataviase Nouvelles, published in 1744 by a Dutch national in Batavia (Jakarta). It was closed by the Dutch administration concerned that it would provide space for criticism of the authoritarian administration.

As a result, strict censorship was put in place, and new publications were discouraged, ensuring that 'the country failed in having newspapers with a substantial history' (Gunaratne 2000: 268). During the Japanese occupation (1942–1945), the media was under the control of the Japanese and used for propaganda purposes. No Dutch media were allowed. The Japanese closed all publications, allowing only a few to reopen. They introduced publishing licence procedures to control the media which were subsequently 'incorporated into the armoury of the independent Indonesian government' and used vigorously by Suharto (Harsono 2000: 79–80). This close control was continued by the Dutch, when they were restored to a shaky position of power by the British after the surrender of the Japanese. In 1945, a third of Indonesia's press disappeared.

Early independence brought some freedoms: under the 1945 constitution the freedom of speech and of the press were provided under the law, and when Independence was granted in 1949, commentators suggest it ushered in 'an era of press freedom plus western liberal democracy' (Sinaga 1989: 27–39). However, this period drew to a close in 1959, when independent Indonesia's founding father President Sukarno introduced the era of 'guided democracy', requiring publication permits under which the press was required to sign an agreement tying them to the government, the opposition press was banned and ANTARA, Indonesia's wire news service, became government controlled.

The move was part of Sukarno's effort to shore up his power, and he defined the mass communication media as a vehicle for the creation of a 'national culture' (Sen and Hill 2000: 11). When television was first introduced in 1962, in order to showcase the Asia Games that year, it was clearly an arm of the government. Taking over where radio left off, Televesi Republik Indonesia (TVRI) was used to communicate government policies and build society (Gunaratne 2000: 270).

But, this period of 'Guided Democracy' was 'characterised by...intense ideological debates' (Sen and Hill 2000: 3). There were heated discussions, particularly in the Jakarta press, reflecting the growing divisions in society and Sukarno's dwindling influence. Debate became increasingly heated until 1965, when the army seized power, finally replacing Sukarno with Suharto in March 1966, and communist papers, Chinese language papers (except one official Chinese daily 'Herian Indonesia') and left wing papers were banned (Gunaratne 2000: 268).

The new order and the control of information

The 'control of information was central to Suharto's hold on power' (Harsono 2000: 78). And where radio had been the tool of the great orator, Sukarno, Suharto used television to create his Indonesia. Satellite served to carry his word to television sets around the nation.

Although the first Press Law passed by the parliament in 1966 provided for press freedom, these were put into the context of the state ideology, *pancasila*.

Suharto's brutal suppression of student protests in 1974 and the closure of newspapers for their coverage of the uprising underlined Suharto's authoritarian attitudes to the flow of information. Suharto's 'mantra' was clear: stability and economic development ahead of democracy and transparency (Harsono 2000: 81).

The New Order tried 'relentlessly' to make Jakarta the centre of the domestic culture and of the perception industries, as part of the centralisation of power under Suharto and the single-minded push to make Jakarta the epicentre of the country not only politically but economically and culturally as well. Turning his will to uniting the country, and centralising power, Suharto tried to prevent regional, ethnic, linguistic and religious differences from taking a political form, by seeking to 'authorise' them (Keeler 1987: 79). In addition, Suharto also created an 'intricate web of relations between the press and the government' (Makarim 1978: 263–264).

Initially, Suharto's family and close allies controlled the privately owned media, but as the industry expanded, a more indirect form of control was necessary. By the 1990s, other groups moved in to control new media operations. Membership of this new family, however, depended on being prepared to operate under 'the constraints imposed by the New Order government' (Hill 1996: 86). Suharto's time in power marked the growth in influence of powerful corporate conglomerates and the political and business influence of powerful families in the country. Indeed, concern about them internally and externally contributed to the fall of the New Order (Robison 2001: 109).

But Suharto also delivered remarkable economic change. During the thirty years between 1966 and 1996, the important economic and social indicators over this period 'far exceeded the expectations of even the most optimistic observers at the beginning of the regime' (Hill 1996: 255). An associated feature of the New Order was 'the emergence of an affluent urban middle class' (Hooker 1993: 3), leading to an expansion in demand for the media: in the 1950s sales of newspapers were about 50,000 copies but by 1973 total circulation was 1.5 million (Suanto 1978: 230).

Television was particularly easy to police. The state broadcaster, TVRI, provided a news monopoly from Jakarta, and even the independent television stations, when they came along after 1995, were all backed by influential conglomerates, and prepared to manipulate their coverage: choice of story, timing of reports, choice of perspective in pictures and quotes, reflected the status quo, producing 'uncontroversial products' (Sen and Hill 2000: 126–131).

The impact of satellite, however, was ambiguous. The same technology that was used to unite Indonesia around Suharto's political and cultural capital, Jakarta, also provided avenues for alternative messages facilitating diversity and division. Unlike Singapore, Indonesia did not ban satellite dishes and, thus, did not attempt to stop people watching foreign television broadcasts, emphasising the porosity of the Indonesian state. In 1996, for example, RTP International, a Portuguese satellite television service, began broadcasting into East Timor. Using transponder space on the largely Chinese-owned AsiaSat 2, the Portuguese government could support East Timor's struggle for self-determination, and the Indonesian authorities were helpless to control its broadcasts. The entry of global networks producing news in Indonesia – CNN, Reuters, BBC, ABN (Australia) and TF-1 (France), only increased competition for viewers, and these carried the pictures of chaos, as the army battled protestors in 1998, into homes in Indonesia and around the world, leading to Suharto's resignation.

The beginning of the end

By the end of the 1990s, the rumblings of the middle class against the overwhelming weight of the New Order were apparent. Suharto moved to suppress dissent, in a time honoured tradition, turning on the media that had the courage to speak the unease the middle class felt. But, technological developments were to play a further role in undermining Suharto and amassing the movement against him. It has been the growth of the Internet in the 1990s that has really complicated Southeast Asia's governmental efforts to control the flow of information, and Indonesia was no exception.

Suharto was keen to continue to deliver economic growth for Indonesia, and being part of the IT revolution was seen as key to this goal. Indonesia had a sophisticated telecommunications system as a result of its early investments in satellite communications, and in 1997, as the Asian financial crisis was about to break over the country, plans for a network and information system (Nusantara-21) were developed, representing the expression of Suharto's vision for the continued development of Indonesia and growth in social prosperity by embracing communication and information technology.

What this vision did not entail, however, was the growing role the alternative media played in the expression of dissent and the organisation of opposition to the Suharto regime. The Internet had a key role in both the fall of Suharto, by helping to coalesce the opposition through the expression of dissent on websites, and, through its role both in the provision of information and in the voting process, the rebuilding of democracy. Indeed, if radio was the communication medium of Indonesian independence, then the Internet might well 'vie for top billing in the fall of Suharto...' (Sen and Hill 2000: 194).

Under Suharto, the Internet, which became accessible in Indonesia from 1995, offered an unfettered, un-scrutinised communication tool and allowed the relatively free flow of information. Post Suharto, the Internet was used in the 1999 and the 2004 elections to provide transparency and credibility for the election process: votes were monitored on the General Elections Commission's Internet site. Those who had used the Internet in the information war against Suharto still see it as a technology of democracy and its further use in the election process was to 'authenticate the newly emerging democracy in their eyes' (Hill 2002: 5).

While Suharto's regime found the Internet difficult to contain, it was the impact of broader media coverage of the reaction to the economic collapse in 1997, which led to his resignation. As the currency collapsed, dropping from 2,400 Rupiah to 17,000 Rupiah to 1 US dollar in January 1998, demonstrators battled with soldiers in the streets of Jakarta. Even the mainstream media found commercial dictates forced their distance from the official voice (Sen and Hill 2000: 132). Local television stations began to broadcast pictures of the protests.

Even the usually conservative TVRI ran eulogies of dead students – 'galvanizing public awareness of the tragedy in Jakarta, and indicating that those at the top were no longer in control' (Harsono 2000: 85–86).

Government and military officials continued to harass and intimidate journalists up to Suharto's resignation and beyond. But the events of May 1998 illustrated the 'failure' of the Suharto regime to understand the international and local media, and the political impact of the media and information technology, as the 'power to control communications became more and more impractical' (Harsono 2000: 86).

Media life after Suharto

Controlling communications may have become more impractical, but it is still something for which many of Indonesia's political and military elite yearn. Whichever way they turn they find a media prepared to criticise the ruling elite, often in terms that shock and awe. In the new media that is free for all, competition has become acute leading not only to greater quality, but also to more sensationalism, from the wide play received by the BBC's Indonesian language programming to the new tabloids with 'speculative and irresponsible' reporting 'spiced up with sex and crime' (Harsono 2000: 88–89). In addition, the limited resources of the local media has encouraged the spread of corruption, intimidation and influence from regional and national political forces. The significant growth of the media since 1998 has not been matched by investment in training or the development of a widespread culture of journalistic professionalism (Scarpello 2002).

While financial constraints began to restrict the further expansion of the industry, even encouraging a dwindling in the number of titles (Idris 2001: 91), new signs emerged of a determination among the political elite to try to reassert control over the country's media. This is partly due to the resistance of the old elite: as with the military and its influence, many of the old faces are still around. Suharto's family still remain influential. His daughter, Tutut, who is said to have political ambitions, owns four television channels including TVI and SCTV (Reporters without Borders 2002), and Suharto's political vehicle, the Golkar Party, remains influential. But, the Megawati regime was also discomforted by criticism in the media. The President worried journalists with her close links to the military (Menon 2001), as did her decision to recreate the post of Minister of Information and to reintroduce to the country's penal code prison sentences for 'slander' (Reporters without Borders 2002). Her attack on the editor of *Rakyat Merdeka* was just part of the evidence that her government was not willing to allow a free and often raucous press to continue its work.

But it was Megawati's attempt to silence the flow of foreign news and information that was telling as to the outlook of the Indonesian authorities. The archaic piece of legislation that the government used, was described by Abdullah Alamudi of Jakarta's Dr Soetomo Press Institute as turning the clock back to 1964, when President Sukarno banned people from listening to foreign broadcasts at the height of the Indonesia–Malaysia confrontation. Amin Said Husni, the deputy head of the parliamentary team drafting the bill, told Reuters, 'We don't want our stations and radio to be foreign kiosks (selling their products)' (Committee for the

Protection of Journalists 2002). Paradoxically it was Sukarno's daughter who was reviving these 'reviled habits' (Scarpello 2002), but they reflect a constant unease with foreign reporting on Indonesia.

Foreign media

Criticism from foreign journalists has often irked Indonesia's political elite, leading to some high-profile expulsions under President Megawati's administration—the first since the fall of Suharto. Like the domestic media, the foreign media faced tight controls for most of Suharto's autocratic, thirty-two-year rule. The Suharto government had welcomed foreign media content as the globalised media sought audiences around Southeast Asia. Suharto saw these products as having a narrow audience and thought it was of little threat to the status quo. Indeed, local broadcasters could fill airtime with US programming, like Dallas, filling space that could have harboured potentially more controversial local products. As the country developed, the availability of these global media products was also seen as part of the modernisation process. Satellite, the symbol of modern Indonesia, brought cable television and foreign channels.

But Suharto remained keenly sensitive to criticism. The Australian news media, in particular, which is 'frank and, at times, confrontational', was seen as ignoring the Indonesian values of respect *halus* and deference *hormat*, and becoming a 'cultural straw man' to be knocked about by the Indonesia government when politically expedient (Kingsbury 1997: 112). In 1975, six Australian journalists were murdered in Timor after ignoring instructions from the military to leave the Island. In 1986, *Sydney Morning Herald* journalist, David Jenkins, was expelled for reporting on the Suharto family wealth. This was followed by a general ban on Australian foreign correspondents, and, although they were slowly readmitted over the next decade, it was made clear they were expected to 'understand the Indonesian government's perspective' (Harsono 2000: 81). The constant presence of foreign, particularly the Australian, media in the Indonesian subconscious led to tensions over East Timor's vote for independence in 1999.

Clearly, the difficulties between Indonesia's political elites and the Western media have stemmed from the Indonesian government's 'disinclination to accept that it could not control external – sometimes critical – commentary' (Kingsbury 1997: 113). This uneasiness with criticism continued through to the government of Megawati Sukarnoputri as, in the post-Suharto era, Indonesia is forced to learn 'how to cope with more intense and sustained attention from the Western media' (Tiffin 2000: 49).

In May 2002, when the government refused to renew a journalist visa for Australian Lindsay Murdoch, concerns about the Megawati administration's attitude to a free press began to gel. The move against the Jakarta correspondent for the *Sydney Morning Herald* and *The Melbourne Age* was said to have come from the National Intelligence Body (BIN), headed by retired General A.M. Hendropriyono, as part of a general resurgence of military influence within the government, and came after Murdoch wrote unfavourable articles about the military's actions in East Timor and Aceh, including revealing a military plan to separate East Timorese children from their parents and bring them to orphanages in Java after East Timor voted overwhelmingly to separate from Indonesia in 1999, claiming Indonesian troops had poured boiling water over a baby who later died in Aceh (Timberlake 2002). It was also a police report from the head of BIN that had the executive editor of the *Rakyat Merdeka* daily charged with defamation.

In the run up to the presidential elections in 2004, the government expelled an American researcher, Ms. Sydney Jones, working for a 'well-respected' think-tank, the Brussels-based International Crisis Group (ICG). Her expulsion was seen as part of the ongoing efforts of President Megawati's government to crack down on its critics, including the detention of peaceful protestors and the conviction for libel of several newspaper editors (*The Economist* 2004: 29). Jones was a long-time source for foreign journalists, and she was known to have very good contacts with some of the radical Islamic groups. Hendropriyono's name emerged again when Jones was expelled. He labelled the organisation's reports on Indonesia, particularly those on Islamic radicalism and the separatism-racked provinces of Aceh and West Papua, as inaccurate, biased and subversive, though he gave no details.

However, some reports by the ICG had clearly embarrassed the military. In a report on operations by Jemaah Islamiyah (JI) and the Christmas Eve bombing in Medan, published in December 2002, the ICG had suggested, although not conclusively, that the Free Aceh Movement, the TNI and JI may be surprising bedfellows. In addition, it recommended that the government strengthen the capacity and coordination of intelligence, with an emphasis on the police rather than the BIN or the TNI, and also pay serious attention to corruption among the police, the military and the immigration service, particularly in connection with the trade in arms and explosives (International Crisis Group 2002).

Indonesia's 'war on terror'

Jones's expulsion was put down partly to politicians looking to score points on the campaign trail (*The Economist* 2004: 29). However, while internal political interests, alongside the efforts to hold Indonesia together, have long been the main focus of the country's political elites, the post 9/11 world is now impinging on developments within Indonesia.

The terrorist attacks on foreign targets in the country, alongside the government's failure to deal effectively with those the West wants to see incarcerated, notably Abu Bakar Ba'asyir (the alleged spiritual leader of JI), is in marked contrast to the efficiency of Indonesia's neighbour, Singapore. The US and the United Nations have blacklisted JI as a terrorist organisation, and the Western powers expect the Indonesian government to root out dangerous militants and shut down any organisation they may belong to or face dire economic and diplomatic repercussions. And yet, internal divisions continue to reduce Indonesia's political scene to a 'Babel of conflicting and sometimes violent factions' (Scarpello 2002).

Indonesia has an image problem. Asia as a whole is seen in the US as a 'risky place, the common explanation was television news images of anti-US protests and Islamic extremists with guns' (Pesek Jr 2003: B2). It is a problem created by the 'TV effect' – where the focus of media attention, in particular television, distorts the daily reality. This is something Indonesia can ill afford, given the importance of the US to its economy. The US is the biggest foreign investor in Southeast Asia, with direct investments totalling nearly US$90 billion, and its third largest export market valued at $US50 billion. And international concern about the security situation in Southeast Asia is very real.

The international media paints a bleak picture of the security situation in Southeast Asia (Clendenning 2004). And with bombs and terrorist training camps continuing to rend the reputation of the country and some of its ASEAN partners, the region looks to be too great a risk for many investors (*Associated Press* 2004). Successive Indonesian governments have closed their eyes to the militant threat, allowing Islamic militias to foment sectarian strife in areas like Maluku and Sulawesi, and security analysts say JI cells are active in Indonesia (McBeth 2002b: 13). The links with the network of al Qaeda terrorists and to 9/11 architect Khalid Shaikh Mohammed, were reinforced by the capture of his Southeast Asian deputy – Indonesian terrorist, Riduan Isamuddin (otherwise known as Hambali), in Thailand in 2003 (Hussain *et al.* 2004: 1–2).

Sydney Jones suggests that it is a wide network that includes 'individuals with well-established political legitimacy' for defying Suharto, blurring the lines between terrorists and political dissidents and Islamic extremists (Wain 2002). In mid-October 2004 a senior police officer, General Ansyaad Mbai, accused the press of giving too much 'visibility' to Indonesia's Islamist activists, and of being responsible for the country's vulnerability to terrorism (Reporters without Borders 2004). The atmosphere of threat encourages self-censorship – especially when reporting on the military and Muslim militants.

However, fears of an Islamist backlash in the run up to the 2004 elections were unfounded. Despite the bombing of the Australian Embassy, Indonesia's first direct presidential election went off relatively peacefully and was praised as a key step in the country's transition to democracy after the downfall of Suharto in 1998. President Yudhoyono is expected to tread carefully given the sensitivity of the Muslim ground and concerns from human rights groups, and in an interview before his inauguration, he made it clear that in his efforts to combat terrorism, he would step up dialogues with Muslim groups to ensure that 'there is no miscommunication'. However, his landslide victory was seen as indicative of popular support for his pledge to fight terror and fix Indonesia's battered economy, and he said that tougher laws might be needed to crack down on Islamic extremism in the country (Pereira 2004). What is clear is that his positioning in the media and his ability to communicate effectively to internal and external audiences will play a key role in the perceived success of this government in the months to come.

Conclusion

The link between the communications media and political change remains ambiguous, even in Indonesia, where the media and the control of information clearly had a role in the creation and the survival of Suharto's Indonesia, as well as the collapse of the President's New Order. While a direct causal link between the media and the fall of Suharto is hard to draw, 'in its pores one could see the impending end' (Sen and Hill 2000: 1).

The part that communications and the flow of information within the state plays in defining that state and creating a meaningful homogeneity is played out in full in Indonesia. As Kellner insists, technological developments and the current round of global economic integration have ensured that the mass communication media and its connected apparatus have become increasingly central to daily life in Asia, even in societies like Indonesia where economic disparities mean the distribution of media products is uneven. And, that this is affecting the perceptions of the political elites with regard to their security and the security of the state, and directly impacting their behaviour, forcing them to look for ways to bring the media back into line and restore the gate keeping role lost to technological development.

The end of the Suharto era brought a dramatic change in media freedom and a growth in the media industry that, itself, has contributed to the emergence of a public sphere and civil society. The new media, in particular, is seen as central in the new democratic process. But, while national level censorship was formally defeated with the collapse of the Suharto regime in May 1998, in this delicately imagined state, elements of the old power elite including the military, business and politicians are seeking to use the media to further their ambitions and interests, as the collapse of the old Suharto system and the highly centralised state authority has 'opened the door for a new struggle to reforge coalitions and build regimes' (Robison 2001: 109).

Indonesia remains an ethnically, socially, economically and religiously diverse country where tensions were held in place by authoritarianism up to 1998 (Scarpello 2002). Today, at the edges of a shrinking state many journalists including the foreign media are under threat. Now, the move to criminalise the work of journalists and the use of defamation laws to silence critics marks a concerted effort by the political elites to regain central control over the flow of information within and across the borders of the state. Internal tensions and external pressures could provide the military with the reasons it needs to move back into the centre of the political stage. Already, new and closer political and business alliances are forming between regional commanders and provincial bosses, as decentralization changes the dynamics of Indonesian politics.

The battle for the control of the media is also affected by the trends that are similarly affecting the media around the world, that of commercialisation and the connected move towards sensationalism, and media concentration remains an obstacle to the existence of true pluralism. But there is a broader struggle going on which has an impact on both the security of Indonesia and on media content, and that is the globalisation of the industry and cross border flows of cultural products. There has been a growth in access to foreign content, both deliberately offered by cable TV and slipping across porous borders. In response to, or at least alongside this wave of cultural products, there is the high-tech mobilization of radical constituencies, whose voices often speak in opposition to globalisation.

These voices are challenging the authority of the centre, as culture becomes a factor in both national security and international relations. Thus, however ambiguous media influence, and flimsy its connections with democracy, the communication nd its electronic forms in particular, are seen as extending their fingers of influence into the national political sphere in various ways, eliciting a response at an elite level to the challenges to traditional forms of power and authority. Thus the information technology that helped to push the Suharto regime from its post, from video machines to mobile text messaging, can serve to 'shake dominant political visions and cultural traditions to the core' (Lull 1995: 114).

In Indonesia's Madrassas and Mosques, the 20 million mobile phones are seen as having more political impact than a plural media, as Afghanistan and Iraq provide kindling for the flames of hate building against the West and the US, in particular. Local anger is joining global hate, whispered in the plotting and scheming, etched on the bullets of resistance, and echoing in the blast of bombs from Bali to Jakarta, and 'South east Asian governments have been floundering in the face of these threats' (*The Economist* 2002a: 23).

As the American 'war on terror' has brought these local tensions onto the global stage, it has complicated efforts to maintain current levels of press freedoms, not only for foreign reporters, but also for their local counterparts. The importance of the media in portraying the image of Indonesia – whether it is seen as a stable, coherent community, or a fractured, disintegrating state beset by Islamic militants, the power elites will want to control these images as they did in the past. As Foreign Minister Hassan Wirayuda made clear, with a globalised media, nothing is purely local anymore: 'every domestic issue has a foreign policy aspect' (Kurniawan 2004).

Writing about Indonesia in 2000, Harold Crouch suggested that the country faced three crucial challenges: the creation of a sustainable and effective political system based on democratic principles and capable of preventing a return of the military to political power, dealing with separatist pressure, and trying to reverse social disintegration, in particular ethnic and religious conflict. Crucial to all these challenges is economic recovery, for 'unless sustained economic recovery can get under way, the long-term prospects of democratisation, national unity and social peace will remain questionable' (Crouch 2000: 132).

The shadows of continued violence, or the return to a more authoritarian government in order to hold the country together (Kingsbury and Aveling 2003: 8), have darkened over the last three years with the solidification of Islamic fundamentalism around the world under the apparent auspices of al Qaeda. But, although internal issues dominate the focus of Indonesia's political elite, the new government clearly understands they have a global audience. With the media key to perceptions, both internal and external, as to whether Indonesia is a viable state where foreign investment and democratic pluralism can flourish, media production and reception will remain a site of contestation for interest groups in Indonesia, just as communications technology will continue to be used to mount challenges to the established authorities. Given that few elements either cultural or legal exist to help protect the freedom the media currently enjoys, like Thailand in 1973, they could prove just as temporary.

Note

1 Later known as Tentara Nasional Indonesia (TNI).

4 The Philippines media

Agent of stability or restraint?

Benjamin Cole

Introduction

The political stability and territorial integrity of the Philippines are threatened by a number of sub-national conflicts, including the worlds longest standing Communist insurgency, a separatist rebellion centred around the Muslim Moro community on the island of Mindanao, as well as terrorist groups with links to al Qaeda, pursuing a mixture of national and regional objectives. Some of these conflicts were drawn into the US 'war on terror' when the US State Department placed the Communist Party of the Philippines (CPP) and its armed wing the New Peoples Army (NPA), as well as the Abu Sayyaf Group (ASG) and the Pentagon Gang (a criminal gang specialising in kidnap for ransom), on its list of 'foreign terrorist organisations' after 11 September 2001. All of the groups and communities that are currently engaged in conflict with the Philippine government are able to exert considerable influence over the media agenda through violence but have struggled to influence media outputs to their advantage. This chapter assesses how the media has reported these conflicts since 2000, the extent to which the various groups and communities engaged in conflict with the government have been able to influence media outputs and the impacts that the media has had on these conflicts.

The Filipino media and the conflicts on Mindanao

The Filipino media is considered to be the freest in Asia, boasting a wide array of print media, TV and radio stations, with the internet also providing a forum for community journalism and political debate. In 2002 there were 3.5 million internet users in the Philippines (CIA 2005), although penetration in the countryside is low for reasons of infrastructure and cost (Flor 2003: 352). Yet this freedom has not always guaranteed independent reporting. Most media inspired political debate in the Philippines reflects the voices of powerful owners or interest groups tied to politics or business interests (McCargo 2003: 20).

Sections of the Filipino media have previously played a major role as agents of political change. Radio Veritas, which is operated by the Catholic Church, is widely credited with having brought down President Marcos in 1986, by mobilising millions of people for anti-Marcos demonstrations. But rather than initiating change, the role of Radio Veritas was to reflect, mediate and facilitate change. Ultimately it was people power and a military revolt which ousted Marcos, not the media (McCargo 2003: 20–21). The internet and text messaging, in conjunction with other mainstream media, are considered to have played a similar facilitating role in the mass protest movement which forced President Estrada from office in 2001 (Pabico 2000). This illustrates the potential role and impact that the media could have on the conflicts in the Philippines.

The quantity of reporting on conflict-related stories is huge and has increased considerably since 2000, but the quality of the reporting is seriously flawed. In 2000 the media was acting as an agent of stability in respect of these conflicts. Its reporting of the Moro rebellion was largely one sided in favour of the government, with many news reports simply reiterating official statements (*Asia Times Online* 2000b). The press did develop some contacts with the ASG, but most reporters were dependent on military and government sources (Quintos de Jesus 2003). There has however been some improvement since then. Studies by the Center for Media Freedom and Responsibility (CMFR), analysing reports in the five highest circulation newspapers, showed that in 2000 roughly three quarters of news articles were government sourced. By 2003 this had fallen to 60 per cent, with more than twice the number of sources being used than was the case in 2000. This included a better distribution of sources, with civil society at over 13 per cent, and almost 35 per cent of articles using more than one source (Pe Benito and Cagoco 2004).

This decline in the reliance on official sources was reflected in the treatment of the different conflicts. The CMFR studies showed that in 2000 the government generally received fairly positive treatment while the ASG and the Moro Islamic Liberation Front (MILF) generally received negative treatment. Barring neutral articles, the 2003 study still showed continued negative treatment for the ASG at 73 per cent and the MILF at 80 per cent, but government policies also received a negative treatment percentage of roughly 68 per cent (Pe Benito and Cagoco 2004). This indicates that sections of the media are gradually adopting a role as an agent of restraint, through monitoring and challenging government policies. Perhaps worried by its declining influence, the army announced in 2004 that it wanted to 'embed' journalists covering the conflicts on Mindanao within its units (Reporters Without Borders 2004).

In 2000, the media was also accused of being superficial and failing in its duty to explain the war. Glenda Gloria, a journalist who has written extensively on the Moro struggle, argued that the media was reporting the conflict as 'nothing but a cock fight – who's losing, who's winning'. The media was not questioning the conflict at the policy level, with nobody asking important questions such as how government policy was being crafted. Instead, Gloria suggested, the public was being given a false notion that the war would end as soon as military victory was achieved (*Asia Times Online* 2000b). This was confirmed by the CMFR, whose studies found that in 2000 just over 1 per cent of stories contained background information, in terms of insights into the history of the violence, details about peace pacts, or meaningful statistics that clarified the bigger picture. By 2003 that figure was close to 5 per cent. This represents a improvement, but almost half of all the reports which contained background information were published in the *Manila Bulletin*, and across all publications the majority of stories were still about the security situation (Pe Benito and Cagoco 2004).

There have also been charges of Islamophobia, from the Muslim community in the media. This has also been corroborated by the CMFR, which has suggested that 'One too many in the Manila press reacted in stereotype and let stereotype color copy and photo selection. One too many journalists let loose "hate-speech" against Muslims' (*Asia Times Online* 2000b). It also found that editorialists often tended to lump 'terrorists' and Muslims together (Reporters without Borders 2004). Filipino journalism has few Muslim practitioners, which might partly explain why editorial policy has not been sensitive to Muslim issues (Quintos de Jesus 2003).

These shortcomings were largely a consequence of flaws in media practice, which included: sensationalism; undue political and corporate influence on the news; and widespread lack of reporting and editorial skills (Quintos de Jesus 2003), whilst corruption also makes it highly partisan and untrustworthy (McCargo 2003: 21). There has generally been a lack of commitment to gathering news on these conflicts. Publishers were reluctant to financially support reporters, forcing many of them to 'embed' with military officials. This resulted in skewed reporting, which viewed the MILF and the ASG as one and the same thing (*Asia Times Online* 2000b). The major TV networks also retain few staff in the region and local bureau are ill-equipped to gather stories and feed them to a national network. When a major story breaks the networks have to bring in staff from Manila who are often unfamiliar with the issues. Jake Maderazo, managing director of the ABS-CBN news channel, admits that Manila newsmen go to Mindanao with preconceived and often erroneous notions about the MILF and the ASG. Few Manila newsmen have a working knowledge of the Moro struggle, and whilst it is incumbent on reporters and editors to research their stories, this has been more the exception than the rule in Mindanao. Lacking the proper tools to effectively evaluate information, some newsmen fell prey to propaganda or simply misread the statements of their sources (Lingao July–September 2000).

To compound the problem, the media seldom called on experts such as academics and civil society leaders who could provide alternative perspectives. As a result, coverage of terrorism does not differ significantly from coverage of criminal violence. The more violent and shocking incidents are reported more prominently (Quintos de Jesus 2003). This was reflected in the way that the media labelled violence. Prior to 2004, most media practitioners used the 'terrorist' label to encompass the actions of guerilla fighters, bandits, kidnappers, arsonists, murderers and terrorists. This ignored the critical distinctions between the different forms of criminal activity and political violence (Teodoro 2003).

These shortcomings were coupled with widespread harassment of the media and attacks on press freedom. Fifty-seven Filipino journalists have been killed since 1986, and none of the murders has been solved. In 2004 alone, seven journalists were murdered, putting the Philippines equal with Colombia as the most dangerous place in the world for journalists to work in. The suspects in these killings included politicians, the military, businessmen, warlords, crime syndicates and rebels

(*Manila Times* 2003d; Reporters Without Borders 2004). Local elites try to influence media outputs through verbal attacks on journalists and physical assaults on media targets. The majority of these incidents appear to be related to media investigations of corruption, but there are incidents related to the conflicts on Mindanao. In May 2004 for instance, the governor of Lanao del Norte province on Mindanao, Imelda Dimaporo, called on President Arroyo to investigate radio DXIC-Iligan for sedition, because it broadcast interviews with the MILF leader, Abdurahman 'Commander Bravo' Macapaar. The governor suggested that its licence should be suspended or withdrawn (Reporters Without Borders 2004).

Despite the improvement in media performance between 2000 and 2003, it had still proven unequal to the task of explaining the complex and multi-faceted character of contemporary political violence to its readers and also to the more urgent task of serving as the advocate of citizen rights (Teodoro 2003). By 2003, elements of the media were increasingly playing a role as agents of restraint, but the media as a whole was still acting as an agent of stability. Since 2003 there have been encouraging signs that the media is still striving to correct these flaws and is gradually improving its performance and increasingly adopting the role of agent of restraint.

The Maoist insurgency

The CPP and its armed wing, the NPA, have waged a thirty-five-year Maoist guerrilla war against the government. The CPP claimed in 2003 that the NPA had deployed fighters in 800 towns in 70 provinces across the country (*Sun Star Davao* 2003), and in 2004 the military estimated the strength of the NPA to be up to 8,000 fighters (*Manila Bulletin* 2004j). Over the years there have been intermittent peace negotiations between the CPP and the government. The negotiations re-started in 2004 after a three-year hiatus but have made little progress. In their dealings with the government the CPP-NPA, along with other revolutionary groups, are united under the banner of the National Democratic Front (NDF).

The CPP-NPA maintain professional relations with members of the media because they see it as a partner in exposing government corruption and abuses (*Sun Star Davao* 2004b). In turn, the media represents both sides of the conflict and remains uncritical of the peace process. The CPP-NPA has full and regular access to all sections of the media, which is often invited to visit NPA camps. As a result, it has a significant influence over media outputs. The *Manila Times* has even suggested that the voice of Gregorio 'Ka Roger' Rosal, the spokesman of the CPP, is so commonplace on the radio that millions of listeners have come to regard it as part of the daily news rather than 'a disturbing presence of a guerrilla openly challenging a government' (*Manila Times* 2003g). Given that the CPP-NPA's support base is largely based in impoverished, hard to reach, rural areas, radio is one of the most important forms of media for communicating its message to its constituency. The print media, especially the Manila broadsheets, and TV are probably of more use in communicating to a wider urban audience which is not the natural constituency of the CPP.

The positive nature of this relationship is reflected in how the media labels the CPP-NPA. The US has labelled both of them as terrorist organisations, and the

EU has done likewise at the prompting of the Arroyo government. The terrorist label is also used by some sections of the Filipino media, particularly provincial newspapers such as the *Mindanao Daily Mirror*, which reports and reflects the views of hard line local politicians such as Rodrigo Duterte, the Mayor of Davao City in Mindanao (*Mindanao Daily Mirror* 2005h). However the broadsheet Manila newspapers generally label the CPP-NPA as guerillas, militants, insurgents or rebels. These labels are not defined, but they are nevertheless useful in differentiating CPP-NPA violence from the terrorist violence of Jemaah Islamiyah (JI) and the ASG, which will be examined later in this chapter. This willingness to differentiate between the nature of different forms of conflict represent a significant advance in the quality of reporting since 2000.

Having direct access to the media enables the CPP-NPA to use its revolutionary propaganda to influence media outputs. One dimension of this has been to exploit media reporting of the root causes of the conflict. These are now so widely accepted that even Arroyo has publicly conceded that poverty has bred many of the insurrections in the Philippines. This gives the CPP-NPA a major advantage in the propaganda war. Arroyo has pledged to bring development to the underdeveloped corners of the Philippines, but it is easy for the CPP-NPA to dismiss this promise as a hollow slogan because in rural areas, poverty, landlessness, government neglect and the stranglehold of elite families and businesses on the economy and political power, remain as real as ever (*Manila Times* 2003g). It is difficult for the government to argue against this convincingly until real change has been delivered. The weakness of the Filipino economy makes this difficult to achieve, but the actions of the government have not made the job any easier. The CPP-NPA has been able to score propaganda points against the government's social and economic policies by citing the administration's policy of freezing wages amid soaring prices, allowing foreign oil companies to raise oil prices with impunity, as well as allowing worsening corruption and criminal activities by government officials (*Sun Star Davao* 2004d).

The NDF argues that

> a just and lasting peace can only be achieved by resolving the roots of the armed conflict, primarily by carrying out land reform and national industrialization.... The Arroyo regime's puppetry to US interests, its worsening corruption and criminal activities, the intensified hardships and oppression of the masses and the brazen use of fascist state violence all justify the intensification of revolutionary armed struggle.
>
> (*Sun Star Davao* 2004d)

This places the blame for the continuation of the war squarely on the government, and sets the stage for the CPP-NPA to publicise what it has done to alleviate these problems. On Mindanao the CPP has briefed the local media about its programme of implementing revolutionary land reform, decreasing land rent, raising the wages of agricultural workers, implementing revolutionary justice, maintaining peace and order and providing health care, education and other public services to the people (*Mindanao Daily Mirror* 2005a).

The CPP-NPA's involvement in the on-off peace negotiations with the government is also a major media story. In August 2004 the NDF chief, Luis Jalandoni, told the Foreign Correspondents Association that the Front did not believe that it could seize power in the near future, and so was prepared to enter a coalition government with Arroyo, even though this would fall short of the goal of a Maoist revolution (*Manila Bulletin* 2004f). Yet this proposal came to nothing when later that month the NDF called off the peace talks, accusing Manila of not doing enough to persuade international governments to remove them from the US list of foreign terrorist organisations (*Manila Bulletin* 2004j). The situation deteriorated even further when military operations by the Armed Forces of the Philippines (AFP) during the 2004 Christmas ceasefire were used by the CPP-NPA as the rationale to publicly declare that a permanent ceasefire with the Arroyo government was impossible (*Sun Star Davao* 2004d).

The CPP-NPA also operates a website which carries news, statements, photographs and other propaganda, as well as offering a forum where people can talk to each other online, and details of how to obtain CPP publications. The website enables the CPP-NPA to publicise a greater amount of propaganda in exactly the way that it wants. For example, it exaggerates the strength of the NPA as twenty-seven battalions of full-time fighters augmented by tens of thousands in the people's militias, and hundreds of thousands in self-defence units of the mass organisations (Philippine Revolution Web Central 2005). The website also enables the CPP-NPA to communicate directly with Filipinos living outside of its rural strongholds, particularly in urban areas. However there is little evidence that the CPP-NPA uses the internet as anything more than an adjunct to support the messages that it publicises in the mainstream media. Neither does it need the internet as an organisational device considering that it has an effective operational command and control system on the ground.

This reporting of the root causes of the conflict as well as CPP-NPA objectives in the mainstream media represents a significant improvement in the quality of media reporting of this conflict, but underlying it, remains a considerable amount of superficial reporting that still reflects the cock fighting analogy that was coined by Glenda Gloria in 2000. This is particularly true in the reporting of the military side of the conflict, with the local media in particular reporting every skirmish between the NPA and the security forces within their locale.

The cock fighting analogy is also reflected in much of the reporting of the political dimension of the conflict. Typical newspaper reports often comprise of government claims followed by CPP-NPA rebuttals in the same piece. In one example from October 2004, Arroyo highlighted 'growing links' between some left wing groups and international terrorist organisations, which prompted her to review her approach to the peace negotiations. Ka Roger replied that Arroyo's claim was 'a figment of her imagination and is based on the rubbish called intelligence reports from the AFP and the Philippine National Police (PNP). Arroyo just wants to divert the people's attention from plunder in the AFP and the entire government' (*Manila Bulletin* 2004g).

Similarly, the government is also forced to use the media to rebut NDF claims. In the battle to retain popular support, the government needs to be seen to be committed to the peace process, and to keep the NDF in the process. In October 2004 it was forced to publicly reiterate its commitment to the peace process after some militants and non-government organisations publicly expressed their doubts about the government's sincerity in advancing the peace process. Arroyo responded by claiming that 'Our commitment to peace has been firm, consistent, and carried out on all fronts. We have a comprehensive peace program that is closely tied up with justice, poverty alleviation, and the fight against terrorism' (*Manila Bulletin* 2004g).

More often than not there is nothing more than this reporting of claim and counter-claim. There is very little analysis or background information to help the reader understand the situation. However it is unclear whether this actually matters greatly to the CPP-NPA, because they have the access to the media that they need and are successfully getting their messages across to the public. It would be helpful to them if the media was more analytical and critical of the government, but the media could equally be more analytical and critical of the CPP-NPA.

The Moro Islamic Liberation Front

The island of Mindanao in the southern Philippines has been the scene of a separatist rebellion by the Island's Muslim population that has lasted three decades, cost hundreds of thousands of lives and stifled development. The rebellion was initially led by the secular Moro National Liberation Front (MNLF), but the more hard line Islamist elements within the MNLF split off to form the MILF in 1977. The MNLF was brought into mainstream politics through a peace agreement in 1996 under which parts of Mindanao became autonomous, but the MILF has continued an armed struggle for full independence, mostly operating in highland and rural areas covered in thick jungle. Since 2002 the MILF has sought a negotiated peace settlement with the government. A ceasefire was agreed, which despite being broken numerous times, still holds. As part of the ceasefire agreement, the former MILF chairman, Salamat Hashim, denounced terrorism and pledged to weed out any terrorists in the MILF ranks (*The Economist* 2003).

As a reflection of its involvement in the peace process, the MILF is labelled by the broadsheet print media as a separatist or rebel organisation. A number of bombings and other violent incidents allegedly perpetrated by MILF troops have been labelled 'acts of terrorism' (*Inq7.net* 2003c,e), and some individual MILF commanders have been labelled as terrorists, but the broadsheet print media and the government have shied away from defining the MILF itself as a terrorist organisation. In contrast, some newspapers such as the tabloid *Mindanao Daily Mirror* and the *Sun Star* have a more ambiguous attitude, labelling the MILF as 'terrorists', but still reporting MILF statements rejecting terrorism.

Reporting of the MILF also shows considerable improvement since 2000. It is the MILF's involvement in the peace process which has had the most direct impact, leading to more background information being provided than was the case in 2000 (Pe Benito and Cagoco 2004). It also enables the MILF to exert some degree of influence over media outputs. It recognises the importance of the media in projecting a positive image of itself and of the need to be committed to the peace process. Therefore it has used the media to publicise the positive steps it has taken to commit itself to the process, particularly the support it has provided the AFP and PNP in tracking down elements of the Pentagon Gang, the ASG and JI operating on its territory.

The media does not, however, fully report all of the causal factors of the conflict. There is a tendency to highlight the economic causes but downplay the political, historical, cultural and religious bases of the rebellion. This is a major shortcoming, but it reflects the government's dual strategy of using military action coupled with development aid to resolve the conflict.

Nevertheless, the MILF's involvement in the peace process means that its views and objectives have to be fully reported. Its primary goal of independence for Mindanao, is a given, but the media has also reported the MILF's justifications for sticking to its absolutist goal. It argues that the political settlement should be just, lasting, comprehensive and acceptable to the Moro people, with independence being the only option which offers all of these things. It has rejected the government's proposal to expand the Autonomous Region of Muslim Mindanao (ARMM), because it has failed to solve the rebellion (*Inq7.net* 2004).

In reporting these objectives, however, the media does not pick up on the MILF's Islamist ideology. In the late 1990s Salamat Hashim publicly stated that the goal of the MILF was to establish an independent Islamist state and to implement Shariah law (Hashim 1998). Many of its political leaders, such as its new Chairman, Ebrahim Murad, fought against the Soviet Union in Afghanistan, and many of them are clerics (*BBC News Online* 2003, 2005). This was highlighted by the Philippine Daily Inquirer in 2000, which noted that, 'According to the MILF's medieval version of Islam and the core belief of Muslim fundamentalism, it is against the word of Allah for a secular state to govern over Muslims' (*Asia Times Online* 2000a). Between 2003 and 2005 however, the media focused on its goal of independence. This is a failure on the part of the media, but it is also a consequence of the MILF deliberately not using its ideology in its propaganda. Its media statements do not use Islamist pharaseology and terminology which might provoke negative reactions from secular Moros, the Christian population, the government and the US. Instead, the organisation primarily comes across in the media as a secular organisation. In the post 9/11 world this serves the added purpose of helping to distance the MILF from Islamist terror groups.

The MILF also uses the internet by operating a website that publishes articles and statements and also offers a forum for online discussion and email addresses to enable direct contact. There is little overt Islamist language on the website, which looks very much like a secular news site. As is the case with the CPP-NPA website, it enables the MILF to communicate directly with Moros and other Filipinos living outside its rural strongholds, particularly in urban areas. Part of the MILF outreach programme has been to disseminate information to non-Muslims about their rights in an Islamic State, in order to try to convince them that they have nothing to fear (Interview with Salamat Hashim 1999). Using the website to present itself as a secular organisation supports that objective. As is the case with the CPP-NPA, there is little evidence that the MILF uses the internet as anything more than an adjunct to support the messages that it publicises in the mainstream media. Neither does it need the internet as an organisational device.

There are, however, other elements within the Moro community who use the internet to disseminate their Islamist ideology. Of these, the Moro Information Agency actively encourages violence. In 2005, its website published a Fatwa from the Moro Islamic Youth Union declaring that it was the duty of all Moros to engage in Jihad against the Filipino government to achieve independence. The Fatwa states that armed conflict is a central element of the Jihad and that those who die in the conflict will be martyrs. However it recognises that the nature of an individual's contribution to the Jihad can vary. Professionals, writers and University students for instance, should use the media to explain the oppression of the Moro people and refute the 'black propaganda' of the government (Fatwa Council of the Moro Youth Union 2005). The full text of the Fatwa is over 3,000 words long, so the advantage of the internet is that it allows the full text of such documents to be accessed without being misquoted, caveated or questioned by the mainstream media.

Despite the improvements in reporting, some sections of the media have still not overcome the shortcomings in their work that were identified in 2000. There is still a considerable amount of one-sidedness. Most opposition to MILF involvement in the peace process is found in the tabloids. These newspapers believe that the government cannot and should not grant independence to Mindanao, which renders the peace process a sham until the MILF relinquishes that objective. This view has been articulated by the *Mindanao Daily Mirror*:

> But what 'peace' is there to talk about? The government has been bending over backwards and stretching its patience to the limit in a bid to have lasting peace in Mindanao. But while members of MILF's peace panel kuno are 'talking' with their counterparts from the government, other MILF terrorists are busy stocking more arms, taking advantage of the lull in skirmishes with government troops.... These Islamic terrorists will only stop wrecking havoc in Mindanao if their ultimate goal is reached: the establishment of an independent and Islamic state from a part, if not the whole, of Mindanao. Will the Christians in the country's second biggest island who outnumber the Muslims five to one allow such thing to happen? NEVER, NEVER, NEVER.
>
> (*Mindanao Daily Mirror* 2005d)

The same publication has also advocated a hard line military approach to the conflict:

> The alleged 'unilateral ceasefire' is a ploy to give the Muslim terrorists a breather, to allow them to restack guns and ammunition. They are on the run what with the military's continued pounding on 'embedded terrorist cells' in Lanao del Norte and other parts of Central Mindanao. So, on with the show...all-out war by the government against the MILF marauders until the last terrorist is either killed or captured. Give them no quarters for they deserve none. To borrow Philippine Star columnist Alex Magno's call, give war a chance.
>
> (*Mindanao Daily Mirror* 2005c)

These reports reflect the attitudes of hard line local politicians such as Emmanuel Pinol, the governor of Cotobato province (*BBC News Online* 2003). Yet the MILF are not without some support in the media, one editorial in the *Sun Star Davao* suggested that

> Compared to the [NDF] the chances of forging a peace accord with the MILF are a lot better. For one thing they're after their own land and are not out to conquer the whole country and impose their own brand of culture, religion and politics – at least that's how it appears so far.
>
> (*Sun Star Davao* 2004a)

There is still a tendency for media reporting of the propaganda war between the MILF and the government to reflect the cock fighting analogy. Many reports merely publish government claims followed by MILF counter-claims, with little analysis. When the ceasefire was broken by skirmishes during 2004 and 2005 the MILF used the media to deny responsibility, or to claim that specific attacks were conducted by renegade elements acting independently (*Inq7.net* 2005a). The more hard line elements of the media question whether it is possible to engage in a peace process with an organisation which still resorts to violence and uses MILF violence as evidence to support the argument for using military force to achieve peace before entering negotiations to find a political solution. In failing to provide analysis or background information, however, the media is doing nothing to explain and clarify the situation.

The biggest problem for the MILF is the persistent reporting of allegations about its links to al Qaeda through the ASG and JI, which could lead to it being labelled a terrorist organisation. While the media reports these allegations, it remains unclear whether the links are at a personal level with individual MILF fighters or whether there are institutional links between the three groups. The MILF has admitted training foreign and local Islamic militants in the past but stresses that this stopped as part of its commitment to the peace process. There is little evidence of institutional links between the two groups, but there are links between individuals in both groups, and perhaps between JI and individual MILF units which are no longer under the control of the MILF high command. And MILF leaders have not denied that there may be individuals within its ranks who subscribe to radical ideas and may have linked up with the JI in defiance of the MILF leadership (*Manila Bulletin* 2004h). This is a major issue but reporting of it has been poor. Both sides of the argument are reported, but allegations from official sources are reported more often than MILF statements, and the media fails to engage in any significant analysis of the issue.

The MILF leadership is sensitive to the consequences of being labelled a terrorist organisation for fear of being isolated, both financially and politically. The government knows this and has used the media to exploit this sensitivity. In May 2003, following a wave of MILF raids and bombings which claimed nearly 100 lives, the government suspended peace negotiations and debated whether to designate the MILF as a terrorist group (*Inq7.net* 2003b). In the end the government chose not to; but it plays a careful game of publicly keeping the pressure on, whilst avoiding taking the irrevocable step of confirming institutional links between the MILF and terrorist organisations, which would have profound repercussions for government relations with the MILF and the future of the peace process.

Whilst the media regularly offers the MILF the opportunity to publicise its rebuttals of these reports, the problem is that official sources are still reported more often than the MILF, putting Arroyo under pressure from hardliners, public opinion, and the US, to take a more militaristic approach to the conflict. Despite the imbalance in reporting, the media largely reflects government policy in high-lighting issues of concern with the MILF but avoiding labelling the MILF as a terrorist organisation whilst it seeks a political solution. The MILF itself has sufficient access to the media to publicise its objectives, but it is still unable to positively influence some of the other key media outputs which are having a detrimental impact on its political standing.

Al Qaeda in the Philippines

In 2003 President Arroyo declared JI, which is commonly considered to be the regional arm of al Qaeda, to be the top national security threat to the country. Al Qaeda has been active in the Philippines since the early 1990s, when Osama bin Laden sent Khaled Sheikh Mohammed, who was later to become the operations chief of al Qaeda, to the Philippines, to try to persuade the various Islamic factions to unite under his banner. That initiative failed, but Khaled and his brother, Ramseh Youssef, who would later be convicted of the 1993 World Trade Centre bombing, were responsible for three bombings in Manila and the bombing of a Philippines Air passenger jet bound for Iran in 1994. These were precursors to the more ambitious 'Oplan Bojinka', which included plans to kill the Pope and blow up twelve US passenger jets over the Pacific. The plan was foiled in 1995 when police investigated a blaze at Youssef's flat (Gunaratna 2003: 175). Hambali, the alleged operations chief of JI, was also active in the Philippines, although most of the bombings sponsored by his network were local in nature, in retaliation to the government's campaign against the MILF and the ASG (*The Economist* 2002).

The most surprising aspect of the Filipino media's reporting of JI is the high profile that it receives. This is primarily the result of reporting briefings from official sources and reflects the tendency that was identified in 2000 for the media to be one sided in favour of the government and to be over-reliant on official sources. In common with other Southeast Asian media, the Filipino media labels the group as terrorists or militants.

Unlike the CPP-NPA and the MILF, the JI does not have direct access to the mainstream Media and does not have a media spokesman or issue media statements. As a result, and despite figuring prominently on the media agenda, therefore, it has limited influence over media outputs. This is particularly evident in its failing to use the Filipino media to publicise its ideology. What little reporting there is of JI's ideology and goals, derives from statements issued by Osama bin Laden or JI leaders in Indonesia. These statements are reported in the broadsheet media such as the *Manila Times*; however they are not reported verbatim. As a result not much sense of the al Qaeda ideology comes through in these reports. In local and community newspapers such as the *Sun Star Davao* there is even less mention of bin Laden's statements. As a result, JI operatives, their sympathisers, and potential supporters, have to rely on the internet to access the full text of al Qaeda statements.

There are indications, however, that media is not the primary means by which JI is spreading its ideology. What seems to be of much greater importance to it is gaining direct access to the fighters of the MILF and the ASG. It is by spreading its ideology by personal contact that JI seems to be finding its recruits or at least influencing them to perpetrate attacks that suit its objectives.

Since 2002 JI has been on the defensive following the arrest or killing of a number of its operatives. Consequently, its recent activities have been low key, mainly using the Philippines as a safe haven and training ground. Most media reports are of the existence of JI cells operating in the country, JI's links to indigenous Filipino groups, alleged JI plans for attacks inside the Philippines, and the killing or arrest of JI members. Even when there are no actual attacks by JI, this constant reporting creates the sense that beneath the surface, JI remains active. More importantly, by constantly reporting the links between al Qaeda, JI, the ASG and the MILF the media is linking these indigenous conflicts to the 'war on terror'. This suits JI's objectives, because it distances these indigenous groups even further from the government.

In reading the numerous reports about JI in the broadsheet Manila-based newspapers, it is difficult to avoid the perception that it has a degree of influence over the media agenda, which is out of proportion to the threat that it poses. It has a much smaller presence in the Philippines than either the ASG, the MILF or the NPA, with only around fifty operatives in central Mindanao in 2004 (*Manila Bulletin* 2004i), and the number of violent attacks or planned attacks attributed to JI is small compared to those of any of the indigenous Filipino groups. Community newspapers such as the *Sun Star* provide a much better balance, because they report the threats that are having a direct impact on their readership, which are predominantly from the NPA, the MILF and the ASG. It seems that every skirmish involving these groups is reported, whilst JI and al Qaeda receive little attention. The high level of attention focused on JI by Manila-based broadsheets seems to be a consequence of the high political profile which Arroyo has accorded the group, which in turn seems to be a direct result of the pressure that the government is under from the US to toe the line in the 'war on terror'.

The Abu Sayyaf Group

Al Qaeda is most closely identified with the most notorious and violent of the indigenous Filipino groups – the ASG. The group broke away from the MNLF in 1991 under the leadership of Abdurajak Abubakar Janjalani, who had been trained in Afghanistan. He was subsequently killed in a gun battle with the police in 1998. The goal of the group was the creation of an independent Islamic state in Mindanao and the Sulu islands (*BBC News Online* 2005). It is notorious for kidnapping Christians and foreigners for ransom, and for the extreme violence that it employs. Among its worst atrocities were the abduction of more than fifty students and teachers on Basilan island in March 2001. Several of the hostages were killed, including a Catholic priest who was tortured and shot in the head. Two months later it seized three Americans and a group of Filipinos from the island of Palawan. Many of the Filipino hostages were recovered after ransoms were paid, but an American hostage was beheaded, and another was killed during a rescue mission in June 2002 (*Manila Bulletin* 2004e). In 2004 the ASG shifted the focus of its activities to bombings, the first of which was the sinking of the Superferry14 in 2004, which left more than a hundred people dead. The government has declared all-out war on the ASG, and since receiving US military assistance, the AFP and PNP had considerable success in reducing its active numbers from 2,000 to 200 between 2001 and 2002 (*The Economist* 2002).

The ASGs relationship with the media is somewhat contradictory. On the one hand it has courted media attention. Coverage of the ASG by Manila dailies increased in both frequency and prominence following the hostage crises of 2000 (*Asia Times Online* 2000b), to the extent that it eclipsed reporting of President Estrada's military offensive against the MILF, despite the fact that the MILF constitutes a much more significant political threat. The main reason for this was the ASG's media strategy. It singled out news organisations for scoops and exclusives, whereas other armed groups are more reticent or rely on their political fronts to deal with the press. Another reason is because stories involving the ASG followed traditional Filipino news values – they had more drama and more excitement, and they were easier to sell and TV exploited the visual elements (Quintos de Jesus 2003). To gain maximum media exposure journalists and TV crews were invited to visit the camps where hostages were being held, and the foreign media were specifically asked to attend in some instances.

However the ASG has also attempted to intimidate the media, and this has included kidnapping journalists. It has also required journalists to pay for access, often robbing them of cash and other possessions whenever they visited ASG camps (*Asia Times Online* 2000b). This raises ethical issues for journalists and also questions about how objective reporters could afford to be if they wanted access to ASG camps. In November 2004, the group was accused of killing Gene Boyd Lumawag, a photo editor for the independent news agency MindaNews, although the National Union of Journalists of the Philippines questioned the military's claim that the ASG was responsible, and the murder remains unsolved (*Manila Times* 2004e).

Even after the big kidnapping incidents, the ASG has remained a major news story in the Philippines, but the majority of this reporting still resembles the cock fighting analogy that Glenda Gloria coined in 2000. The majority of reports about the ASG consist of warnings by the security forces of impending attacks and a steady trickle of stories related to skirmishes and the killing or capture of ASG fighters. This may be because the government is winning the military conflict with the ASG, but there is also no peace process to draw attention away from the military side of the conflict. As a result, the ASG has been unable to significantly influence media outputs since 2001, despite being able to force itself onto the media agenda.

There is hardly any reporting linking ASG violence to its root causes in the lawless environment on Basilan island. These causes include grinding poverty, a gun culture, and local government that lacks legitimacy. Christians who migrated to the province control the economy whilst Muslims remain poor. This has enabled the ASG to convince recruits that the Christians are depriving Muslims of life's barest essentials. The group made similar progress in Sulu province on Jolo island, which is among the Philippines' ten poorest provinces (Gloria 2000).

The ASG itself has also failed to use the media to articulate its ideology and objectives, which is another reason why reporting of the ASG has not developed much beyond the cock fighting analogy. Successive governments have been uncertain about how to view the group. Under the Ramos administration, the Intelligence Service of the AFP described the ASG as no more than a kidnap gang, whilst the PNP claimed that the group was part of the global spread of Islamic fundamentalism. Whilst under the Estrada administration the government viewed the ASG as part of a single Muslim movement engaged in armed struggle against the state, with the goal of establishing a separate Islamic state through terror (Gloria 2000). In recent years, however, the media labels the ASG as either 'terrorists', or 'bandits', and sometimes as 'militants' or a 'Muslim extremist group'.

The group has periodically demanded the release of Ramseh Youssef and other al Qaeda figures who have been jailed in the US (Gunaratna 2003: 180), but the media primarily focuses on the ASG's actions, rather than its objectives. Its only goal that is given any real attention is the ransoms that it has demanded for hostages. When hostages have been murdered, it seems to have been because a ransom was not paid or purely to instil terror, rather than for ideological reasons. This fits with the labelling of the ASG as a bandit group, which has neither political nor social objectives. Part of the reason for its failure to communicate any political goals is because it has lost its ideological compass. Its founder, Abdurajak Janjalani, was well schooled in a fundamentalist interpretation of Islam, and he instilled the belief in his recruits that Jihad was their personal responsibility, and that non-believers had to be killed or driven out of Mindanao. His successor, Khaddafy Janjalani lacked any strong ideological or religious convictions. Whereas Abdurajak could spend a whole day discussing Islam, a police official who interrogated Khaddafy in jail described him as someone '. . . who knows nothing when it comes to ideology' (Gloria 2000).

By the time of the Basilan kidnappings in 2000 the indications were that the ASG did not know what it wanted or how to articulate the problems of the Moro community. The kidnappers at first demanded only rice and food. When they allowed the media to interview the hostages, their leader, Commander Robot, took the opportunity to declare that the kidnappers were mujahideen who respected the Geneva Convention and would not harm civilians, journalists and medical personnel. Yet these statements are no substitute for a clearly articulated political and social agenda in winning popular support. Although on Jolo, where another faction were holding a group of largely foreign captives, they first asked for money and then followed this with a demand for implementation of fishing laws and the obsolete 1976 Tripoli Agreement between the Marcos government and the MNLF (Gloria 2000).

The ASG relies primarily on violence and the threat of terror to intimidate public opinion, and the extremity of the violence that it employs is guaranteed to secure media attention. In an interview aired by radio station DXRZ in 2003, ASG spokesman Abu Solaiman said the group 'will be your worst nightmares. We will let you feel the fear and the raging fury very deep inside us' (*Mindanao Daily Mirror* 2005b). The previous year had witnessed one of its worst excesses when footage of a soldier being beheaded was aired on prime-time newscasts. The Standards Authority of the Kapisanan ng mga Brodkaster ng Pilipinas (KBP), censured the four networks involved in a strongly worded decision which read,

> The grisly beheading scenes … constitute a flagrant, shocking, sickening and insensitive display of graphic and horrifying violence which has no place on Philippine television, or elsewhere, and can find no shield under the free speech provision of the Constitution or respondents' responsibility to inform the public on news or current events. The questioned footages are utterly offensive, absolutely dehumanizing, and completely devoid of any redeeming quality. They are unfit for public consumption, whether primetime or otherwise, in newscasts or other program modes.
>
> (Chua 2003)

The four stations were deluged with complaints, showing both public repugnance for their giving the ASG propaganda and also popular opposition to the ASG. However the ASG's inability to articulate any political objectives effectively devalues these actions to the level of being gratuitous violence.

The ASG's attempts to influence media outputs have intensified since 2001, because the group has been on the defensive and media attention has focused on the successes of the security forces. It attempted to re-brand itself by renaming itself 'Al-Rakatul Islamiah' and claiming that it was a group of rational armed men fighting for a legitimate cause. It also re-directed its violence and ratcheted up the scale of its attacks. This was reflected in the bombing of Superferry 14 and its alleged plans for a 'Madrid level' bombing in 2004.[1] Persistent media reports in 2004 that ASG cells had moved into Manila came amid suggestions that it was planning to intensify attacks on civilian targets in order to show to the government and international terrorist groups that it was still a force to reckon with (*Manila Times* 2004c). Janjalani also issued a statement which claimed that the group had an endless list of suicide bombers ready to be deployed against undisclosed targets (*Manila Times* 2004a). Despite these efforts the media still universally refers to the group as the ASG and still labels it as a bandit group.

Its inability to articulate any coherent ideological goals, coupled with its gratuitous use of violence, has meant that the ASG's use of the media has failed to win it any measure of popular support among the Muslim population. Instead, media reporting perpetuates the image of the group's lack of popular support. Nash Pangadapun, secretary general of Maradeka, a federation of Moro civil society groups, told the *Manila Bulletin* that the Moro people were tired of the ASG, because they were suffering persecution, oppression and discrimination due to its 'hijacking' of Islam and its values of tolerance, co-existence, justice, fairness, sincerity and honesty (*Manila Bulletin* 2004c). Regular reporting of the displacement and killing of civilians in battles with the AFP focuses popular discontent on the negative impact that the ASG is having on the Muslim community, and has effectively isolated the ASG (Gloria 2000). Unlike the MILF and the CPP-NPA, the ASG has not shown any ability to develop and adapt its relations with the media or to influence media outputs. As a consequence, the nature of the reporting of the ASG still largely reflects the shortcomings that were highlighted in 2000.

The military and the media: hyping the terror threat

One of the main criticisms of the Filipino media's reporting of these conflicts in 2000 was the way it used briefings from official sources. The media's handling of official sources has improved since then, but the majority of reporting still tends to be skewed in favour of official sources. On the face of it this perpetuates the primary role of media as an agent of stability. The situation is complicated by the existence of divisions within the government and the security forces over how to deal with these conflicts. As a result, political turf battles are frequently played out in the media. Elements of the military favour a more hard line military approach than President Arroyo and are in a powerful position to influence media outputs through briefings on operational issues. The MILF in particular has complained about AFP misinformation in the media, and the Filipino media has been unable to avoid being dragged into these political turf battles. Therefore sections of the administration are attempting to use the media as an agent of change, in respect of government policy.

These political turf battles were evident when the MILF proposed a temporary ceasefire in 2003. Arroyo welcomed it as a positive development, but Defence Secretary Angelo Reyes rejected it on the grounds that the MILF could use it to regroup. Major General Roy Kyamko, head of the army's Southern Command, also saw the ceasefire declaration as a tactical move that had been forced upon the MILF by heavy losses. Unlike Arroyo, they preferred to continue military operations to achieve a military victory (*Inq7.net* 2003d). It is indicative of the power of the Military that it feels able to use the media to challenge the President in this way. The problem for Arroyo is that she is politically indebted to the AFP and is fearful of suffering the same fate as former President Estrada, who was forced from office in 2001 after the AFP withdrew its support (Trillanes 2001).

The main way in which these elements of the AFP attempt to undermine the peace process with the MILF and force a change in government policy is to persistently brief the media with intelligence reports about actual and alleged links between the MILF, JI, the ASG and the Pentagon gang, often implying that these links are institutional in nature. But it is often difficult to distinguish one group from another when they all operate in the same geographical area and many of them are related to each other, either by kinship or erstwhile comradeship (Rimban 2003). After a kidnapping incident by the ASG on the island of Sipadan in 2000, police and military intelligence agents drafted separate internal briefs suggesting that the incident was the spark for a united front of 'Islamic extremists' in the Philippines, Indonesia and Malaysia. This assessment proved to be wrong, and could be interpreted as a deliberate attempt to hype up the threat in order to justify increased military action (Gloria 2000).

The AFP has also influenced media outputs through its assessment of responsibility for terrorist incidents. Its attempts to manipulate these assessments have led to a number of public fiascos. The most notable was the bomb attack on Davao City airport in March 2003, which was initially claimed by the ASG in a telephone interview with ABS-CBN. Almost immediately the Defence Secretary Angelo T. Reyes dismissed the claim on the grounds that the ASG does not operate in Davao (*Manila Times* 2003b). The MILF denied involvement but a number of its senior commanders were subsequently accused of the bombing. The charges threatened to de-rail the peace process until they were finally withdrawn in 2004 due to a lack of evidence. The media was justifiably critical of the government's handling of this incident. The *Manila Times* argued that it had given the MILF the upper hand in the propaganda war, because it could be used as proof that the MILF was not linked to terrorism, and also displayed a lack of sincerity on the part of the government in the peace process (*Manila Times* 2004d).

The AFP finds a receptive audience for these messages amongst those tabloids which label the MILF as a terrorist organisation, and favour a military response to the conflict. But there are serious concerns that even the broadsheet press rely too heavily on AFP and PNP briefings, often reporting them verbatim, even when their contents cannot be verified. The inability or unwillingness of the media to analyse or caveat the briefings that it receives from official sources is a serious deficiency, although the media does give the MILF the opportunity to comment on some of these briefings. In 2004 for instance, when the *Sun Star Davao* reported comments by Ebrahim Murad that there would be no peace with Manila if sections of the military continued to make allegations that the MILF sheltered JI militants, he suggested that 'frankly, we feel there are people in government who don't want peace in Mindanao' (*Sun Star Davao* 2004c). But merely reporting these claims and counter-claims does not clarify the situation and is not a real substitute for thorough and independent analysis of the issues.

Nevertheless, there have been encouraging signs that some sections of the media oppose the change to more hardline military solutions and are increasingly taking on the role of an agent of restraint, notably the internet news site *Inq7.net*. Following a massive military assault on the MILF in February 2003, *Inq7.net* attacked the influence of 'hawks' in the AFP and the administration. The AFP had initially justified the assault by claiming that the MILF was harbouring members of the Pentagon Gang but subsequently admitted that the real target was the MILF itself. The rationale was an allegation that it was massing its forces in violation of the ceasefire, but there are other political mechanisms to address such problems.

The use of military force was interpreted as being evidence of the hawks becoming increasingly powerful and of their desire to force the MILF out of the resource-rich Liguasan Marsh, in order to secure access for big investors (*Inq7.net* 2003a). A subsequent editorial went even further by claiming that the whole military strategy for dealing with the MILF had been a failure and that it was actually a number of political and diplomatic factors which had forced the MILF to the negotiating table (*Inq7.net* 2003d).

Some sections of the media have also reported stories that the AFP could have hyped up terror threats for its own purposes. In 2004, Senate Minority Leader, Aquilino Pimentel Jr, requested that the AFP present proof of an alleged plot by members of the MILF with links to JI, to blow up the US embassy in Manila, in order to remove any suspicion that it was a ploy to draw public attention away from a congressional probe on corruption in the military (*Manila Bulletin* 2004h). Some sections of the media have also displayed some sense of even handedness by reporting briefings from conflicting government sources (*Manila Times* 2003e). However these examples are overwhelmed by the preponderence of reports based on AFP briefings, over which the media continues to routinely suspend its critical faculties. Yet this has not facilitated change in government policy because the majority of the media also reflects the official government policy of pursuing political solutions with the MILF and the CPP-NPA.

The Filipino media and US interventionism

By placing the ASG, the CPP-NPA, JI and the Pentagon Gang on its list of foreign terrorist organisations, the US has identified the Philippines as one of the main battlegrounds of its 'war on terror' in Asia. In turn, President Arroyo is completely committed to the 'war', even to the extent of supporting the invasion of Iraq on the grounds that Iraqi weapons of mass destruction might find their way to the ASG or the MILF, although her popularity has suffered as a result (Coronel 2003). The closeness of the Bush–Arroyo relationship means that US views and objectives in the 'war on terror' are central to Filipino government policy and are widely reported in the media. The US is often reported in a favourable fashion, including direct reporting of President Bush. Addressing a joint session of the Philippine Congress in 2003, Bush promised to help bring the ASG to justice, to work with all Southeast Asian nations to destroy the JI, and committed US development assistance to Mindano once peace had been established. He called the US–Philippine military alliance 'a rock of stability in the Pacific'. The *Manila Times* commented that

> these pronouncements come across as genuine and sincere. And they are
> exactly what many Filipinos want to hear. His message is clear and reassuring: 'The United States and the Philippines are warm friends. We cherish that
> friendship, and we will keep it strong'.
>
> (*Manila Times* 2003f; *Mindanao Daily*
> *Mirror* 2005f)

Despite this, Arroyo's approach to dealing with the Philippines' indigenous conflicts often does not fit neatly into US policy in the 'war on terror'. The US seeks to highlight links between al Qaeda and local groups throughout Asia in order to build a picture of a regional and global terror threat. It is these actual and perceived links to al Qaeda that underpin a US policy towards the various conflicts in the Philippines that borders on interventionism and at times brings it into conflict with the Filipino government. The US has attempted to use the media to exert public pressure on Arroyo to pursue a more hard line policy that fits with its vision of the 'war on terror'. The US embassy in Manila regularly briefs the Filipino media on how the conflicts in the Philippines fit into the 'war on terror'. One of the ways it does this is to hype-up the al Qaeda threat in the Philippines. In 2004 for instance, US Ambassador, Francis Ricciardone, issued a statement that JI training camps in the Philippines posed a danger not just to Southeast Asia but to the world at large (*Manila Bulletin* 2004d), and US defense officials also briefed journalists that JI had become the biggest terrorist threat to the Philippines (*Mindanao Daily Mirror* 2005g). Yet JI perpetrates fewer violent attacks in the Philippines than any other combatant group currently operating in the country and is not known to have been involved in any attacks outside Southeast Asia.

The US also attempts to link indigenous Filipino groups with JI in order to bring them all within the ambit of the 'war on terror', even though it accepts that it is 'rogue factions' within the MILF and MNLF which have links to terrorism (*Mindanao Daily Mirror* 2005g). In 2004 for instance, Ricciardone questioned MILF denials that it shelters foreign militants, as well as the sincerity of its offer to help the government fight JI (*Manila Bulletin* 2004d). The following year he expressed doubts about the sincerity of the MILF to resume peace talks and suggested that the MILF should rid itself of members who were alleged to be connected with JI: 'The United States is confused with the MILF. Are they people who welcome terrorist bombers from the Jemaah Islamiyah? Are they killers who bomb markets or otherwise? They have to make their position clear' (*Manila Bulletin* 2005b). This contrasts markedly with the views of the Filipino government, as expressed by Foreign Affairs Secretary Alberto Romulo, who stated that the government trusts the MILF leadership (*Manila Bulletin* 2005b; *Mindanao Daily Mirror* 2005f), and Eduardo Ermita, a presidential adviser on the peace talks with the MILF, who has stated that al Qaeda has no contacts in the Philippines apart from with the ASG (Suh 2001).

The statements issued by the US Embassy in Manila often reflect more deep seated concerns in Washington about the Philippines' handling of the 'war on terror', which are also reported back in the Philippines. In a particularly damaging instance in 2004, the *Manila Times* reported on a story from the New York Times that the Filipino government had received a diplomatic reproach from Washington for not doing enough to root out terrorist groups. A Western diplomat suggested to the New York Times that Manila had been 'in a state of denial' about the terrorist threat, following a US assessment that an alliance had formed between JI, the ASG and the MILF (*Manila Times* 2004b). This assessment completely misrepresents the nature of the links between these three groups and gives no credit for the military successes against the ASG since 2001. The article shows the US trying to pressure Arroyo into pursuing a more hard line policy, even though a political solution is the only way of achieving a lasting peace with the MILF. Yet the Filipino media offered only weak criticism of what was said in the New York Times article.

The CPP and the MILF have attempted to exploit anti-US sentiment within the country, particularly the historical antipathy towards the US in Mindanao, in order to discredit the government. In 2003 for instance, the CPP spokesman, Ka Roger, warned that the inclusion of the CPP-NPA in the US list of terrorist organisations was a prelude to US military intervention in the Philippines (*Manila Times* 2003a). Ka Roger has also denounced the US for trying to blackmail the MILF into signing a peace deal with the government by threatening to include it on its list of foreign terrorist organisations and of attempting to blackmail the CPP-NPA by threatening to only remove it from the list if it submits to the government in the peace process (*Manila Bulletin* 2003a).

But despite these occasional outbursts in the media, the negative impact of US interventionism is not a theme that is pursued in the media to any great extent and is more than matched by reporting that is supportive of the presence of US troops. The propaganda value that the CPP-NPA can potentially generate from it illustrates the shortsightedness of US policy, but the media has helped to create a favourable climate for the reception of US messages by linking indigenous Filipino conflicts to the 'war on terror'. In addition, widespread public antipathy towards the MILF, JI, ASG and the CPP-NPA means that US interventionism is not as politically damaging to the government as it could be.

Conclusion: media impacts

The mainstream media has made some significant progress in improving the quality of its reporting of these conflicts. There is now a more even-handed approach to reporting the MILF and the CPP-NPA, which both have full access to the mainstream media. Prior to 2004 the media had exacerbated the sense of marginalisation felt by different cultural and religious groups, especially the Muslim community, through its negative stereotyping and profiling. Headlines regularly identified 'Muslim bandits' and 'Muslim kidnappers' (Quintos de Jesus 2003). By 2004 however, such headlines had largely disappeared from newspapers such as the *Manila Times, Manila Bulletin* and *Inq7.net*, although those headlines will have left a lasting legacy which will not be easily reversed. But nevertheless there are still some major shortcomings. Reporting of the JI and ASG is still one sided, and the cock fighting analogy is still prevalent to varying degrees in reporting the military dimensions of all of these conflicts. These shortcomings are exacerbated by a lack of analysis of key issues and an unquestioning reliance on official sources.

It is often assumed that an independent media, together with the new media, will act as an agent of change, but this has not been the case with these conflicts, although some elements of the Filipino media have increasingly fulfilled the role of agent of restraint. The improvements in media performance have been most beneficial to the CPP-NPA and the MILF, which have both been able to influence media outputs to some extent. Yet despite occasionally being able to politically discomfit the government, the practical impact of this reporting has been limited. It has not helped to generate mass popular support for any of these groups and has not generated any pressure on the government to make significant concessions to any of them.

The media has had a bigger impact in terms of de-legitimising the ASG by perpetuating its status as a bandit organisation, downplaying its Islamist ideology, and publicising its violence as being gratuitous by failing to make the connection with its root causes. The nature of this reporting both reflects and reinforces the predominant view of the ASG within the government and Filipino society, and even within the Muslim community, where the group remains marginalised. This is partly a result of the ASG's lack of sophistication in handling the media, but it is also a consequence of media hostility towards the group, which was reflected in its unwillingness to accept the ASG's attempt to re-brand itself. The internet seems to have had no impact in terms of challenging these preconceptions. As a consequence, ASG violence has had little impact in terms of generating popular support or forcing concessions from the government.

The media has also helped to create a perception that the threat from JI is probably greater than it actually is. This has had impact in terms of rooting indigenous conflicts within the 'war on terror' in the public consciousness and building public support for a more hard line military response in dealing with the group.

Perhaps the most positive media impact lies in how it differentiates between the MILF and the CPP-NPA, on the one hand, as secessionist or revolutionary groups, and the ASG and JI, on the other hand, as terrorist groups. This helps to support the political and public perception that negotiated solutions might be found to resolve the conflicts with the MILF and the CPP-NPA. This search for negotiated solutions is threatened by the most negative impact of this reporting – the media's tendency to identify indigenous conflicts with the 'war on terror'. Although for the time being at least, the media is not firmly rooting these conflicts within the 'war on terror'. However it is unclear whether the media is making these distinctions between the groups independently, or is just reflecting the views of the government, which currently sees negotiations as the way to secure a lasting peace with the CPP-NPA and the MILF. Therefore, it is difficult to determine the full extent of the progress that the media has made since 2000, or whether it continues to merely reflect the views of the government of the day.

Note

1 This refers to the bombs on commuter trains and train stations in the Spanish city of Madrid in 2004, which killed nearly 200 people, al Qaeda was blamed for the attacks.

5 Shooting the messenger?

Political violence, Gujarat 2002 and the Indian news media

Prasun Sonwalkar

'Communalism becoming news is not dangerous. News becoming communal is.'
(A poster of the Delhi Union of Journalists)

Introduction

This chapter presents an example of how journalists negotiate political minefields and face criticism for the simple reason that their output may go against dominant political interests. I focus on the coverage of the political violence in the western Indian state of Gujarat in the spring of 2002 – which was widely seen as a pogrom against Muslims – and explore some of the ethical, political and professional dilemmas faced by journalists covering such events. Gujarat, the land of Gandhi, is likely to remain in the news for some time for the events of 2002, when mobs went on a rampage against Muslims and perpetrated some of the most gory acts of violence since India's independence in 1947. The nature of the news coverage made as much news as the acts of political violence themselves.

My starting point is to propose that political violence, and even parliamentary politics, can no longer be imagined without examining the ways in which they are communicated. Several events of political violence can be best understood as spectacles on television. CNN's coverage that brought the 1991 Gulf War to our drawing rooms was perceived by many as a video game war or a Hollywood movie. The defining image of September 11 for millions outside New York is the spectacular television footage of the planes ploughing into the twin towers. Political violence makes for riveting television, which partly explains why news organizations around the world invest millions covering wars and conflicts. In 2003, the coverage of the Iraq conflict by 'embedded journalists' made as much news as the conflict itself. On such occasions, the medium itself becomes the message.

The symbiotic relationship between the media and terrorism/political violence has been the subject of several studies (Schmid and de Graaf 1982; Schlesinger et al. 1983; Schlesinger 1991; Weimann and Winn 1993). There is a constant struggle between state and non-state actors to ensure that their versions are prominently covered by the news media. Given the close relationship between the news media and political violence, Hansen's (2004: 19) notion of 'politics as permanent performance' is useful to understand and unpack major contemporary events.

Acts of political violence should be viewed as political performance enacted by state and non-state actors. Such acts do not take place in a vacuum, but within political frameworks that privilege or marginalize the pursuit of certain ideologies, values and beliefs. Violence is central to a democratic framework that sees the state having legal control over organized violence (police, army, security forces and vigilantes of ruling parties). In Hansen's words, political performance 'comprises the construction of images and spectacles, forms of speech, dress and public behaviour that promotes the identity of a movement or party, defines its members and promotes its cause or worldview' (2004: 23).

This formulation is particularly useful in multicultural societies that witness constant tension between majorities and minorities, widely constituted as 'insiders' and 'outsiders', or as 'us' and 'them'. In such contexts, the macro-dimensions of religion, community, language and ethnicity are played out at the micro level as politics of permanent performance. Most acts of political violence take place between *unequal* groups or actors, which places the news media in a piquant situation: both sides court journalists, but they may be despised too if their professional output does not fit within contending frames. It is not uncommon for dominant political actors to hail the news media when convenient and to heap flak on them when they do not toe the 'party line'. They become damned if they report and damned if they don't. It is also not uncommon for dominant political forces, including their supporters in the news media, to brand or stereotype journalists who may not be amenable to toe the 'party line'. In media and political circles in London or Delhi or elsewhere, the political inclination of most journalists is known. The problem arises when a journalist with no ostensible allegiance towards any party or ideology comes to be branded simply because his or her output does not fit into certain political frames.

The chapter is also informed by my personal experience of covering the activities of the Hindutva forces, including several defining events, for *The Times of India* and other publications between 1988 and 1999.[1] Some of the events I covered were based in Gujarat or had strong connections with the state. I have some experience of the damned-if-you-cover-damned-if-you-don't conundrum. The very act of reporting that the Hindutva forces were making waves through their grassroots political mobilization in Gujarat in 1990 invited opprobrium from some ideologically driven journalist colleagues and others. It betrayed the hope that by merely not reporting certain political events, somehow, the growth of certain ideologies would be prevented. It also implied that the English-language press had overweening status in a country of 1 billion plus people, of whom barely a small but influential minority uses the English language.

When journalists face sustained criticism from political actors, many ask the question: are the news media responsible for political violence or do they merely report political violence? That the Hindutva forces went on to wield power in New Delhi in the late 1990s and become one of the poles of Indian politics – despite trenchant criticism in the English-language press over the years – suggests a disjuncture between the spaces that English-language journalists inhabit and the vast non-English reality in India. As Smith (1980: 160) observed, 'India is a country with an intellectual elite which is perhaps further alienated from its own masses than that of any other developing country'. India's English-language press is closely implicated with the values of the political and social elites, most of them exposed to western ideas of modernity. On the other hand, the non-English language press is considered to reflect more adequately the life situation of the vast majority that is unfamiliar with the English language and western values. This juncture within the Indian media was also evident during the coverage of Gujarat 2002 – widely dubbed as India's first communal riot for the satellite television era.

The events reflected and reinforced a politics that, since the late 1980s, had been enacted as 'permanent performance' on a stage carefully nurtured by the pro-Hindutva forces. As Hansen observed,

> Democracy in India has produced a culture of politics that is incredibly fluid, situational and dynamic – where stable constituencies, alliances, equations and ideological principles are in constant flux and redefinition. In such a culture it is those who can create a collective mood, or the illusion of a collectivity driven by a mood – both highly ephemeral phenomena – that can set political agendas at least for some time ... To perform this type of politics depends, therefore, on the ability to stage public performances, to use and employ a range of registers that can generate authority, and put the power of rumours, myth and other cultural registers to effective use.
>
> (Hansen 2004: 23)

Politics and political violence in India are framed against the shifting quicksands of religion, caste, community, language, gender, region and individuals belonging to influential groups or families. As Nandy (1970: 58) observed, 'It is possible to interpret the political process in India as a continuing attempt to reconcile older categories of thought and social character to the demands of nation-building and political culture as a complex of continuities'. Generating collective moods, particularly during elections, has been a key method of political mobilization. More often than not, such mobilization also involves violence – indeed, violence has been central to electoral politics in northern states such as Bihar and Uttar Pradesh.

But before setting out an overview of contemporary Hindutva-oriented politics, it is important to set out definitions of some key terms used in the discourse:

- *Sangh parivar* This is the umbrella term used for various organizations owing allegiance to the Hindutva ideology. These organizations – such as the Vishwa Hindu Parishad (VHP; World Hindu Council) and the Bajrang Dal (an organization of young devotees of Lord Hanuman, considered a symbol of physical strength and power) – have been formed by, and work under the close supervision of, the Rashtriya Swayamsevak Sangh (RSS), or the national volunteers association. 'Parivar' is the Hindi word for family and 'sangh parivar' refers to the family of organizations spawned by the RSS.
- *BJP* Bharatiya Janata Party, which literally means Indian People's Party. It is the political front of the 'sangh parivar', and strives to capture political power while aiming at reviving the Hindu social order and traditions in order to reinforce and distinctively establish the dominance of Hindus in India.

- *'Kar sevaks'* Literally, this means religious workers. The term has been widely used for the thousands of supporters who volunteer to help in the construction of a temple to the Hindu god, Lord Ram, at Ayodhya in North India. The 'kar sevaks' were accused of demolishing the Babri mosque at Ayodhya on 6 December 1992, which set off a rash of Hindu–Muslim clashes in India.

Hindutva and Gujarat

Gujarat is better known as the birthplace of Gandhi, the apostle of peace. But here, Hindu–Muslim clashes have been endemic – the state has the worst record of Hindu–Muslim clashes in the country since India's independence in 1947 (Varshney 2002: 97–98). Three Gujarat towns have been particularly prone to Hindu–Muslim clashes: Ahmedabad, Vadodara and Godhra. Since the early 1980s, the state has been one of the major areas where Hindutva forces have focused their attention. Political adversaries of the 'sangh parivar' allege that such forces have treated Gujarat as a 'Hindutva laboratory' to conduct political, social and cultural experiments in order to replicate them in other parts of India.

As Shah (1998: 244) observed,

> The Sangh Parivar has disseminated Hindutva ideology in Gujarat over many decades. The party (BJP) and its allies have built the organization brick by brick. It began to reap the benefits of these endeavours in the early 1990s and captured power in 1995.

After the BJP won an overwhelming majority in the state elections in December 2002, months after the pogrom against Muslims, there was much speculation in the media that the BJP would adopt the 'Gujarat formula' to win power in other states in the country.

Over the years, Gujarat has been turned into a Hindutva powerhouse that the BJP and the 'sangh parivar' often tap into for human and material resources for activities in other parts of India. Gujarat is one of India's most prosperous states; people of the state are known for their business acumen and spirit of enterprise. The factor of 'long distance nationalism' also plays a role, with prosperous Gujaratis in Britain, the US and elsewhere generously contributing funds to organizations of the 'sangh parivar'. It is also a fact that in several cities in Gujarat, Hindus and Muslims are linked together in trade relations, bound by economic compulsions and the Gujarati language and culture. Hindutva supporters from Gujarat have been in the forefront of the BJP's political mobilization. From the late 1980s onwards, the BJP openly joined other organizations of the 'sangh parivar' such as the VHP and the Bajrang Dal to create a national mood for the construction of a temple in honour of Lord Ram at Ayodhya, at precisely the same spot where the Babri mosque stood.

Ayodhya has a prominent place in the myths and mists of Hinduism, mainly in the ancient religious text, the Ramayana. The 'sangh parivar's argument has been that a Ram temple had existed at the very spot on which the Mughal emperor Babur built the Babri mosque in the sixteenth century to humiliate the Hindus and that the mosque needed to be replaced by a grand temple of Lord Ram. In the late 1980s, before the mosque was demolished, the 'sangh parivar' unleashed nation-wide campaigns to mobilize people in favour of the temple and effectively used the mosque as a symbol of a variety of (real and imaginary) grievances suffered by the Hindus. Hindutva elements argued that the Muslim community had been favoured and appeased by the Congress party that had mostly ruled independent India. In Gujarat, as Chattarji (2004: 114) argued, there was a 'mythic construction of wronged Hindu majorities now wreaking vengeance to reverse centuries of Muslim barbarism and atrocity, and the media is shocked at government complicity'.

The mosque was demolished by 'kar sevaks' in a frenzy on 6 December 1992. The issue has since remained on and off the political agenda even as the BJP and its allies, for the first time, went on to win political power in New Delhi under the moderate BJP leader, Atal Bihari Vajpayee (the BJP-led government had a brief tenure between May and June 1996 and was then in office between March 1998 and May 2004). During the clashes in Gujarat in 2002, the BJP was in power in Gujarat as well as in New Delhi. Several of the BJP's allies in the government did not support the Ayodhya agenda, and the compulsions of power forced the Vajpayee government to tone down its Hindutva rhetoric and try to build a political consensus on constructing the temple in Ayodhya. However, this consensus was hard to reach, since most political parties in India are opposed to Hindutva-oriented politics. The issue continues to simmer in political discourse and tortuous legal proceedings, while the VHP continues its work to sculpt pillars and other material to be used when – and if – the construction of the temple is legally allowed to begin.

It was against this backdrop that the infamous events occurred in Gujarat in February–March 2002. It all began on 27 February, when the Sabarmati Express train carrying 'kar sevaks' was returning home from Ayodhya. They were returning from a political ceremony organized by the VHP as part of its campaign to construct the temple. At around 8 am, the train pulled out of the Godhra station in Gujarat on the last leg of what was to be dubbed as 'one of the most catastrophic rail journeys of post-Partition India' (Varadarajan 2002a: 3). As the train left the station, it was stoned by an angry mob and some 20 minutes later, one of the coaches was burned to cinders along with 58 passengers, many of them later identified as members of the 'sangh parivar'. Why the mob gathered and attacked the train has been the subject of much speculation and mystery. Inquiries into the Godhra tragedy were yet to deliver their final conclusions in early 2005. The identity of the mob was not immediately known but local Hindutva leaders promptly declared that the attackers were Muslims, and that the community needed to be taught a lesson. Retaliation for the Godhra tragedy was swift with politically mobilized mobs launching fierce attacks on Muslims in several parts of the state. Narendra Modi, Chief Minister of the Gujarat government and a leading member of the 'sangh parivar', tried to justify the attacks on helpless Muslims in Newtonian terms: every action has an equal and opposite reaction.

From 27 February there was barbarous violence for over forty days, as revenge against the killing of 'kar sevaks' in Godhra. The official figure of Muslims killed was 800 but the unofficial figure was over 2,000. As many as 200,000 people were displaced because their homes had been burnt or looted. Property belonging to Muslims worth millions of rupees was destroyed while the police and the state administration controlled by the BJP were accused of passivity, if not complicity. Sustained adverse coverage of the Gujarat's government's role in handling the violence played a major role in the federal government intervening to bring the violence to an end. The federal government, even while being critical of the coverage, acted and put pressure on the local government, particularly when India started getting bad press in the international news media.

It is important to note that since the Hindu–Muslim violence accompanying the partition of India in 1947, other incidents of political violence on such a scale have taken place. The BJP and the Hindutva forces have not been the only ones practising such politics. The Congress party, which was in power in New Delhi in 1984, resorted to similar principles and actions when Sikh guards assassinated Prime Minister Indira Gandhi. The incident led to targeted attacks against the Sikh community in New Delhi and other parts of north India as revenge for the killing of Indira Gandhi. Congress Party leaders and workers were allegedly armed with voters' lists to identify the location of Sikhs, who were attacked almost all over India, but mainly in the northern states. After the Babri mosque was demolished in 1992, Hindu and Muslim groups clashed in Mumbai and elsewhere, resulting in a large number of deaths across India.

During every such episode of mass killings, the role of the state has come in for much criticism. The state is seen as complicit in such acts of mass political violence. As Varshney observed,

> (No) amount of critique since 1947 has yet brought about *durable changes* in the behaviour of the state on Hindu–Muslim relations. Even if Narendra Modi, Gujarat's Chief Minister at the time of the communal violence . . . were to fall tomorrow, the bigger questions of Indian politics on Hindu–Muslims relations would remain.
>
> (2002: xi; emphasis in original)

Over the years, despite several inquiries, most of the perpetrators of the gory events of 1984, 1992 and 2002 have remained unpunished.

If the political violence in Gujarat in 2002 and its aftermath signified dubious 'continuity' with earlier episodes, a notable 'change' was the way in which the news media covered the events. For the first time, due to the proliferation of satellite television since the early 1990s, and the bold and independent coverage of Gujarat 2002, the news media emerged as prominent players in the political discourse. As Rajagopal (2001) observed, since the mid-1980s, when Doordarshan, the state-owned television network, telecast serials based on the ancient religious texts of Ramayana and Mahabharata, television had reshaped the context in which Indian politics was 'conceived, enacted and understood'.

The next section examines the coverage of Gujarat 2002 primarily through four lenses:

- the breakdown of long-held ethical norms in Indian journalism about not identifying victims and attackers by religion;
- the use of flak by the Hindutva forces to discipline the media;

- the pro-Hindutva bias of sections of the mass circulation Gujarati-language press; and
- the dangers and problems faced by journalists while covering the Gujarat events.

In several respects, the coverage marked a significant departure from the way the Indian news media had approached Hindu–Muslim relations since 1947. It also highlighted the disjuncture between the English-language press and the influential sections of the Gujarati-language press.

India's first television riot

For the first time in the history of covering Hindu–Muslim clashes, 'violence was carried live' on television (Ninan 2002) as television cameras brought home graphic images to viewers in Gujarat and elsewhere. There was no live coverage of the attacks against Sikhs in 1984 or of the 1992 Hindu–Muslim clashes in Mumbai and elsewhere. It was then the era of print, and television news reporting was years away. It was only in 1996, when STAR News – the first of the 24-hour news channels – was launched, that television news added a visual dimension to politics, political violence and the public sphere in India.[2] In 2005, the television newscape had turned dense, with several 24-hour news channels broadcasting in different languages, drawing more people and regions into the public sphere and rejuvenating local networks of culture, politics and economy. The proliferation of satellite television also sparked off an intensely competitive brand of journalism. During the Gujarat events, there was a large presence of journalists and television crews in the streets, each trying to outdo the other, as politically mobilized mobs attacked Muslim men, women (including pregnant women), children and their property. Reporting the clashes, often live, made for riveting television, the likes of which the Indian audience had never been exposed to.

The coverage by the print media – English and Gujarati-language – also made news when sections of the press (Gujarati-language dailies *Sandesh* and *Gujarat Samachar*) covered the events from a pro-Hindutva perspective while other sections (*The Times of India, Indian Express*) were severely critical of the attacks against Muslims. The Godhra incident occurred on 27 February and was reported extensively the next day. But news channels and newspaper editors devoted more time and space to the Union Budget that was presented in the Indian parliament in New Delhi on 28 February. The budget coverage pushed Godhra to the margins, and it was further relegated in the news columns when large-scale retaliation against Muslims began in others parts of the state.

Ethics: medium is the message

Since the 1950s and 1960s, the Indian news media followed a set of guidelines formulated by the Press Council of India, a quasi-judicial watchdog organization, stipulating that the identity of victims or attackers should not be mentioned in news reports to prevent further escalation of communal violence. The guidelines were drawn up against the backdrop of colonial India's partition into independent India and Pakistan in 1947 and the tense Hindu–Muslim relations that accompanied it. There was as yet no television, and, until the transistor revolution of the 1970s, even radio was confined to the affluent sections of society. When Gandhi was shot dead on 30 January 1948, the second sentence on All India Radio's news bulletin was that the killer was not a Muslim.[3] The editor of the bulletin wanted to nip any rumours in the bud, and the speedy announcement that Gandhi's assailant was not a Muslim prevented attacks against the millions of Muslims that had chosen not to migrate to the new (Islamic) state of Pakistan.

But the ban on naming communities in the news media never really worked. The identity of the victims and attackers was all too evident when news reports used euphemistic phrases such as 'members of a particular community' or 'members of the minority community' (meaning Muslims) or 'members of the majority community' (meaning Hindus). For decades, both the privately owned press and the government controlled electronic media adhered to the guidelines. Varadarajan (1999: 160–229) argued that the convention of not identifying communities

> works to increase the sense of suspicion and anxiety amongst ordinary citizens not just in riot-affected areas but also elsewhere in the country...people tend to assume that the victims are 'their own' while their attackers are 'the other'.

While covering Gujarat 2002, television journalists openly identified the attackers and victims in their voice-overs as the footage showed graphic images of violence. As Phillip observed

> When the television camera focuses on a riotous mob or its victims, it leaves little to the imagination of the viewers... The ban on naming the communities was a fit case for review, although with the advent of television it has become redundant. Questions also remain whether the guidelines are applicable to the electronic media...(The) argument that the violence in Gujarat would have been worse if the media, particularly electronic, had not aroused public opinion against the killing spree through focused and sustained reporting cannot be dismissed out of hand.
>
> (Phillip 2002)

Television coverage of the events made it impossible to adhere to the Press Council guidelines. Television journalists such as Rajdeep Sardesai and Barkha Dutt of STAR News identified attackers and victims as 'Hindus' and 'Muslims'. However, as Varadarajan (2002b: 275) pointed out, it was improper to use the term 'Hindus' to describe what was usually a politically mobilized mob: 'The discourse of communal riots had no room to acknowledge that some Hindus brought together by political or economic motivation to attack Muslims at large cannot really be referred to as "the Hindus" or even as "some Hindus" ' (2002b: 275). Naming the attackers as 'Hindus' also concealed the reality that the overwhelming majority of Indians who happen to be categorized as Hindus – practising or non-practising – have been vociferous in their criticism of the attacks against Muslims.

Referring to the practice of not naming communities, Sardesai observed that

> no one is quite sure who initiated this practice, but … it does seem a bit like obfuscation, and an attempt to inject a false blandness to the harsh and grim reality of a communal riot. If a shop of a Bohra Muslim has been attacked, should that be disguised by suggesting that a shop belonging to 'a member of a minority within the minority community' was attacked?
>
> (2002a)

As Barkha Dutt stated, 'Naming the community under siege in Gujarat was moot to the story. In fact it was *the* story, revealing as it did a prejudiced administrative and political system that was happy to just stand by and watch' (2002, emphasis in original). The press also abandoned its earlier restraint: 'Newspapers were both sensational and fairly upfront about identifying the communities involved' (Ninan 2002). Some newspapers published from other parts of India adhered to the guidelines, but many, including the English-language *The Asian Age*, named the Muslim victims.

L.K. Advani, deputy prime minister at the time and a leading figure in the Hindutva mobilization, used the US media's coverage of the September 11 attacks to criticize the way the Gujarat events were being reported by the Indian media. He asked the media to draw lessons from the coverage of September 11 – displaying media sensitivity towards victims and their families – and suggested that 'sometimes, speaking the truth may not be an act of responsibility' (*The Telegraph* 2002). He was against the graphic coverage of the violence on the grounds that it could inflame passions elsewhere. A former journalist, Advani recalled the practice of not naming communities, and remarked, 'But now all that has been flouted' (*The Telegraph* 2002).

The open identification of communities involved during the Gujarat events sets a precedent for the reporting of Hindu–Muslim clashes in the future. However, such identification is unlikely to be adopted across the news media, mainly because of the deep-rooted convention of not naming the religion of those involved, and because of the criticism – or flak – that the coverage of Gujarat 2002 attracted. Also, the original motivation that led to the Press Council of India formulating the guidelines – to prevent escalation of violence – remains valid.

Hindutva flak: disciplining the media

Bold and independent coverage by the news media invites flak from political actors who are shown in a bad light. Criticizing the BJP and Hindutva forces severely for their role in the Gujarat events got STAR News and English-language newspapers such as *The Times of India* and the *Indian Express* bad press. As journalists who covered the political activities of the Hindutva forces over the last two decades are well aware, one of the methods of disciplining the media is through physical violence. When the Babri mosque was being demolished on 6 December 1992, several journalists suffered injuries when they were attacked by 'kar sevaks' and many had their cameras broken.

As Herman and Chomsky observed, flak is often used by political elites to discipline the media:

> It (flak) may take the form of letters, telegrams, phone calls, petitions, lawsuits, and other modes of complaint, threat, and punitive action. It may be organized centrally or locally, or it may consist of the entirely independent actions of individuals. If flak is produced on a large scale, or by individuals or groups with substantial resources, it can be both uncomfortable and costly to the media … If certain kinds of fact, position, or program are thought likely to elicit flak, this prospect can be a deterrent.
>
> (Herman and Chomsky 1988: 26)

The BJP was in power in Gujarat and New Delhi during the clashes. After the initial days of violence, when the coverage of the attacks against Muslims started reflecting badly on the BJP governments, its leaders came down heavily on journalists. A day after Prime Minister Vajpayee's televised address to the nation on 3 March, regretting the 'disgraceful' violence in Gujarat, he told a group of concerned citizens that the news media were presenting 'exaggerated' accounts of the situation (*The Times of India* 2002a).

The BJP and the Gujarat government singled out STAR News and banned cable operators from showing it in the state. Soon, viewers in Ahmedabad – the state capital and the scene of some of the worst violence – were met with blank television screens. Other channels were also banned, including two local channels in Surat, MY TV and Channel Surat. In Rajkot, the police banned the publication of special supplements of three Gujarati dailies. Cable operators received calls from local officials in Ahmedabad and elsewhere to black out STAR News, Zee News, CNN and Aaj Tak (*The Times of India* 2002b). Dossiers and 'hitlists' on journalists were reportedly prepared while 'those channels and newspapers who are critical of the chief minister are not invited to his press conferences and denied the basic right to information by the state apparatus' (Sardesai 2004).

The main complaint of the BJP and its allies was that the news media did not criticize those responsible for the Godhra train tragedy in which 'kar sevaks' were the victims. This, however, was less than true because every channel and newspaper had covered the Godhra tragedy extensively, but follow-ups on subsequent days were overtaken by the Union Budget on 28 February and the retaliation unleashed on Muslims in Ahmedabad and other parts of Gujarat. Another complaint was that the news media 'inflamed communal passions' by providing graphic television coverage of the events. Journalists and others critical of the attacks against Muslims countered this by saying that the level of violence would have been much worse if the news media had not sounded the alarm through their graphic coverage.

The BJP and its allies also used the technique of branding to discipline the media. Journalists who criticized the attacks on Muslims were dubbed as the 'Marxist-Mullah combine' and the 'secular Taliban'. A group of angry Hindutva supporters told members of the Editors Guild of India who visited Gujarat to inquire into the media side of the events that news channels and the English-language national press had defamed the Hindu community with one-sided coverage: 'They only listen to Muslims and ignore the Hindus', the team was told (Patel *et al.* 2002). Sardesai pointed out the predicament faced by journalists while covering the events:

> (If) any reporter, whether print or television, sees large-scale violence being committed, is the journalist to ignore the hard reality and merely present the facts as seen through government binoculars? If the chief minister says that the situation is returning to normal even while reports are streaming in of continuing violence in several parts of the state, are not the lies to be exposed? And if the government insists that the army is out on the street when the fact is that the army has been kept on stand-by and is waiting for transport trucks, whose version is to be broadcast?
>
> (Sardesai 2002a)

In India, the state has been the biggest source of news and journalists routinely use information disseminated by officials. But, as Sardesai pointed out, the situation becomes unclear for journalists when the government itself – with its vast powers – is openly seen to be on the side of the mob. The government used its formidable powers to discipline the critical news media by a variety of methods: outright banning of news channels or publications; withholding access to information and advertisements; and severe criticism. Dominant political forces may also distribute largesse and heap praise on journalists and news outlets perceived to be favourable to their interests. Gujarat Chief Minister Modi applauded *Sandesh*, the Gujarati-language newspaper that had published several rumours and false reports with a pronounced anti-Muslim and pro-Hindutva bias. In a letter to the newspaper's editor, Modi wrote:

> The newspapers of the state played a decisive role as a link between the people and the government. You have served the humanity in a big way... It is the state government's primary duty to restore peace, security and communal harmony when violence takes place... The timely measures taken by the government turned out to be effective and normalcy was returned within a short period. It is noteworthy that the newspapers of Gujarat gave their full support to the state government in undertaking this difficult task. I am happy to note that your newspaper exercised restraint during the communal disturbances in the wake of the Godhra incident. I am grateful to you.
>
> (cited in Varadarajan 2002b: 286)

Modi, who once took a course in New York on media management, is considered one of the most media-savvy politicians in India. However, he turned selective in providing access and information to journalists and refused to interact with journalists from the English-language press. The accreditation of local journalists critical of his politics was not renewed, and he made it difficult for journalists to access centres of information such as the legislative assembly. He refused to meet the press and also instructed his ministers not to meet journalists, unless he permitted them to do so. Several local newspapers faced reduced advertising support from the government while some had court cases slapped against them. A senior Gujarat police official told an Ahmedabad-based journalist of the *Indian*

Express: 'Darshan, you are blacklisted' (Desai 2004: 228). Journalists of the English-language press were dubbed as members of the 'secular Taliban'.

Faced with the concerted campaign of criticism, Sardesai, one of the key targets of Hindutva forces for his coverage of Gujarat 2002, admitted: 'The sheer viciousness of the campaign has pushed the media on the defensive...The messenger has been shot again' (2002a).

Objectivity and bias in the press

The graphic coverage by television channels hit the headlines, but the nature of the press coverage also made news. The team of the Editors Guild of India met several editors, journalists, Chief Minister Modi and others and concluded that the English-language national press and sections of the Gujarati media, barring notable offenders, played an exemplary role. The charge of the BJP and its allies that graphic coverage by the news media was a major aggravating factor in the situation, the team concluded, was 'specious, self-serving and must be dismissed' (Patel *et al.* 2002). The team observed:

> (Our) finding is that the prompt and extensive portrayal by sections of the local press and national media of the untold horrors visited on innocent people in the wake of the Godhra carnage was a saving grace. The exposure of the supine if not complicit attitude of the State and manifest outpourings of communal hatred, stirred the conscience of the nation, compelled remedial action, howsoever defensively and belatedly...However, the role of sections of the Gujarati media, especially the *Gujarat Samachar* and more notably *Sandesh*, was provocative, irresponsible and blatantly violative of all accepted norms of media ethics. This cannot be lightly passed over.
>
> (Patel *et al.* 2002)

Being the largest selling dailies in the state, coverage by the *Gujarat Samachar* ('Gujarat News'; circulation: 810,000) and *Sandesh* ('Message'; circulation: 705,000) had considerable impact. The editors' team found several instances of distorted and false reporting in the two dailies, but the team also found that because of *Sandesh*'s pro-Hindutva stand, its circulation rose by 150,000 copies. A study of the *Sandesh* coverage found that when Muslims were at fault, names were mentioned and perpetrators clearly identified. But when Muslims were the victims of murderers, arsonists, looters etc., the attackers remained unnamed. The study concluded:

> No sources were quoted for headlines, even when they were simply lifted from speeches by VHP leaders. Headlines were also misleading, and often followed up by reports that did not substantiate, and even negated the headlines completely...The anti-minority stand was obvious in the slant in news reporting.
>
> (PUCL 2002)

Sandesh used headlines to 'provoke, communalize and terrorise people' (PUCL 2002). On 28 February, the main headline read: '70 Hindus Burnt Alive in Godhra'. Another report on the front page said: 'Avenge Blood with Blood', which was actually a quote from a statement issued by a VHP leader, but the newspaper simply used the words as a headline. On 6 March, the headline was: 'Hindus Beware: Haj Pilgrims return with a Deadly Conspiracy', when the fact was that hundreds of terrified Haj pilgrims had returned to Gujarat under the protection of a police escort. The study found that most news reports of the post-Godhra violence in *Sandesh* began with the sentence: 'In the continuing spiral of communal rioting that broke out as a reaction to the "demonic/barbaric, etc. Godhra incident..." '. The study observed: 'The denunciatory adjectives used liberally to describe the Godhra incident were strikingly absent in reporting the subsequent genocide' (PUCL 2002).

The study found that the *Gujarat Samachar* also played a role in heightening tensions. But unlike *Sandesh*, it did not devote all its space to 'hawkish and inflammatory reportage in the first few weeks, and did carry reports highlighting communal harmony' (PUCL 2002). *Gujarat Today*, a Gujarati-language daily started by Muslim liberals, was praised for its balanced and restrained reporting of the events.

> The paper was... temperate in its language and eschewed shrill and potentially provocative matter. It regularly carried items highlighting interdependence of communities and incidents of help and cooperation extending across community barriers. It investigated incidents and carried detailed information that did not appear in other newspapers. Overall, our analysis suggests that *Gujarat Today* played a responsible and positive role during the violence in the state, for which it deserves to be commended.
>
> (PUCL 2002)

Gujarat Today's sober coverage stood out amidst the dominant pro-Hindutva news discourse of the Gujarati-language press. The editors' team interviewed editors of several newspapers, including those of *Gujarat Samachar* and *Sandesh*. In its report, the team mentioned the example of a banner headline in *Sandesh* that the breasts of two Hindu women had been chopped off by mobs during the Godhra incident – a report that was subsequently proved to be false. The newspaper's editor told the team that the information was from the local police. But this was contradicted and the contradiction appeared in the rival *Gujarat Samachar*. The *Sandesh* editor told the team that it was the paper's policy 'not to carry corrections and clarifications' (Patel *et al.* 2002). The Press Council of India subsequently censured both the newspapers 'for the infraction of the norms of journalistic conduct' (Prerna 2003).

The two English-language national newspapers, *The Times of India* and the *Indian Express*, publish editions from Gujarat. A clear divide was evident between the news content of these English-language newspapers and the two Gujarati-language newspapers. While the former was trenchant in its criticism of chief minister Modi, the state government and the Hindutva forces, the two Gujarati-language dailies espoused the cause of Hindutva. Desai, an Ahmedabad-based correspondent on the *Indian Express*, wrote

> Today, all the people who once used to look at me with respect question me and abuse me. They do this because I represented a publication whose medium is

English and because I reported human misery in its right perspective ... A friend said: 'All of you from the English language media have tarnished the image of Gujarat'... Today, the 'common man' in Gujarat hates the English language media. The Gujarati language media hates the English language media. Even a section of the English language media hates the English language media.

(Desai 2004: 228)

Journalists' experience of covering Gujarat violence

Journalists, particularly those critical of the Hindutva forces, had been subjected to much criticism, threats, violence and worse over the years. As noted earlier, journalists were attacked by 'kar sevaks' while the Babri mosque was being demolished in Ayodhya. The story was repeated in Gujarat. During a peace meeting organized at Gandhi's Sabarmati Ashram in April 2002, when the level of violence had come down, nearly a dozen journalists were attacked by the police and Hindutva supporters. Sharma (2002) chronicled several such instances:

- Sonal Kellog, a woman reporter of *The Asian Age*, and a male reporter from a Surat-based newspaper, were pounced upon by the police when they went into the Ahmedabad inner city to interview women who had been attacked.
- Raju Chiniwala, a photographer for *Sandesh* in Surat, was caught by a mob. They poured kerosene and petrol on him and were about to set him on fire when a police van arrived on the scene.
- Bhargav Parikh, News coordinator for Zee News, was beaten up by a mob in Ahmedabad while the channel's cameraman, Tejas Gondalia, had his camera smashed and was beaten up.
- Parish Joshi, photographer for the *Indian Express* in Rajkot, was pushed around by a mob, the roll in his camera removed and his camera smashed.
- Sudhir Vyas of *The Times of India* in Rajkot was beaten up by the police.
- Tanvir Siddiqui, senior reporter for the *Indian Express* and Javed Raja, senior photographer for the newspaper, could not go out to report because anti-Muslim mobs were roaming the streets.

Being a journalist in a conflict zone once lent a degree of immunity to the person. This is no longer the case. In fact, the presence of journalists with their still and television cameras now makes them visible and easy targets. Television journalists enjoy a high profile due to regular appearances on the screen. They are recognized on the streets and, depending on the timing and context, are greeted or derided. Sardesai and Dutt, prominent television journalists for STAR News, stood out for their bold and independent reporting.

They each recounted some of their experiences of covering Gujarat 2002. Sardesai wrote:

Amidst the kaleidoscope of images that one has encountered during the Gujarat violence ... one incident stands out. We had just finished interviewing the Gujarat chief minister at his residence in Gandhinagar shortly before midnight. As we were driving back to Ahmedabad, we were stopped by a mob of around 30 to 40 'trishul' (trident) and lathi (stick)-wielding youth. They asked us our names, our religious identity and wanted to inspect our cameras. We desperately tried to flash our press credentials, but before we could react, one youth climbed on the bonnet of our Tata Sumo and proceeded to smash our windscreen. Claiming that if any one of us belonged to the minority community we would be killed, our identities were closely inspected. Then, after the car's side window was also smashed, we were allowed to leave, but only after we had joined the chorus in chanting 'Jai Shri Ram' ('Hail Lord Ram').

(Sardesai 2002b)

Dutt described the attack even more vividly:

They came swooping down on us like vultures lunging at a carcass. There were at least 20 of them, faces remarkably indistinguishable. In fact, frenzied though these men may have been on your TV screens, they had an almost robotic, rehearsed air about them as they thrust their gleaming swords into our windshield and barked: 'What's your religion?' There was only one answer to that. 'Hindu', I said (aware that an articulation of my agnostic beliefs would guarantee the unspeakable), privately cringing for my cameraperson Ajmal Jami. What would we do if he were asked to produce an identity card? For the rest of the journey we mentally made up false names for him, and avoided addressing him in public.

An educated man stopped our crew on the streets of Vadodara, and excitedly leapt out of his car. 'You're doing a good job, madam', he said almost kindly, 'but why don't you ask the Muslims of Gujarat to apologise for Godhra?' By this time my patience had run thin. 'I agree, sir', I said, trying to sound calm, 'but will all the Hindus of Gujarat also say sorry for the 600 Muslims who have been killed?' 'It's not the same', he declared, before stomping off.

(Dutt 2002)

Journalists negotiate a minefield of situations while covering conflict. Their own religious and cultural identities are often called into question – even if it is not to their liking. The culture of intolerance of dissent or the mere presence of reporters results in the messenger himself or herself becoming a target of attack.

Conclusion

The events of Gujarat 2002 acquire salience when viewed as part of Gujarat Chief Minister Modi's politics as permanent performance. It was widely dubbed as India's first riot for the satellite TV era, but it was less a riot than a pogrom. The attacks against Muslims were clinically one-sided, much as the 1984 attacks against the Sikhs had been. In the era of satellite television, the news media can help highlight abuse of power and acts of passivity or complicity in acts of political violence. Journalists face serious questions in such situations: How should they use information provided by the government? How credible is such information when journalists witness a different reality? And what implications do such contours of power geometry have for democracy, citizenship and multiculturalism?

The coverage of Gujarat 2002 marked a departure in the way the Indian media approached communal clashes. It also highlighted the disjuncture in the news cultures of the English-language news media and the non-English variety. Windmiller (1954: 313–315) observed that 'India's English language press is the only national press and it is paramount in the world of Indian journalism', but it is also true that this was one of the many instances when the English-language press' disconnect with the wider Indian realities showed up. It will be incorrect to generalize that the entire English-language press is balanced and impartial or that the non-English language press is biased and one-sided. There are instances of biased reporting in the former and instances of impartial reporting by the latter. But during events of such magnitude – such as the events after the mosque demolition in Ayodhya – influential sections of the non-English language press are known to have provided biased coverage while major sections of the English-language press made efforts to provide critical reporting by covering different versions.

In the era of media proliferation, the importance of the news media has increased, going by the flak unleashed by dominant political groups. The proliferation of television channels and growing viewership, rising literacy and the increasing circulation of newspapers indicates that barring notable exceptions of blatant bias, the Indian news media will continue to play the role of a watchdog in the world's largest democracy. Since the early 1990s, there are apprehensions that the news media will not be able to highlight the abuse of power or signify weaknesses in society due to the gnawing march of corporatisation (Sonwalkar 2002). But the bold and independent coverage of Gujarat 2002 provides ground for some hope because Indian journalism's ability to hold the state accountable, when power is abused, has not been obliterated by infotainment – yet. The coverage was marked by state-sponsored efforts to intimidate and censor, but these had little impact. Censoring ensured that the message of government complicity was well and truly conveyed to the larger audience, within and beyond Gujarat – due to the experience of censorship during the Emergency of 1975–1977, the popular perception being that censorship is imposed when the state wants to prevent citizens from knowing facts.

Notes

1 Hindutva stands for Hindu-ness but is widely used as a synonym for political Hinduism that seeks to win political power on the basis of India's Hindu majority. Hindutva supporters conflate 'Hindu' with 'Indian' and seek to build a *de facto* Hindu nation, if not a *de jure* theocratic state. In the Indian context, such politics is often referred to as 'communalism', which refers to the organized politics of hostility and antagonism between members of religious communities – in this case, between Hindus and Muslims.
2 Launched in 1996, Rupert Murdoch's STAR News enjoyed much credibility as its news content was provided, until March 2003, by NDTV, a respected Indian production house headed by Prannoy Roy, who had built a reputation on Indian television over a decade covering elections, budgets and foreign events. After March 2003, the channel set up its own editorial infrastructure.
3 Gandhi was shot dead by Nathuram Godse, a Hindu.

6 Uyghur separatism and nationalism in Xinjiang[1]

Michael Dillon

Introduction

Xinjiang is the contested region of north western China that borders on
Kazakhstan, Kyrgyzstan, Tajikistan, Pakistan and Afghanistan. With an area of
over 1,600,000 square kilometres, almost three times the size of France, it is the
largest administrative area in China. It is administered by the People's Republic
of China (PRC) as the Xinjiang Uyghur Autonomous Region, *Xinjiang Weiwuer
zizhiqu*. But this is considered to be illegitimate to many of the Uyghur and other
non-Han (that is non-Chinese) population, who refer to it as Eastern Turkistan, or
Sharqi Türkistan in the Uyghur language. The Uyghurs, after whom the region is
named, are the single largest ethnic group in Xinjiang, although their dominance
has been threatened by the growing migration of Han Chinese from the east of the
PRC since the 1950s. The Uyghurs are a Turkic people who have been Muslims
since at least the fifteenth century, and their language is closely related to that of
the Uzbeks and distantly to other Turkish languages including Kazakh and
Kyrgyz and remotely to the Turkish of Turkey.

Historically, Xinjiang has been the region of Central Asia closest to China but
that does not mean, as the Chinese authorities often claim, that it has always been
part of China. It had a diplomatic relationship with the Chinese empire for centuries through the 'tribute system', the arrangement under which smaller and
weaker states sent regular missions to the Chinese capital, bearing gifts of 'tribute' and nominally subordinating themselves to the emperor of China while for
all practical purposes remaining independent. The last imperial dynasty of China,
the Qing (1644–1911), which was Manchu rather than Chinese, was one of the
most aggressively expansionist ruling houses in China's history and in the late
eighteenth century it began a process of consolidating its control over its frontier
regions. The Turkic-speaking Western Regions, *Xiyu*, were integrated into the
Qing empire and given the name of Xinjiang (new frontier). Xinjiang became a
regular province of China in 1884 after the Manchus defeated Yakub Beg, a military leader from Khokand who had established an independent Turkic regime at
Kashghar in the far south-west of the region. Since 1884 there has been tension
between control by China and local, mainly Turkic, resistance. Independent
governments were installed in Kashghar in the 1930s and in Yining (Ghulja) in

the north-west of the region in the 1940s and the tradition of these self-governing administrations lives on in the thinking of many Uyghurs in twenty-first century Xinjiang, including those who have been involved, directly or indirectly, in separatist movements.

Media coverage of Xinjiang has been inconsistent. The conflict between Beijing and the Uyghurs has featured only rarely in the western media when there have been major disturbances. In China, there has been regular reporting of positive news, particularly where it supports the picture of successful economic development that the government wishes to present. Coverage of separatist activities was extremely rare until the 1990s when there was press and television coverage of the trials of those accused of separatist activities. The political case for independence is never allowed to appear in the official media in China, and virtually the entire media remains under state control. There is an alternative source of information on Xinjiang in the newsletters and, more recently, the websites of Uyghur organizations based outside of Xinjiang, but these do not have the resources of professional press and television organizations and their access to first hand information is often limited.

Political control

Political control at the local level in traditional Xinjiang was inextricably bound up with the religious hierarchy. A combined secular and religious bureaucracy controlled the towns and villages and Islamic law played an important role: the Chinese imperial presence was limited to Urumqi and garrison towns. After the collapse of the empire in 1911 warlords ruled Xinjiang as they did in China proper. With nationalist attempts to reunify China in the 1920s, Han Chinese governors were imposed by Beijing, but they ruled partly through the old mixed system of administration and Xinjiang remained effectively an independent political unit until 1949.

The government of the PRC was determined to treat Xinjiang just like any other province of China. It was brought under military control in 1949 and its first political leaders were Wang Zhen and Wang Enmao, both long-standing senior officers in the People's Liberation Army (PLA) and both ethnic Han Chinese. Land reform policies in the 1950s, under which land owned by landlords and religious foundations was requisitioned and redistributed throughout China, undermined the economic basis for the political control that the mosques and other Islamic foundations had exercised. The 'Anti-Rightist' campaigns of 1957 and the Great Leap Forward mobilisation of 1958, which affected the whole of China, were targeted in Xinjiang at breaking down the authority of the religious structures once and for all.

Xinjiang was designated an Autonomous Region (AR) on 1 October 1955. Other ARs were Tibet, Inner Mongolia, Ningxia and the largely Zhuang region of Guangxi. The AR concept was an attempt to give formal recognition to the fact that there were major ethnic and religious differences between these areas and the predominantly Han population of China proper. Minority politicians were promoted to senior positions in the regional governments, but, on the whole, real power remained in the hands of the predominantly Han Chinese officials of the Communist Party (CCP), and ethnic minority cadres often faced tough tests of loyalty.

Xinjiang has an extra layer of politico-economic administration that is not found in any other region of China. The Xinjiang Production and Construction Corps (XPCC) was created in 1954 from (largely Han) units of the PLA when they were demobilised. It runs farms and reclamation projects, and through its militia and prison system plays an important role in the security of the border region. Its status is equivalent to that of a province. XPCC bases have been the target of attacks by separatist groups, partly because they have weapons and ammunition and partly because they are a symbol of Beijing's control in the region.

Social trends

The migration into Xinjiang of mainly Han Chinese from the east has created a complex multi-layered society in which the distribution of economic benefits, power and privilege is very unequal. Poor rural Uyghurs are at the bottom of the social hierarchy whilst the government, party and military bureaucracies, which are mostly but not exclusively Han, have a monopoly of political authority and access to the lion's share of better quality housing, well-paid employment and consumer goods.

In between the two are the educated Uyghurs, often fluent both in their own language and Chinese, who have in many cases moved to the cities and play a role in the upper echelons of Xinjiang society. They might be doctors, engineers, teachers, journalists or academic researchers. Their upward social mobility has, in part, been due to the policies of the CCP which has in relatively liberal times, encouraged young Uyghurs into mainstream careers. This has ensured a presence of non-Han Chinese in key areas of Xinjiang society but at some cost to those who have taken on this role. At best, they are viewed with considerable suspicion by those who have remained in solely Uyghur communities. At worst, they are seen as collaborators with an occupying power and traitors to the Uyghur people and have been physically attacked and some even killed. The same is also true of the Kyrgyz, Kazakh and other Muslim communities in Xinjiang.

Before the collapse of the Soviet Union, even educated Uyghurs were largely dependent on the state-controlled media for their information, but some international media are now accessible to the population of Xinjiang. Radio Moscow did broadcast in Uyghur and Kazakh during the Soviet era, although Russian is in any case a language that is widely spoken in the northern border areas of Xinjiang where there is a long-standing Russian minority population. However, these broadcasts were primarily for propaganda purposes and were not highly valued in the region. The BBC broadcasts in Uzbek, which is close enough to Uyghur to be useful to the population of Xinjiang. Radio Free Asia has an Uyghur language service which broadcasts regular programmes of news, current affairs and cultural matters relating to Xinjiang and China. Although the station eschews support for separatism, its very existence is anathema to the Beijing government which regards its broadcasts as unwarranted outside interference in its internal affairs. The imprisonment of the successful Uyghur businesswoman and social activist, Rebiya Kadir, who was awarded the Norwegian Rafto Prize in 2004, was in part a consequence of her personal connections with Radio Free Asia. She was released in March 2005.

Ethnic and religious issues

Social differentiation and social conflict is, needless to say, complicated by the ethnic and religious background of the various communities. Han Chinese come from a society which traditionally adhered to two main religions, Buddhism and Daoism, which were practised throughout China, and to a wide range of local beliefs and religious associations which focused on local deities, temples and ancestral shrines. Organised religion in China had suffered a serious blow during the years of war and civil war in the 1930s and 1940s, and it was one of the main targets of the CCP when it took power in 1949. Religion in general was attacked as feudal superstition especially during the more radical periods of the Great Leap Forward (1958) and the Cultural Revolution (1966–1976), but the CCP did make some concessions to the religious practices of ethnic minorities (Dillon 2001: 5–6). For many young Han Chinese, educated in state-run schools, religion is seen as backward and at least partly responsible for slowing China's progress. Some others may belong to Christian communities (either official or underground), which have seen a resurgence since the 1980s. There is likely to be little sympathy towards Islam, which many Hans regard as an alien creed, viewing its mosques with disdain and even revulsion.

For the non-Chinese population of Xinjiang, Islam is an essential part of their identity, and, in the last resort, they are likely to define or identify themselves primarily as Muslims in spite of the linguistic differences between them. The PRC has sought to regulate Islam by imposing a national regulatory body, the Chinese Islamic Association, and by requiring all mosques and madrassas (religious schools, which play a key role in the education of the faithful and the training of clergy) to register with local officials. Unregistered mosques and madrassas have been the target of government campaigns and have frequently been forced to close down.[2]

Some Imams and their communities, mainly from the most orthodox mainstream Sunni tradition in Xinjiang have accepted this level of state control, but other groups have not. There is a long tradition in Xinjiang of Sufi orders which operate outside the mainstream mosque network (although their members may also attend the mosques). They are organised in a hierarchical system with the leadership being transmitted hereditarily whenever possible. This hereditary succession and their practices, which centre around direct communication between the individual Sufi and Allah through the silent or vocal acknowledgement of Allah (*dhikr*) accompanied by ritual dancing or chanting, depending on the particular order, have separated them from mainstream Islam and brought them into conflict with its authorities. Sufism is not, of course, a phenomenon found only in

Xinjiang. It exists throughout the Islamic world: the whirling dervishes of the Mevlevi Sufis of Turkey are the most familiar to westerners but it is particularly strong in Iran where it originated and in Central Asia and is an important part of the religious life of the Hui (Chinese speaking) Muslims of Ningxia and Gansu in north-west China (Dillon 1999: 113–129). Sufism is also one of the most overtly political forms of Islam and since the 1950s separatist groups in Xinjiang have often been influenced by Sufi masters (Xu 1999: 72–93).

In Xinjiang, Sufis have formed part of the opposition to state sponsored Islam and many have been responsible for attacks on senior Imams who are members of national or local committees of the Chinese Islamic Association and are therefore seen by some as collaborators.

The religious picture in Xinjiang is further complicated by ethnic diversity. Parts of the region have more Kazakhs or Kyrgyz than Uyghurs, and, where resources permit, these communities will worship in their own mosques. Chinese speaking Hui Muslims in Xinjiang also have their own mosques, and these are further subdivided into mosques for the separate Hui communities which originated in different parts of China.

The Hui are in an intermediate and often difficult position between the Han Chinese and Turkic Muslims. As Muslims they are frequently distrusted by the Han, while as Chinese speakers they are not considered to be proper Muslims by the Turkic communities. Depending on the time and place, they have acted as intermediaries, spokesmen for 'moderate Islam', or religio-political activists who can merge into the background when violent conflict erupts, as they are often indistinguishable physically from the Han Chinese.

Separatist movements

The separatist movements in Xinjiang which Beijing has identified as the major threat to national unity and stability have emerged from this ethnic and religious conflict. Separatism is not a new phenomenon in China, and it is not confined to Xinjiang: the internationally recognised movement to demand independence for Tibet and the less familiar campaign for independence in Inner Mongolia are the other most significant separatist struggles within the PRC.

Resistance to Chinese rule and the wish to create or retain an independent Muslim state predate the CCP by over a hundred years. The military administration of the Manchu Qing dynasty (1644–1911) which took control of the region in the eighteenth century encountered constant political and religious opposition, often allied to Islamic forces from the neighbouring Khanate of Kokand (in present day Uzbekistan). *Jihads* or religious struggles against the Qing were declared as early as 1820, and in the 1860s Kashghar was controlled by the forces of Yakub Beg who declared an independent state which was finally annihilated by the forces of the Qing in 1878.

Although contemporary separatists may invoke the name of Yakub Beg, their real inspiration is the Eastern Turkistan Republic (ETR) which controlled the north western part of Xinjiang around the city of Yining/Ghulja between 1944 and

1949.[3] To some extent it was a multi-ethnic regime but the basis for its appeal was Islam and Turkish nationalism. When the CCP took control of Xinjiang in 1949, the ETR administration surrendered to the PLA and was incorporated into the PRC, but support for genuine independence persisted.

Resistance by Eastern Turkistan loyalists, or separatists as Beijing would prefer to call them, continued into the 1950s. It took the form of small activist units which launched attacks on police and military barracks to obtain weapons and conducted armed robberies to obtain funds. These groups were frequently associated with Sufi orders and this religious connection was important in their attempts to win popular support and convert small scale insurgencies into large scale resistance. The Sufis used their network of connections to visit mosques in order to rally support for the cause. Members of the Sufi orders were invited to meetings where they swore an oath on the Qur'an to resist the infidel Chinese and support a *jihad* to install a Muslim regime. The first major resistance to the CCP after 1949, the 1954 rising in Khotan, which featured an attack on a prison camp in Karakash, was mounted almost entirely by adherents of the Sufi brotherhoods. These activities were suppressed by local police and troops and the militia of the XPCC. But the idea of an independent Eastern Turkistan Republic did not disappear; it later resurfaced in the Eastern Turkistan People's Party (ETPP) during the chaotic years of the Cultural Revolution in the late 1960s. Beijing claims that the ETPP was simply a creation of the Soviet Union with which the PRC had been in dispute since the late 1950s, but it is clear that there was considerable local support for independence (Xu 1999: 94–101).

After the death of Mao Zedong in September 1976 and the re-emergence of Deng Xiaoping as the single most important political figure in the PRC leadership, China's economic and social structures began to be liberalised. Partly as a result of this, separatist activity began to re-emerge in Xinjiang. The first recorded major incidents were clashes between different social and ethnic groups in Aksu in the west of the region and in Kashghar in the south-west, both in 1980. The collapse of the Soviet Union in December 1991 and the emergence of independent Muslim states in Kazakhstan, Kyrgyzstan and Uzbekistan fuelled expectations that the establishment of an independent East Turkistan state was imminent, and there were further acts of insurgency throughout the region in the years that followed.

Xinjiang and the former soviet Central Asia

The Kazakhs and Kyrgyz of Xinjiang are from the same ethnic background as their counterparts in Kazakhstan and Kyrgyzstan. There are Uyghur communities in both of these former Soviet central Asian republics; the Uyghurs are closely related to the Uzbeks of Uzbekistan and there are Uzbek communities in other parts of central Asia including Xinjiang. The Uyghur and Uzbek languages are extremely close and the two people share a common literary and cultural tradition. Many independent analysts consider that they are essentially the same people although both Uyghurs and Uzbeks prefer to maintain the distinction between the two communities.

It follows therefore, that, although Xinjiang is firmly under the administrative control of the PCR, its most important social and cultural bonds are with the

Turkic peoples to the north and west of the Karakorum mountains. These bonds were severed during the Sino-Soviet dispute which lasted from 1960 (or even earlier) until Mikhail Gorbachev's ill-fated visit to Beijing, during protests by students and citizens which were suppressed by the PLA, on 4 June 1989. The mass migration of Kazakhs, Uyghurs and others from north western Xinjiang into Kazakhstan in 1962 prompted China to seal its borders and contact between China and its western neighbours was minimal for decades.

The collapse of the Soviet Union in 1991 and the creation of the new sovereign states of Kazakhstan, Kyrgyzstan and Uzbekistan changed cross border relations dramatically. China needed to forge diplomatic relations with the new states, and discussions on long standing border demarcation issues and troop reduction began almost immediately. The border routes across the mountains were opened to trade: informally they opened straightaway, but officially they were authorised from 1992 onwards. Families and communities, which had had little contact for many years, renewed their acquaintance and trade developed at a rapid pace.

The new links were not restricted to commerce. Religious connections were also renewed and there were exchanges of political views. Independent Turkic Islamic states were immensely attractive to Uyghurs who looked to them for assistance in their own bid for independence. Initially there appeared to be serious and genuine support from other Turkic states, including Turkey, but as China's confidence in dealing with its Central Asian neighbours grew, Beijing made it perfectly clear that this support would be treated as unwarranted interference in China's internal affairs and would not be tolerated. Beijing negotiated with the stick of its overwhelming military superiority and the carrot of lucrative trade and energy deals, and persuaded the Central Asian states that they should curb any political activities by their own Uyghur communities or on behalf of Uyghurs in China. The new Central Asian governments readily complied. They were concerned about the threat to their own stability from political Islamist movements (particularly in Uzbekistan and Kyrgyzstan). The demise of communist regimes in Central Asia had led not to the hoped for democratisation of the region but to the emergence of authoritarian governments based partly on pre-Soviet clan and regional ties and partly on Soviet political culture. Although there was still distrust of China, they shared many common values.

As part of the attack on separatists, both within China and across the border, a campaign was instigated to demonise them as criminals. Press reporting of trials of Uyghurs frequently included separatist activities in a list of charges that also referred to crimes such as armed robbery, murder and rape. In the minds of the reader, in particular the Han Chinese reader, the implication was quite clear: there was no legitimate political support for independence only the criminal activities of separatists.

Shanghai Co-operation Organisation

As China developed relations with its Central Asian neighbours and Russia following the break-up of the Soviet Union, bilateral meetings on border and trade issues were found to be inadequate to deal with the changing geopolitical environment of east and Central Asia. Political Islam became more powerful in Afghanistan and Tajikistan and was perceived as a threat to the new governments of Uzbekistan and Kyrgyzstan: consequently, all of the regional powers discerned a common interest in combating this new force.

The first meeting of what was to become a major regional grouping took place in Shanghai in 1996 when the foreign ministers of China, Russia, Kazakhstan, Kyrgyzstan and Tajikistan met to discuss common concerns. An agenda was constructed around border security, combating insurgent Islamic forces and the smuggling of Islamic literature, weapons and narcotics. The grouping which met regularly came to be known as the Shanghai Five, but was renamed the Shanghai Co-operation Organisation in June 2001 when Uzbekistan was admitted. The name change being sufficiently flexible to allow for the admission of other members, although Pakistan, the only other state being seriously considered for membership, was not permitted to join as there were serious doubts about the Islamabad government's relationship with political Islamist groups.

Repression and western development

Beijing's strategy in dealing with the problem of ethnic separatism in Xinjiang since the early 1990s has been twofold. On the one hand, there has been the severest repression of any unofficial religious activity and any political activity that could be classified as separatist. On the other, there has been a recognition that poverty and underdevelopment lie at the root of the region's social problems, and programmes to alleviate poverty have been initiated from time to time. In the new realism that followed the death of Mao Zedong in 1976, it was publicly acknowledged in the media that under previous strategies of economic development, the west of China, including Xinjiang, had been neglected. This could conveniently be blamed on the 'Gang of Four' after their arrest in 1976 and trial in 1980–1981.

Beijing's initial response to the deepening conflict was to launch the Strike Hard campaign in 1996. Nationally, this campaign was said to be targeted at crime in general but in ethnic minority areas, the priority being clearly to suppress any manifestation of separatism. Mass arrests, short and long-term administrative detention, the seizure of unauthorised Islamic printed or recorded materials and a clampdown on unregistered and therefore illegal mosques and madrassas were all employed in order to root out separatism. Political re-education campaigns have also been used to persuade Islamic clerics that they should be more active in supporting the CCP's policy on religion, and to give support to registered mosques and Imams and isolate unregistered radical groups. Although this had the desired effect of curbing overt manifestations of separatist or Islamist protest, it did not kill off the sentiment which gave rise to them. Paramilitary separatist units continued to attack police and military bases.

Ever since Deng Xiaoping announced the policy of 'reform and opening' in 1978 and encouraged foreign investment to assist in the modernisation of China's economy, development has been uneven. The Special Economic Zones in which foreign investment was first permitted, beginning with Shenzhen, were in the south and Southeast of China, coastal areas that had already benefited from development during the Treaty Port era of the late nineteenth and early twentieth centuries. The economic development of these areas in the provinces of Guangdong, Fujian, Zhejiang and the city of Shanghai became the phenomenon of the 1980s and 1990s. As capital moved to these areas, so did labour, and China experienced a migration of population unlike any it had seen for over a century. In contrast, poor and underdeveloped areas in the west suffered even more from a lack of investment.

The decision to tackle the problem of the relative underdevelopment in the whole of China's western provinces led to the policy of the Great Development of the Western Regions (*Xibu da kaifa*) which was launched in 2000 in Chengdu, the capital of Sichuan province. The Western Development policy was targeted at the whole of the west, not just Xinjiang and this includes Ningxia, Gansu and Qinghai. The choice of provinces and regions to be included is somewhat controversial as it includes relatively prosperous localities such as Sichuan province in addition to genuinely impoverished areas, and the strategy requires considerable investment from abroad if it is to succeed.

The economy of the west of China is clearly in desperate need of development although improvements in the infrastructure, primarily road and rail links and urban construction have taken place over the last ten years. However the development plan treats the west as one homogeneous region and does not take into account its ethnic and religious diversity: this is likely to lead to conflict if it appears that economic development will benefit one group (i.e. the Han) rather than others.

Ethnic and religious conflict in the 1990s

Throughout the 1990s, political violence gradually spread throughout the region, partly evolving out of the internal dynamics of Xinjiang's political, social and ethnic structure and partly in response to the cataclysmic break up of the Soviet Union and the formation of new states by the predominantly Turkic peoples across the border from Xinjiang. As the decade progressed, the conflict became more acute and better organised.

The crucial events which determined the region's slide into conflict and violence were the riots of April 1990 at the height of the spring ploughing season at Baren in the Kizilsu Kyrgyz Autonomous Prefecture in southern Xinjiang. Baren is some 50 kilometres to the south-west of the great trading centre of Kashghar, it borders the Kashghar counties of Shufu, Shule and Yengihisar (Yingjisha) and is close to the Pamir mountain range which forms China's border with Afghanistan. A group of men attending prayers at a mosque on 5 April began criticising CCP policies towards ethnic minorities, including regulations on birth control, nuclear weapons testing at Lop Nur, and the export of Xinjiang's resources to 'inland China'. This developed into a mass protest with some activists calling for a *jihad* to drive the Han non-believers out of Xinjiang and to establish an East Turkistan state. One hundred police officers sent to quell the riot were overpowered and their weapons and ammunition stolen. Disturbances continued on 6 April with rioters firing small arms and throwing bombs at police and officials who were surrounding them and blowing up part of the local government building. According to the official account of the events, the rising was finally suppressed by the Public Security Bureau, People's Armed Police from the Kashghar garrison and militia units, but there were also reports that 1,000 regular PLA troops were brought in, and local politicians later visited injured soldiers in hospital to thank them for their part in suppressing the rising.

The next major incident occurred in June 1993 when a bomb exploded in Kashghar. Government buildings were damaged and as many as ten people were killed or injured in what was seen as a calculated attack on the representatives of the provincial government in the city (*BBC Summary of World Broadcasts* 1993). Émigré sources reported several bomb attacks in southern Xinjiang during 1993 and claimed that martial law had been declared in Kashghar city. Song Hanliang, the CCP Secretary for Xinjiang is reported to have visited Kashghar and is quoted as telling a multi-ethnic meeting of cadres that, 'Nationalist separatists form the main danger to the stability of our region, Xinjiang is a land with rich underground resources, our main task in Xinjiang is to keep the stability so the other parts of China could develop smoothly' (*Eastern Turkistan Dispatch* 1993a: 4). More detailed reports appeared in the German press, which stated that the explosion was apparently caused by 'a well-trained commando' which used a large quantity of explosives that tore a hole 7 metres long in the facade of the government's agricultural building in Kashghar. The report included a photograph of the damage. A second explosion occurred on 4 August and further bombs were planted in five different cities. Leaflets calling for independence and the cessation of Chinese migration into Xinjiang were distributed. Kazakhs in the Yili region[4] of north western Xinjiang also clashed with Chinese security forces during the summer of 1993 with some demonstrators demanding that they be allowed to become a republic in the CIS. There were also reports of an attack by Uyghur farmers on Han Chinese labourers who had been brought in to work in an oilfield in Karghalik in the Altishahr. An assassination attempt on the chairman of the Xinjiang Regional People's Congress, Amdun Nyaz, was also reported in July (*Eastern Turkistan Dispatch* 1993: 1–3).

There was further serious unrest in six towns in the Yili region in April 1995. On 22 April, as many as 50,000 people were reported to have taken part in rallies and demonstrations against Chinese rule in the towns of Mongolkure (Zhaosu), Tekes, Künes (Xinyuan) Gongliu, Qapqal and Nilka which surround Yining/Ghulja, the administrative capital, and are close to the border with Kazakhstan. Demonstrators were contacted through the mosques and the informal networks of extended family and Sufi orders that bypasses the official channels of communication. Contact was often by personal approaches and word of mouth, as written communications could be dangerous and even telephone conversations might be monitored. The climax of the agitation came on 24 April with strikes by as many as 100,000 workers, teachers and shopkeepers. Demonstrators handed in petitions to local authorities and called for the end of Chinese rule in the Ghulja region and its incorporation into Kazakhstan. They carried banners with slogans including 'Establish a Kazakh State', 'End Communist Rule in Xinjiang' and 'Long Live Uyghur Xinjiang'. More than 3,000 residents of Zhaosu and Gongliu are said to have surrounded local government offices, driven lorries at police stations and stolen guns and police vehicles. The local government offices in Zhaosu are reported to have been completely ransacked. Public Security Bureau police and People's Armed Police Units dispersed the crowd with armoured vehicles but were faced with return fire from light machine guns manufactured in the former Soviet Union. Military units from Ghulja and Bole were sent to the two towns to restore order. Zhaosu was placed under curfew on 25 April and over eighty people suspected of involvement in the disorder were arrested. As many as 220 people may have been killed or injured and over 8,500 rounds of ammunition were fired.

The towns of Nilka and Qapqal experienced equally serious disturbances. Demonstrations on 22 April were followed by a sit-down protest at the offices of the municipal government on the 23 April and strikes on the 24 April, during which water, electricity and gas supplies were cut off. Crowds surrounded the government offices on the 25 April, breaking into them in the afternoon and into the Public Security headquarters and People's Armed Police barracks in the evening. As many as 3,000 demonstrators surrounded the local military base, demanding Chinese withdrawal from Xinjiang and the establishment of an independent state of Uyghuristan. Troops fired back and issued an ultimatum that if the demonstrators did not depart by nine o'clock in the evening, they would take further action: in return the demonstrators demanded that police who had opened fire be prosecuted.

In the town of Khotan, a demonstration began on 7 July 1995 after reports circulated among local Muslims that an Imam at the Baytulla mosque had been arrested. Several hundred members of his congregation went to the local police and government offices to demand his release and a disturbance broke out when this was refused. The fifty or so officers and men of the People's Armed Police who were stationed there were reinforced by large numbers of armed troops and police and there were many injuries to protesters, police and government officials. There were arrests on the day and in the weeks that followed, and over 20 people were imprisoned after trials that took place in September of the same year (Amnesty International 1999).

Between February and April 1996 there were a number of serious incidents in four counties of the Aksu region, which is approximately half way between Kashghar and Urumqi. They all had links with the separatist struggle and were almost certainly connected. On 10 February four men dressed in old-style police uniforms and carrying pistols, drove a Beijing 2020 jeep to Bozidun farm in Wensu county where they robbed six herding families. They stole hunting rifles, ammunition, gunpowder, telescopes and over ¥4,000 Renminbi in cash. The local border police were called, and two police officers and one of the robbers died in the subsequent gun battle. This was reported as a crime but was almost certainly an operation by separatists to secure funds and weapons.

The motivations and ideologies of those involved in the demonstrations were quite complex. Underlying it was the resentment at what was seen by many as the unjustified occupation of their ancestral territory by the Chinese who were not only not Uyghurs but also were not Muslims. Memories of the independent government of the 1940s were still strong as were family connections to those who had served in those governments. There is no doubt that there was a highly developed sense of Uyghur or Eastern Turkistani nationalism, although it is difficult to document this precisely as it could only be expressed in private, in clandestine publications, or in illegal and therefore dangerous (potentially fatal) activities. The religious component of the resistance was always there and linked the demonstrators with the risings of the 1950s. The discourse of the demonstrators was frequently expressed in Islamic terms, but at this stage the movement itself was more nationalist than Islamist.

These disturbances were barely reported in the Chinese media at the time. Short reports appeared in *Xinjiang Daily* and on the state-controlled radio broadcasts from Urumqi and news of these filtered out to the west via the émigré Uyghur community.

The Yining/Ghulja rising of February 1997

The insurrection of February 1997 in Yining/Ghulja was by far the most serious of all the confrontations between the Uyghurs and the Chinese state. From the point of view of the authorities, the 'beating, smashing and looting' (*da za qiang*) incident on 5 February was no accident but had been planned for many years with the object of splitting the motherland. Since 1995, separatists across the region had been operating as the Eastern Turkistan Islamic Party of God (*Dong Tujuesitan Yisilan Zhenzhudang*) and its leader, Payzulla, together with a number of other key figures had frequently been to the Yili region. They had also sent more than twenty members from southern Xinjiang to Yili to preach *jihad* and develop their organisation there. In January 1996, Payzulla sent people into the villages of Yining and the rural counties attached to it to establish a training camp. In January and February, supporters were sent to establish secret contacts, and it was decided that there would be street demonstrations on the twenty-seventh day of Ramadan (5 February). Abuduleilili, Abudumijiti and other key members claimed that,

> We are going on to the streets to carry out religious propaganda openly. Whether we succeed or fail it will still be a success. Everyone can enter paradise. If we go to prison we will still have Allah's blessing and protection and those left outside will carry on the work.

On 4 February, Abudumijiti passed on to his supporters by word of mouth, the slogans that were to be inscribed on the banners to be carried during the demonstrations, and the time and the place where the demonstrators were to meet and the route were finalised (Xu 1999: 177–178).

On 5 February at 10:30am Beijing time, hundreds of young Uyghurs came out onto the streets holding banners in Arabic script with two slogans. One read, 'It has begun', the other, 'Fight the unbelievers with all our might using the Qur'an as a weapon'. They gathered as the Tashilaipukai market on Victory Road and made their way along Red Flag road, Stalin Street and Liberation Road 'in an illegal demonstration'. By the time they reached the Great Western Bridge (Xidaqiao) their numbers had risen to over three hundred and as they walked they chanted, 'Don't pay taxes' and 'We want nothing from the government' (Xu 1999: 178). This is a fair reflection of the attitude of many Uyghurs who prefer to run their own businesses, avoid working for the state, and have as little as possible to do with what they regard as an alien and oppressive government. It was not until ten in the evening, Beijing time, that the police tactics of dividing the demonstrators and arresting the ringleaders brought the protests to an end (Xu 1999:178–179).

The political leadership in Xinjiang tried strenuously to play down reports that casualties in Yining were more serious than had officially been admitted. In particular Wang Lequan, the CCP Secretary in Xinjiang, who was furious and agitated according to the *Sing Tao Daily*, denied that 400 people including as many as 300 Uyghurs had died in the riots. The *Xinjiang Daily* on 11 March called for continuing class struggle against the separatists and once again blamed 'hostile foreign forces' for taking advantage of the changes that had followed the collapse of the Soviet Union and trying to 'split' China (*BBC Summary of World Broadcasts* 1997). These concerns were echoed by Tomur Dawamat, a former Xinjiang regional chairman and later Vice Chairman of the central organisation the Standing Committee of the National People's Congress, China's parliamentary body.

Since the Yining/Ghuilja riots of 1997, such serious and overt confrontation between large groups of Uyghurs and the Chinese state has died down, primarily because of the repression associated with the Strike Hard campaign, which has been extended. It is unlikely, however, that confrontation on this scale is over for all time. The underlying causes of conflict have not been addressed and the benefits of economic development are only likely to alleviate the problem to a limited degree and may in some ways exacerbate it as the social exclusion of those Uyghurs who are not assimilated into Chinese society becomes more acute.

Conflict for the time being is left to small groups of activists, operating illegally and underground, some of them armed. The degree of support that they enjoy from the majority of the Uyghur population is extremely difficult to assess given the severity of possible reprisals from the state. There is evidence that some Uyghurs have been prepared to inform on others to the Chinese authorities. But there is also evidence that there is powerful resentment in certain families and specific regions at the execution and imprisonment of activists and this is likely to provide the impetus for new recruits to paramilitary and other separatist groups.

Large-scale conflict is likely to recur from time to time in different places and may be sparked off by local, probably unpredictable, grievances. The Xinjiang authorities with the support of troops from the Lanzhou Military Region will deploy such forces as are necessary to suppress the conflict; there will be further arrests and the closure of more mosques and schools, and this will stoke up further resentment and increase the potential for more conflict in the future.

The authorities will continue to pursue militant armed groups and will, in all probability, eliminate some of them. Other groups are likely to replace them and given the challenging terrain of Xinjiang and the unreliability of Chinese intelligence gathering in the Uyghur community, not all of them will be wiped out. Some degree of long term low intensity conflict is very likely and could include armed attacks on security forces, armed robberies and sabotage.

The impact of 11 September 2001 and the 'war on terror'

China reacted to the attacks on New York and Washington by restricting the access of foreigners to Xinjiang, which has a 70 kilometre border with Afghanistan, and by declaring that separatism in Xinjiang was a terrorist phenomenon and that China should be given *carte blanche* to deal with it as the authorities saw fit. This provoked international concern from Human Rights quarters including the UN High Commissioner for Human Rights, Mary Robinson. Although the anti-terrorist rhetoric has remained, China has actually done very little that is new to suppress separatism in Xinjiang, it has largely continued with the policies that it began in 1996 with the Strike Hard campaign. China was clearly using the cover of the 'war on terror' to clamp down on Islam *per se* in Xinjiang and implied that the Uyghurs' struggle for independence was nothing other than the activities of a branch of al Qaeda. As has been demonstrated however, the Uyghur movement predates al Qaeda by many decades at least and any connection is tenuous and difficult, if not impossible, to prove.

Rohan Gunaratana has repeated suggestions that the militancy dates from the return to China of Uyghurs sent to Afghanistan by the Chinese government or the PLA to assist, or at least liaise with, the *mujahidin* who were resisting the Soviet invasion of 1979 (Gunaratana 2002: 172–173). While this would have been entirely consistent with China's interests at that late stage of the Sino-Soviet dispute, there has, not surprisingly, never been any clearly documented evidence that this took place. The presence of Uyghurs in Mazar-e-Sharif at the end of the war in Afghanistan in 2002, and the detention of twenty-two of them in the US detention centre at Guantanamo Bay in Cuba is, however, a matter of fact. Some of these Uyghurs may have been trained in camps on the Afghanistan–Pakistan border that were supported by al Qaeda and there are reports of others who have escaped from Xinjiang and moved through Central Asia and Afghanistan to the 'tribal areas' of Pakistan, notably Hasan Mehsum who was shot dead in south Waziristan on 2 October 2003.

Nevertheless, the Chinese government has stated explicitly that its opposition to separatism in Xinjiang is part of the 'war on terror'. At a press briefing in Shanghai on the occasion of the Asia-Pacific Economic Cooperation meeting in October 2001, Zhu Bangguo, speaking on behalf of the Ministry of Foreign Affairs, identified Eastern Turkistan forces as part of the global terrorist movement that the US-led coalition was fighting. Later that month, the Foreign Minister, Tang Jiaxuan, alleged that Uyghur separatists in Xinjiang had close links with Osama bin Laden and that some militants had been trained in al Qaeda training camps in Afghanistan. Many Uyghurs were outraged that their entire community was being maligned by these assertions.

Even more difficult to assess is the long-term impact of the presence of US troops in Central Asia. During the Cold War the deployment of American forces in this region was completely unthinkable as it was under the absolute control of the Soviet Union. Since 1991, Russia has seen itself as the one outside power with a legitimate interest in the region, and this has been recognised by its inclusion in the Shanghai Cooperation Organisation. Central Asian states were initially reluctant to accept US and allied troops on their territory in the war against the Taleban, but in the long term some limited military contact will almost certainly be maintained as part of Uzbekistan and Kyrgyzstan's resistance to the rise of political Islam in the Ferghana valley.

The first deputy interior minister of Kyrgyzstan welcomed the presence of US troops in his country when they were allowed to use Manas airport and suggested that members of the coalition might have a long-term future in Kyrgyzstan, 'if the situation in the region deteriorates' (*Vecherny Bishkek* 2001). Two hundred US servicemen had arrived at Manas by 25 December 2001 and were preparing to establish a more permanent base in Kyrgyzstan (*Public Education Radio TV, Bishkek* 2001). The initial agreement for the US presence was for one year, but even at that stage local commentators thought it was likely to be for longer (*Komsomolskaya Pravda v Kyrgyzstane* 2002). Discussions on the establishment of a US military presence in Kazakhstan also took place in January 2002 (*Kazakh TV* 2002). Both China and Russia are concerned at this threat to their influence and to the overall balance of power in Central Asia.

China also benefited from the 'war on terror' by offering its support to the US-led coalition in return for an agreement under which the Eastern Turkistan Islamic Movement (ETIM), which Beijing had identified in 2002 as the main 'terrorist' group operating in Xinjiang, would be proscribed by the international community. It was accused of having links with al Qaeda and was blacklisted by the US and the United Nations.

In December 2003 Beijing published the names of what it claimed were the main Xinjiang 'terrorist' groups. A Statement by Zhao Yongshen of the Ministry of Public Security listed ETIM, the Eastern Turkistan Liberation Organisation, the World Uyghur Youth Congress and the East Turkistan Information Centre. The last of these is based in Munich and is essentially an émigré propaganda organisation.

Also in December 2003, China announced the death of Hasan Mehsum *alias* Abu Muhammad Al-Turkestani, who was identified as the leader of ETIM and who had apparently been shot and killed in south Waziristan, a region of Pakistan on the border with Afghanistan on 2 October 2003. It was not made clear whether he had been killed by Pakistani troops or by US troops in a joint operation. Information provided by official Chinese sources about Mehsum was sketchy and contradictory. They claimed that he had been arrested in Xinjiang in 1993 and spent three years in a labour camp but that he was linked with a series of bombings in China in 1995.

Terrorist activities and sabotage in Xinjiang

Although overt and public resistance to Chinese rule has effectively been suppressed since the 1997 demonstrations in Yining/Ghulja, the activities of small militant groups continue, and these activities are likely to become more widespread and more daring as long as there are no alternative means of expressing separatist sentiments. During the late 1990s émigré sources reported that militant groups within Xinjiang were trying to set up urban guerrilla units to bring their struggle to the cities, which apart from Urumqi and on one occasion Beijing, had not been affected by separatist violence. To date, this has not happened, but it remains a possibility for the next decade as it would be one way of dramatically bringing home to the population of China the seriousness with which separatists in Xinjiang regard their struggle for independence. There could therefore be further bomb attacks in cities in Xinjiang other than Urumqi and in major cities throughout the rest of China. Large and relatively cosmopolitan cities like Shanghai and Guangzhou where there is already a small but significant Uyghur population are potential targets for this kind of attack. The public security forces are already on the alert for this kind of attack and from time to time groups of Uyghurs in cities in China proper have been rounded up and arrested and sometimes sent back to Xinjiang or at least sent out of the cities in which they have been working, usually as traders. The reporting of these attacks, or danger of these attacks, became more open in the period after 11 September 2001 and was reinforced by word of mouth and the informal system of communication that the CCP has maintained in its network of organisations since 1949.

Sabotage has also been one of the tactics of the more militant groups of separatists, although it is extremely difficult to assess the effect that this sabotage has had because the authorities are very reluctant to attribute damage to separatist activities. From time to time there have been disruptions to rail and road communications and it has been suggested by émigré organisations that these were as a result of bombs or other kinds of damage to the track or rolling stock but the government has frequently attributed these to natural conditions such as excessive rainfall, snow or landslips. The prevention and detection of sabotage is clearly one of the priorities for the public security forces in Xinjiang as this is where it is most likely to occur. This would tie up the resources of the police and the security units of the XPCC.

Xinjiang separatism and the media

Media coverage of the conflict in Xinjiang has been patchy, to say the least. The Western media have largely ignored the issue, with the exception of a few articles in the quality press, a documentary on Channel 4 and an occasional mention in television news bulletins. Part of the reason for this is the genuine difficulty of obtaining anything remotely resembling accurate information on what is still a remote and inaccessible region. The Chinese government has strongly discouraged journalists from visiting Xinjiang and for many years, western journalists based in Beijing were not allowed to visit the region at all on pain of losing their accreditation. Carefully managed visits by groups of journalists have been arranged by the authorities since China's declaration of its support for the 'war on terror', in an attempt to garner international support for the suppression of East Turkistan sentiment, but access to ordinary Uyghurs, particularly those living in outlying areas, has been severely restricted. The Uyghurs' struggle for independence has never in any case been a popular one, whereas the Tibetan cause which has a very similar rationale seems to have won almost universal acceptance.

The Chinese official media, which is of course state-controlled, has clearly run into considerable difficulties in its coverage of the conflict. Until relatively recently there was no coverage at all in the main national press *People's Daily* and *Guangming Daily* (the preferred daily newspaper of the intelligentsia) or Chinese Central Television which, when it ran stories about Xinjiang, concentrated almost entirely on positive economic successes in the time-honoured fashion. Even in the provincial daily newspaper *Xinjiang Daily*, little space was devoted to the separatist issue in an attempt to marginalise it and underplay its significance. This changed during the 1990s when from time to time, there were reports of court cases against Uyghurs convicted of crimes linked to separatist activities that were intended to serve as a warning to others. This also applies to the broadcast media, in particular Xinjiang Radio, broadcasting from Urumqi.

Local newspapers in Xinjiang below the provincial level, which are published in Chinese and Uyghur editions, are a much better source of detailed information on separatist activities seen from the point of view of the Chinese government. However, for that very reason their circulation is restricted and they are classified as *neibu* (internal) which means that they were for the eyes of party cadres and selected trusted outsiders only. This classification was formerly very common throughout the whole of China, for newspapers, other periodicals and books and there were even higher levels of classified documents which could only be read by the most senior party officials, but the system gradually fell into abeyance in the 1980s as the 'reform and opening' programme inspired by Deng Xiaoping developed and has effectively ended with the exception of genuinely secret material which refers to national defence and to sensitive areas such as Xinjiang. The attitude of the Beijing authorities to these *neibu* publications can be gauged by the eight-year prison sentence that Rabiya Kadeer received for sending state secrets abroad – these were runs of *Kashghar Daily* sent to her husband in the United States. Local television, especially the channels that broadcast in Uyghur (and in Kazakh in northern Xinjiang) also cover separatist issues as a warning to the populace not to become involved. The trials and the sentences handed down are reported, and often accompanied by footage of the humiliated 'criminals', heads bowed being led away to prison or to execution. Long-term residents of Xinjiang confirm, however, that they have never seen detailed coverage of major disturbances broadcast on local television in the region.

Since the upsurge of the separatist movement in the 1990s, the silence on the issue has been broken by a number of books published in Chinese which have taken a very confident attitude towards Beijing's suppression of the Uyghurs and have in doing so provided an unprecedented amount of detailed information both about the separatist movement and the methods used by Beijng to contain it. The most influential of these is *Guojia liyi gaoyu yiqi* (*The interest of the state is greater than anything*) by Ma Dazheng, which was published in Urumqi in 2003 and, as its title suggests, is an uncompromising condemnation of the separatists.

There is no independent media in Xinjiang. All Uyghur language publications have to be whetted by the authorities or they are deemed to be illegal, and although there was a relatively liberal period in the 1980s and 1990s there has since been a crack down and sensitive or controversial books or journals cannot be published. Oppositionist material does circulate clandestinely in Uyghur, often via the mosques and the unregulated madrassas. Some of this is produced locally but much material is also imported in the form of video and audiotapes, which are subject to searches and confiscation by the Chinese authorities. Much of this material is religious in nature: it reflects, and may have contributed, to the growing Islamist trend in the Uyghur independence movement.

Émigré Uyghur publications have been an important conduit for alternative sources of information about the lives of people in Xinjiang. As these have been produced by scattered communities, often with few resources, they have been ephemeral and of varied quality. Émigré organisations also have a number of different functions and responsibilities, including the development of support agencies for their own communities, the preservation and transmission of Uyghur language and culture within their community, and the dissemination of news from Xinjiang. The *Eastern Turkistan Information* (*Bulletin*) was published from May 1991 by the Eastern Turkistan Union in Europe from its base in Munich until 1996 and the *Eastern Turkistan Dispatch* appeared infrequently from an address in Lausanne, Switzerland. Both carried reports on abuses of human rights and the repression of unauthorised Islam by the Chinese authorities in Xinjiang. Difficulties with access to contacts inside Xinjiang and a reluctance to analyse the independence movement objectively make them problematic as primary sources. Towards the end of the 1990s the growth in the availability of the internet made it possible for these hardcopy sheets to be replaced by web sites.

The internet is becoming more widely available in Xinjiang, but not to the same extent as in the more prosperous areas of east and Southeast China. Detailed data are not available, but it is clear that relatively few individuals have personal internet connections at home. There are internet cafes, including a long-established one in Kashghar, but these are subject to regular monitoring by the Public Security Bureau and there is in any case regular filtering of internet content throughout the whole of China. Because of this the internet has not been used as a major vehicle for transmitting information about the separatist cause, but it has increased the availability of information from outside Xinjiang. Uyghurs have developed special fonts for the version of Persi-Arabic script that is used in Xinjiang for computers and the web so that in itself is not a barrier to electronic communication.

Although the media has played a role in the development of the independence movement in Xinjiang, it has not been a major consideration. Since the movement is illegal and all of its operations are clandestine, it has no access to the mainstream state controlled media in China. Uyghurs have continued to rely on grass roots organisations, family and religious networks to disseminate their ideas and to mobilise people for demonstrations. Access to the foreign media to present the case for an independent Eastern Turkistan has often proved dangerous and the repercussions on the Uyghurs have been severe The informal exchange of ideas and underground contacts is likely to continue as their main method of communication rather than any of the mass media.

Notes

1 Dillon, M. (2004) *Xinjiang: China's Muslim Far Northwest*, London, RoutledgeCurzon, pp. xiv and 201 treats these issues in more detail. An earlier version of this chapter was given at the conference on *Xinjiang: Central Asia or China?* Heyns Room, The Faculty Club, University of California, Berkeley, CA on 13 March 2004.
2 All other religions in China are subject to similar restrictions especially those with foreign connections including Christianity.
3 Yining is the Chinese name for the city known as Ghulja in Uyghur.
4 In Chinese, Yili, (Ili in Russian), the name of the river that runs through the area and out into Kazakhstan is used of the region in general, while the main city and garrison town is called Yining in Chinese and Ghulja in Uyghur and Kazakh.

Conclusion

Benjamin Cole

Non-state combatants and the media in Asia

The analysis in this book has demonstrated that groups and minority communities engaged in, or suffering from, violent political activity across Asia are attempting to access the media. They attempt to use the media for broadly similar purposes: to highlight their grievances; to publicise their objectives or ideology; to publicise their violence as a means to intimidate public, elite and political opinion; and to build popular support both within and outside of their natural constituency, including international support from governments or other militant groups. The ability of any group or community to achieve these purposes depends upon the nature and extent of the reporting of their conflict, and in Asia this varies widely.

Virtually all of these groups and communities have been able to successfully access the media and influence its agendas, through using violence. However the level of access that different groups and minority communities have to the mainstream media varies widely between states and even between different groups within the same state. Since most of these governments work to deny these groups and communities access to the media and attempt to control media outputs, the level of access that each group or community has is primarily determined by the extent of media freedom in each state. At one end of the spectrum, the Filipino media gives the spokesmen of the Moro Islamic Liberation Front (MILF) and the Communist Party of the Philippines-New Peoples Army (CPP-NPA) extensive access, and similarly the majority of the Indian media reported the politically inspired anti-Muslim violence in Gujarat objectively. At the other end of the spectrum China has the most restrictive media, giving the Xinjiang separatist movement no direct access. Indonesia is an interesting anomaly because Jemaah Islamiyah (JI) has successfully publicised its messages in the mainstream Indonesian media, but local elites and the military have denied similar access to the Free Aceh Movement (GAM). But whatever level of access any of these groups has, it is far outweighed by the access accorded to their respective governments and other elites.

The level of access that a group or community has also tends to vary between different sections of the media, which can have a significant impact on determining which audiences see their messages. In Gujarat for instance, the bulk of the media reported the violence boldly and independently, but the two local newspapers which were most likely to have been read by those sections of the Hindu community, who formed the politically mobilised mob, had a heavy pro-Hindutva bias. This would have limited the ability of the media as a whole to act as a restraining influence on those perpetrating the violence. Similarly, in the Philippines the most objective reporting of the various conflicts is generally found in the broadsheet Manila newspapers, but it is the local newspapers and tabloids, whose reporting of these conflicts generally has the most flaws, which are probably most widely read by the communities in the conflict areas.

This makes it imperative for groups and communities themselves to proactively seek access to the media, but different groups have displayed different levels of professionalism in their media relations. Some groups such as the Abu Sayyaf Group (ASG) are proactive in seeking media attention, whilst others such as the JI and Kumpulan Militan Malaysia (KMM) are more reactive in letting the media report their activities. Some have simply been more professional than others in cultivating media contacts, tailoring their violence to ensure maximum media coverage, using media spokesmen, and issuing media statements.

All of these groups and communities rely on the mainstream media as the primary medium for communicating their messages. Television remains the most powerful medium, and in the Philippines, the ASG, the CPP-NPA and the MILF have all allowed TV to film in their camps, whereas JI in Indonesia has perpetrated spectacular attacks that make a dramatic impact on TV. One medium which tends to be overlooked is radio. In poor rural communities across Asia, radio may well be much more significant than it is in the West. Radio Veritas played a key role as a facilitator in the ousting of President Marcos in the Philippines, and all of the groups currently engaged in conflict with the Filipino government, with the exception of JI, make extensive use of radio stations to publicise their media statements.

Given the lack of media freedom in the region, the internet offers an alternative source of news and views, especially for people and communities which have lost faith in the mainstream media. Internet reporting is a source of dissident viewpoints and news throughout the region. In Indonesia the internet has already played an important role as a facilitator in mobilising people power to topple one government. The majority of the groups and communities referred to in this book use the internet, but it seems to be primarily as a supplement to their use of mainstream media. There may be structural reasons for this since many of them are operating within communities where internet access is limited. But there is also evidence from states such as Malaysia that the internet is not wholly trusted as a source of news and information (*The Straits Times interactive* 2004). It is al Qaeda and its local affiliates that seem to rely on the internet the most because of the need to communicate transnationally.

The Xinjiang separatist movement also illustrates the potential of alternative 'old' media such as privately produced newsletters, as well as video and audiotapes, and other literature, which are smuggled into China from neighbouring states. These have been used to spread the separatist message and, on occasion, to mobilise large numbers of people. However there are inherent problems in distributing such material clandestinely, which works to limit its accessibility.

Through using violence to access the mainstream media, the majority of the groups and communities covered by this book have demonstrated an ability to set the media agenda. Using violence is a particularly effective device in the short term, and provided these groups and communities can sustain a consistent level of violence, it can enable them to exert influence over the media agenda for prolonged periods of time. But violence is a fairly blunt instrument for setting the media agenda. It can ensure access, but it does not guarantee the necessary influence over media outputs. It is significant that none of these groups and communities, with the partial exception of the Hindu rioters in Gujarat, has really been able to use the root causes of their violence, their objectives, or their ideologies, to control the media agenda and positively influence its outputs. In Gujarat, the Hindu rioters were only able to achieve this to a limited extent through the two local newspapers which supported their ideology. Gaining publicity for these issues is supposed to flow from setting the media agenda through violence, but this is often not the case because reporting tends to focus in on the act of violence. Instead, governments and the other vested interests which exercise influence over the media in these states, have a much higher level of control over its outputs. As a result, only a few of the groups and communities covered by this book, such as the CPP-NPA and the MILF in the Philippines, are able to exert even limited influence over media outputs.

The media and the 'war on terror' in Asia

One of the main goals of the US media strategy in the wake of 9/11 was to control the international media agenda on 'terrorism' and 'counter-terrorism', particularly through transnational media providers such as CNN. This strategy has had some success in Asia because one of the most disturbing features of the reporting of indigenous conflicts by the mainstream national media in China and the Philippines, is the way that it links those conflicts with the 'war on terror'. This reporting gives an erroneous impression of these conflicts, raising issues about the legitimacy of the causes that the various groups and communities are fighting for, and helping to generate expectations over how to deal with them.

In contrast, the media in Malaysia and Indonesia, under the influence of their respective governments, have worked to de-link their indigenous conflicts from the 'war on terror', despite the fact that the US has tried to draw both states into the 'war', by putting JI and the KMM on its list of foreign terrorist organisations. This reflects the opposition of these two states to the wider 'war on terror' but also a desire to downplay the threat of Islamic extremism within their borders. This illustrates the limitations of the globalised media for disseminating US messages.

Despite its best efforts therefore, the US has failed to win the 'battle of ideas' with al Qaeda in Asia, because its counter-terror messages and its perspective on the wars in Afghanistan and Iraq are rarely reported directly in the Asian media. This is largely because with the possible exception of the Philippines, the US media has been discredited in the states covered by this book, due to the inherent nationalism and bias in its reporting of the 'war on terror'. The inability of the US media to convince sceptical audiences in Asia of the justifiability of US policies threatens to exacerbate existing anti-American sentiment across the region, creating an environment which militant groups might be able to exploit. If for no other reason than this, Malaysia and Indonesia are trying to distance their counter-terrorism policies from the 'war on terror'.

As a consequence of the lack of credibility of its own media, the US needs to disseminate its counter-terrorism messages through the national media of each country, but it has few levers to do this. In all of the states covered by this book, US policies in the 'war on terror' are widely and routinely criticised. Nowhere is this more apparent than in Malaysia, where the reporting of the conflicts in Iraq, the occupied Palestinian territories and Chechnya is supportive of the fighters and critical of the US. This undermines the core messages that the US is trying to get across in its global media strategy, and in generating sympathy for the causes that militants champion it has the potential to generate popular support for militant groups and ideologies.

But despite this, the US shares common interests with regional governments in wishing to see sub-state conflicts suppressed, which is why even Malaysia and Indonesia have been partners for the US in hunting down al Qaeda. It is this common interest which is driving local media outputs to reflect US objectives in the 'war on terror' to a greater or lesser extent. In some states the mainstream media defines indigenous conflicts within the context of the 'war on terror' by highlighting the links between al Qaeda and indigenous conflicts, which in turn creates implicit linkages between the reporting of these conflicts and generic reporting of the 'war on terror.' This is sometimes a deliberate policy on the part of governments in order to obtain international support for the repression of those groups and communities. China was successful in getting the East Turkistan Islamic Movement onto the State Department list of foreign terrorist organisations, despite it having only limited links to al Qaeda. While the Philippines actively lobbied the EU to have the CPP-NPA designated as a terrorist organisation. The influence of the 'war on terror' is now so pervasive, that even Malaysia, which does not link its indigenous conflicts with the 'war', is much less criticised for using the Internal Security Act (ISA) after 9/11, despite persistent allegations that it is being used to suppress legitimate political dissent.

In the freer media in the region, the origins of this failure, or deliberate bias, are also a result of deficiencies in media practice. In particular, reporters often fail to question and assess the material that they receive from official sources, such as whether links between al Qaeda and indigenous groups are institutional or at an individual level, and whether any links are strategic in nature or for purely tactical purposes. A key issue that is frequently not picked up by the media is that the majority of the groups in these states do not share al Qaeda's pan-Islamic ideology. This is particularly evident in the Philippines, where the Arroyo government is trying to disentangle its policy towards the CPP-NPA and the MILF from US policy in the 'war on terror', but under the influence of the AFP and the US, the mainstream media is constantly highlighting MILF links with JI.

The influence of the mainstream media in some states in perpetuating the norms of the 'war on terror' and linking indigenous conflicts into the 'war' for national political reasons has some profound implications. First, the solutions to most of these conflicts are predominantly national in nature, but the nature of media reporting gives the impression that defeating al Qaeda militarily is the key, when it is not. This is one of the great fallacies of the 'war on terror' but the mainstream media in these states generally tends to perpetuate it. Second, it alienates potential support from the international community. The potential benefits of international political support for some of the conflicts mentioned in this book were illustrated when Indonesia was forced to grant independence for East Timor under pressure from the international community. However the international community were not seriously engaged in any of these conflicts prior to 9/11, so the effect of this reporting is probably to stifle any future support that might have come from the international community.

A number of groups have recognised the consequences of being dragged into the 'war on terror' and have attempted to distance themselves from al Qaeda and terrorism. In Indonesia, Ayip Syafruddin, chairman of the Communication Forum, a group associated with the militant group Laskar Jihad stated that 'We have nothing to do with Osama Bin Laden... We have no contact with them. We have a different vision'. Similarly GAM insists it has no links with outside groups (Suh 2001). Whilst in the Philippines, the MILF has publicly renounced terrorism but is still fighting a running battle in the media over whether, and how, it is linked to JI. It is indicative of the pervasive nature of the 'war on terror', however, that even though the Indonesian media and government do not portray the conflict in Aceh as part of the 'war', the West has shown itself to be eager to support Jakarta's efforts to quell the conflict.

Media impacts: the media as an agent of change or stability

The impact of the media on the conflicts identified in this book has been varied but generally limited. In particular, there does not appear to be any correlation between media outputs and the spread of militant ideologies, and neither has media reporting generated widespread public or political pressure to accede to the demands of any of these groups. Even where the media has articulated the root causes of violence and the objectives of combatant groups and communities, there does not appear to be any widening of those conflicts. The possible exception is in Gujarat, where local pro-Hindutva newspapers have complemented the work of the sangh parivar in spreading the Hindutva ideology.

The same is true with the reporting of al Qaeda's messages. Despite the failure of the US media to win the 'battle of ideas', al Qaeda has also discovered the limitations of the globalised media for influencing the reporting of conflicts at national level. There is little evidence of al Qaeda's pan-Islamist ideology gaining a significant foothold in the Muslim populations of Indonesia, Malaysia, or the Philippines. Bin Laden has also failed to co-opt any of these indigenous conflicts into his global 'jihad'. This is reflected in the fact that virtually none of the indigenous groups exploit al Qaeda's messages in their own communications with the media, and there is no apparent increase in either the number of citizens of these countries joining al Qaeda or JI, or of Muslims from outside of the region arriving to join indigenous groups. Islamist groups continue to recruit new members, but they remain a small minority. Similarly, its impact on the development of passive support for militant Islamism also seems to be minimal. In Malaysia for instance, support for the Islamist party PAS has diminished significantly since 2001.

This illustrates the limitations of the media as a vehicle for shaping public opinion in communities which are not receptive to particular messages or ideologies. There is some evidence of increased Islamism in Xinjiang, but that seems to be as a result of local activists disseminating alternative media sources.

Instead, the mainstream media predominantly acts as an agent of social and political stability by reflecting and reinforcing the views of governments and majority populations. The majority view of Islam within most Muslim populations in Southeast Asia is pragmatic and moderate. Whilst dissident and militant viewpoints are reported, the mainstream media overwhelmingly reflects and reinforces a moderate view of Islam. In those states dealing with separatist movements, the mainstream media takes a nationalistic line in support of maintaining the territorial integrity of the state.

In Malaysia for instance, limited media criticism of the government coupled with its use of the media to co-opt Islam serves to reassure public opinion that its concerns about oppressed Muslims overseas and the US 'war on terror' are being addressed. At a more general level, militant causes and objectives have been assimilated into the mainstream political debate. Whilst this might generate broad sympathy for some militant objectives in Malaysian society, it has not fostered a causal link to militant action. The Malaysian government, in common with other regional governments, has generally used the media to scare the public about extremist 'threats', and this has strengthened public support for counter-terrorism. Across the region there remains a disjunction between popular opposition to the 'war on terror' as articulated in the media, and active support for militant groups.

Whilst the majority of the national media are acting as agents of stability in relation to these conflicts, sections of the media in some countries are acting as agents of restraint in challenging government policies. In Malaysia there is some questioning of the government's use of the ISA, although it has had no impact on government policy. The Filipino media also comes close to fulfilling a monitoring role, but even there, the pervasive influence of government sources on media outputs coupled with deficiencies in media practice, means that whilst some publications, or journalists, are acting as agents of restraint, the majority are still acting as agents of stability.

Only in Gujarat has the media acted as a facilitator of change. This is evident both in the role of some sections of the local media in spreading the Hindutva ideology and fanning the violence in 2002, and also in the role which other sections of the media played in forcing the federal government to intervene to bring the violence to an end.

Nevertheless, media reporting had positive and negative impacts for groups engaged in conflict with government. In the Philippines for instance, the identification of the MILF and the CPP-NPA as rebel or revolutionary groups, and their differentiation from JI and the ASG, is important in maintaining public support for the government's political approach to dealing with the MILF and the CPP-NPA. The Malaysian and Filipino media have also had a major role in de-legitimising the KMM and ASG respectively, by denying the theological justification for their actions.

In contrast, the campaigns by the mainstream media in Indonesia and China to de-legitimize the GAM and the Xinjiang separatist movement respectively, have not had any appreciable impact in undermining support for these causes within the Acehnese and Uyghur communities. Again, this illustrates the limitations of the media in being able to shape opinion in communities which are not receptive to particular messages.

The internet has the potential to act as an agent of change in the region, and as a facilitator for protest movements, but that potential remains unfulfilled in these conflicts. Minority communities and militant groups across Asia are using the internet as a means of by-passing the media gatekeepers, and governments are finding it increasingly difficult to police the net. It has been suggested that the new media allows those on the periphery to develop and consolidate power, and ultimately to challenge the authority of the centre (Majod 1999: 81), and as regimes toppled in Thailand and Indonesia in the 1990s, the global communication media was increasingly identified as an important cause of regional political upheaval in Southeast Asia (Atkins 1999: 420).

Yet the impact of the internet should not be overstated. In the instances where it has facilitated political change, there was already widespread popular discontent with those governments, centreing around the issues of democracy and anti-corruption. In the Philippines, limited internet penetration suggests that it was not the internet which generated the mass popular discontent with the Estrada administration, whilst in Indonesia the fall of Suharto was as much a consequence of the mainstream media broadcasting images of protests over the 1997 economic collapse as it was the mobilisation of mass opinion through the internet. The parallels between these incidents and the conflicts covered by this book are limited, because the groups and communities engaged in violence with their governments do not have mass popular support, and neither have the root causes of those conflicts generated mass popular support sufficient to enable the media to facilitate change. By itself, the internet has not proven that it is capable of generating a mass movement capable of forcing political change. Its limitations are reflected in the fact that despite hosting a large number of websites publicising militant Islamist ideologies and causes, and militants being active in chat rooms and on message boards, significant numbers of people in the states covered by this book have not been infected with those militant ideologies. It is also illustrated by the inability of Xinjiang émigré groups to effectively use the internet to gather and disseminate information.

It must not be forgotten that people are not passive receptors for messages on minority causes and militant ideologies, and the internet is a melting pot for a wide variety of different belief systems and viewpoints. Studies have shown that when accessing information online, people typically browse from multiple sources, thereby reducing the influence of single sources, and online audiences typically go to news sites to get more information about subjects that interest them rather than to seek general enlightenment (Budha 2003: 79). The internet is therefore a potential facilitator in the spread of popular support for minority causes and militant ideologies, but it does not guarantee it.

Instead, the main influence of the internet on these conflicts can be seen as a complement to reporting by the mainstream media. In the Philippines for instance, the MILF and CPP-NPA do not need to rely on the internet because they have excellent access to the mainstream media. People are also more likely to come into contact with al Qaeda ideology via reports in the mainstream media, in the first instance. The internet is useful as a source of further information on militant ideologies for those whose interest has already been aroused by other factors.

Evidence of the limited significance of the media can also be seen in those conflicts where groups and communities rely on other, traditional mechanisms to achieve their purposes. The Xinjiang separatist movement, for instance, has been able to use community and religious networks to mobilise large numbers of people, and publicises its cause through those same networks as well as through illegal publications. Similarly, the violence in Gujarat was largely initiated, organised and driven by grass roots political activists and networks. Recruiting, indoctrination and fund-raising for many groups is still largely carried out through traditional means such as in Mosques, educational establishments, and through community networks, personal contacts, as well as clan and family ties. This also discredits the notion that by not reporting certain political events and issues, the growth of certain ideologies would be prevented.

The pervasive nature of government media controls, coupled with the deep seated deficiencies in media practice across the region, suggests that the role of the media in any of these conflicts is unlikely to change dramatically in the near future, although there may be a gradual shift in some states towards more elements of the media acting as an agent of restraint. As a result, any positive impact for the groups and communities engaged in these conflicts is likely to remain small.

Bibliography

Abayah, A.C. (2004, 16 September) 'Aimez-Vous Bush?', *Manila Standard*.

Abdoolcarim, Z. and Mitton, R. (2001, November 16) 'Face-Off', *Asiaweek.com*. Online available: www.asiaweek.com/asiaweek/magzine/dateline/0,8782,183538 (accessed 3 July 2004).

Abrahamian, E. (2003) 'The US Media, Huntington and September 11', *Third World Quarterly*, 24, no. 3: 529–544.

Agovino, T. (2003, 25 March) 'NYSE Revokes Credentials for Al-Jazeera', *Editor & Publisher*.

Ahmad, A. (2003) 'Contextualizing Conflict: The US "War on Terrorism"', in D.K. Thussu and D. Freedman (eds) *War and the Media: Reporting Conflict 24/7*, London: Sage Publications.

Aktan, G. (2004, 15 May) 'Denigration and Democratization', *Turkish Daily News*.

Allan, S. and Zellizer, B. (2004) 'Rules of Engagement', in S. Allan and B. Zelizer (eds) *Reporting War: Journalism in Wartime*, London: Routledge.

Alterman, E. (2003) *What Liberal Media? The Truth about Bias and the News*, New York: Basic Books.

Amnesty International. (1999) *People's Republic of China: Gross Violations of Human Rights in the Xinjiang Uighur Autonomous Region*. Online available: http://web.amnesty.org/library/index/ENGASA170181999 (accessed 30 April 2005).

Anderson, B. (2000) 'From Imagined Communities: Reflections on the Origin and Spread of Nationalism', in M. McKeon (ed.) *The Theory of the Novel: A Historical Approach*, Baltimore, MD and London: John Hopkins University Press.

Asia Times Online. (2000a, 7 March) 'The Net Result of Mahathir's Move Against the Press'. Online available: http://www.atimes.com/media/BC07Ce01.html (accessed 10 March 2005).

Asia Times Online. (2000b, 10 June) 'Economic Roots of Philippines' Muslim Unrest'. Online available: http://www.atimes.com/se-asia/BF10Ae01.html (accessed 3 March 2005).

Asia Times Online. (2000c, 5 July) 'Press a Casualty in Mindanao Conflict'. Online available: http://www.atimes.com/se-asia/BG05Ae01.html (accessed 3 March 2005).

Asia Times Online. (2002a, 23 October) 'Terror Link Shakes Malaysian Coalition'. Online available: http://www.atimes.com/atimes/Southeast_Asia/DJ23Ae07.html (accessed 2 July 2004).

Asia Times Online. (2002b, 3 December) 'Media: Casualty in Malaysia's War on Terror?', Online available: http://atimes01.atimes.com/atimes/Southeast_Asia/DL03Ae03.html (accessed 2 July 2004).

Asia Times Online. (2003, 1 November) 'Uproar Over Anti-terror Center in Malaysia'. Online available: http://www.atimes.com/atimes/Southeast_Asia/FC10Ae05.html (accessed 2 July 2004).

Asian Media and Communication Bulletin. (2002), 'Thailand, Indonesia, and East Timor: Journalists warn of Threats to Press Freedom', 32, no. 5, September–October.

Asian Media and Communication Bulletin. (2004, Jan–Feb), 'Indonesian Officials too Sensitive to Media Criticism', *Jakarta Post.*

Associated Press. (2003, 12 November) 'APME Requests Pentagon Halt Harassment of Media in Iraq'.

Associated Press. (2004, 4 October) Bambang Wins Indon Presidential Poll, *Straits Times Online.* Online available: http://straitstimes.asia1.com.sg/latest/story/0,4390, 276090,00.html? (accessed 4 October 2004).

Association for Progressive Communications. (2003, 4 April) 'Statement Opposing Actions against the Online Presence of Middle East News Agency, Al-Jazeera'.

Atkins, W.S. (1999) *The Battle for Broadcasting: Politics of the New Media in Southeast Asia in the 1990's,* Sydney: University of Sydney Department of Government Public Administration.

Aufderheide, P. (2004) 'Big Media and Little Media: The Journalistic Informal Sector During the Invasion of Iraq', in S. Allan and B. Zelizer (eds) *Reporting War: Journalism in Wartime,* London: Routledge.

Ayoob, M. (1992) *The Third World Security Predicament: State Making, Regional Conflict, and the International System,* Boulder, CO: Lynne Rienner.

Ayoob, M. (1995) *The Third World Security Predicament: State Making, Regional Conflict, and the International System,* Boulder, CO: Lynne Reinner.

Barkin, S.M. (2003) *American Television News: The Media Marketplace and the Public Interest,* Armonk, NY: M. E. Sharpe.

BBC Monitoring International Reports. (2004a, 28 July) 'BBC Monitoring Quotes from Malaysian Press'.

BBC Monitoring International Reports. (2004b, 30 April) 'Rafsanjani says "Total Censorship" of Casualties in US Media'.

BBC News Online. (2003a, 6 May) 'The Philippines' MILF rebels'. Online available: http://news.bbc.co.uk/1/hi/world/asia-pacific/3003809.stm (accessed 3 March 2005).

BBC News Online. (2003b, 16 June) 'Poll Suggests World Hostile to US'. Online available: http://news.bbc.co.uk/1/hi/world/americas/2994924.stm (accessed 10 March 2005).

BBC News Online. (2003c, 12 September) 'Malaysia's PAS Backs Bombers'. Online available: http://news.bbc.co.uk/1/hi/world/asia-pacific/3104394 (accessed 12 September 2003).

BBC News Online. (2003d, 11 November) 'Malaysian "Militant" Students Held'. Online available: http://news.bbc.co.uk/1/hi/world/asia-pacific/3259339.stm (accessed 11 November 2003).

BBC News Online. (2003e, 12 November) 'Islamic Plan Unveiled for Malaysia'. Online available: http://news.bbc.co.uk/1/hi/world/asia-pacific/3263785.stm (accessed 12 November 2003).

BBC News Online. (2004a, 16 January) 'Malaysian Activists Test New PM'. Online available: http://news.bbc.co.uk/1/hi/world/asia-pacific/3402173.stm (accessed 16 January 2004).

BBC News Online. (2004b, 14 May) 'Malaysia Targets Terror Websites'. Online available: http://news.bbc.co.uk/1/hi/world/asia-pacific/3714277.stm (accessed 14 May 2004).

BBC News Online. (2004c, 14 July) 'Militants Weave Web of Terror'. Online available: http://news.bbc.co.uk/1/hi/technology/3889841.stm (accessed 14 July 2004).

BBC News Online. (2004d, 13 September) 'Jemaah Islamiah Still a Threat'. Online available: http://news.bbc.co.uk/1/hi/world/asia-pacific/2983612.stm (accessed 13 September, 2004).

BBC News Online. (2004e, 6 October) 'A Web Wise Terror Network'. Online available: http://news.bbc.co.uk/1/hi/world/3716908.stm (accessed 6 October 2004).

BBC News Online. (2005, 10 February) 'Guide to the Philippines Conflict'. Online available: http://news.bbc.co.uk/1/hi/world/asia-pacific/1695576.stm#mnlf (accessed 3 March 2005).

BBC Summary of World Broadcasts. (1993, July) Far East 1724.

BBC Summary of World Broadcasts. (1997, 18 March) Far East 2870.

Beinin, J. (2003) 'The Israelization of American Middle East Policy Discourse'. *Social Text*, 75: 125–139.

Benaim, D., Visesh, K. and Priyanka, M. (2003, 21 April) 'TV's Conflicted Experts', *The Nation*: 6–7.

Berkowitz, B. (2003, 28 August) 'Wounded, Weary and Disappeared', *TomPaine.com*. Online available: http://www.tompaine.com/feature2.cfm/ID/8736 (accessed 10 March 2005).

Bernama. (2002a, 3 November) 'Maintain Unity in Face of Terrorism: Samy'. Online available: http://www.dailyexpress.com.my/news.cfm?NewsID=14763 (accessed 12 August 2004).

Bernama. (2002b, 6 December) 'Groups Using Terrorism to Set Up Islamic State a Confused Lot: PM'. Online available: http://www.dailyexpress.com.my/news.cfm?NewsID=15488 (accessed 12 August 2004).

Bernama. (2003a, 10 July) 'Ulamas Guidance Key to Restore Glory of Islam, Says Dr M'. Online available: http://www.bernama.com/bernama/v3/news.php?id=3214 (accessed 7 July 2004).

Bernama. (2003b, 10 July) 'M'sia Does Not Accept Islamic Terrorism, Says Abdullah'. Online available: http://www.bernama.com/bernama/v3/news.php?id=3292 (accessed 7 July 2004).

Bernama. (2003c, 24 November) 'Freedom For Four ISA Students'. Online available: http://www.bernama.com (accessed 7 July 2004).

Bernama. (2003d, 25 November) 'Nik Aziz Wants Remaining ISA Detainees Tried In Open Court'. Online available: http://www.bernama.com (accessed 7 July 2004).

Bernama. (2004, 2 April) Four Ex-Members Admit Jemaah Islamiah Is Deviant. Online available: http://www.bernama.com (accessed 7 July 2004).

Bernstein, R. and the Staff of *The New York Times* (2002) *Out of the Blue: The Story of September 11, 2001 from Jihad to Ground Zero*, New York: Times Books.

Blondel, J. (1969) *An Introduction to Government*, New York: Anchor.

Bosse, E. and Palast, G. (2003, 17 March) 'Anybody Using this First Amendment?', *AlterNet.org*. Online available: http://www.alternet.org/story/15404 (accessed 10 March 2005).

Boyd-Barrett, O. (2004) 'Understanding: The Second Casualty', in S. Allan and B. Zelizer (eds) *Reporting War: Journalism in Wartime*, London: Routledge.

Brown, J. (2004) 'Changing Minds, Winning Peace: Reconsidering the Djerejian Report'. *American Diplomacy*. Online available: http://www.unc.edu/depts/diplomat/ (accessed 10 March 2005).

Brynen, R. (2002) 'Cluster-Bombs and Sandcastles: Kramer on the Future of Middle East Studies in America', *Middle East Journal*, 56, no. 2: 323–328.

Budha, K. (2003) 'Content and Continuity: Online News in Asia', in M. Rao (ed.) *News Media and New Media*, Singapore: Select Books.

Burston, J. (2003) 'War and the Entertainment Industries: New Research Priorities in an Era of Cyber-Patriotism', in D.K. Thussu and D. Freedman (eds) *War and the Media: Reporting Conflict 24/7*, London: Sage Publications.

Byrne, C. (2003a, 1 May) 'Al-Jazeera Returns to NY Stock Exchange', *Guardian*.

Byrne, C. (2003b, 29 October) '*Simpsons* Parody Upset Fox News, Says Groening', *Guardian*.

Carr, D. (2003, 25 March) 'Reporting Reflects Anxiety', *New York Times*.

Center for Arts and Culture. (2004) *Cultural Diplomacy: Recommendations and Research*. Arlington, VA: Center for Arts and Culture. Online available: http://www.culturalpolicy .org/pdf/CulturalDiplomacy.pdf (accessed 10 March 2005).

Center for Constitutional Rights. (2003, 24 March) 'CCR Says US Government Hypocritical on Application of Geneva Conventions'.

Chattarji, S. (2004) 'Media Representations of the Kargil War and the Gujarat Riots', *Sarai Reader: Crisis/Media*.

Chester, J. (2002) 'Strict Scrutiny: Why Journalists Should be Concerned about New Federal Industry Media Deregulation Proposals', *Harvard International Journal of Press/Politics*, 7, no. 2: 105–115.

Chua, Y.T. (2003, January–March) 'Checking the Airwaves', *i Magazine*, IX, no. 1. Online available: http://www.pcij.org/imag/Media/kbp2.html (accessed 2 February 2005).

CIA. (2004) *The World Factbook: Indonesia*. Online available: http://www.cia.gov/cia/ publications/factbook/geos/my.html (accessed 8 November 2004).

CIA. (2005a) *The World Factbook: The Philippines*. Online available: http:// www.cia.gov/cia/publications/factbook/geos/rp.html#Comm (accessed 8 March 2005).

CIA. (2005b) *The World Factbook: Malaysia*. Online available: http://www.cia.gov/ cia/publications/factbook/geos/my.html (accessed 8 March 2005).

Clark, J. and McChesney, B. (2001, 24 September) 'Nattering Networks: How Mass Media Fails Democracy', *LiP*. Online available: http://www.lipmagazine.org/articles/ featclark_138_p.htm (accessed 10 March 2005).

Claussen, D.S. (2004) *Anti-Intellectualism in American Media: Magazines & Higher Education*, New York: Peter Lang.

Clendenning, A. (June 21, 2004) 'Port security still off course', *Washington Times*. Online available: http://www.washtimes.com/business/20040620-095247-3779r.htm (accessed 9 November 2004).

Committee for the Protection of Journalists. (2002, 6 September) 'CPJ alarmed by broadcast bill'. Online available: http://www.cpj.org/protests/02ltrs/Indo06sept02pl.html (accessed 8 March 2005).

Coronel, S. (2003, April–June) 'The Problem With Gloria', *i Magazine*, IX, no. 2. Online available: http://www.pcij.org/imag/PublicEye/gloria3.html (accessed 2 February 2005).

Council on Foreign Relations. (2003) *Finding America's Voice: A Strategy for Reinvigorating U.S. Public Diplomacy*, New York.

Crouch, H. (2000) 'Indonesia: Democratisation and the Threat of Disintegration', *Southeast Asian Affairs Year Book, 2000*, Singapore: ISEAS.

Davidson, L. (2002) 'Ivory Towers on Sand: The Failure of Middle Eastern Studies in America', *Middle East Policy*, 9, no. 3: 148–152.

Della Carva, M.R. (2003, 2 April) 'Iraq gets Sympathetic Press Around the World'. *USA Today*.

D'Entremont, J. (2003) 'Clear and Present Danger'. *Index on Censorship*, 32, no. 3: 124–128.

Desai, D. (2004) 'Massacres and the Media: A Field Reporter Looks Back on Gujarat 2002', *Sarai Reader: Crisis/Media*.

Desker, B. (2002) 'After Bali, Will Indonesia Act?' This article was published under IDSS Commentaries in October 2002. Online available: http://www.ntu.edu.sg/idss/ Perspective/Research_050226.htm (accessed 8 March 2005).

Dillon, M. (1999) *China's Muslim Hui Community: Migration, Settlement and Sects*, Richmond, VA: Curzon.

Dillon, M. (2001) *Religious Minorities and China*, London: Minority Rights Group.

Dillon, M. (2004) *Xinjiang: China's Muslim Far Northwest*, London: RoutledgeCurzon.

Dolny, M. (2003, July/August) 'Spectrum Narrows Further in 2002: Progressive, Domestic Think Tanks see Drop'. *EXTRA!Update*. Online available: http://www.fair.org/ index.php?page=1149 (accessed 10 March 2005).

Donnan, S. (2004, 28 October) 'Trial of Radical Cleric to test Indonesian Resolve on Terrorism', *Financial Times*.

Donnan, S. (2005, 26/27 February) 'Read All About Lads' Mags in Jakarta', *Financial Times*.

Dutt, B. (2002, 25 March) 'Covert Riots and the Media', *Outlook*.

Dyer, G. (2005, 20 January) 'Another Target of America's Paranoia', *South China Morning Post*.

Eastern Turkistan Dispatch. (European Edition) (1993a, October), 1, no. 4: 4.

Eastern Turkistan Dispatch. (1993b, November), 1, no. 5: 1–3, citing in part *Der Spiegel*, (1993, September 13): 1–3.

The Economist. (2002a, 3 August) 'The Elusive Enemy'.

The Economist. (2002b, 19 October) 'Special Report: The War On Terror'.

The Economist. (2003c, 16 November), 'Indestructible Golkar'.

The Economist. (2003a, 11 January) 'Screen Test'.

The Economist. (2003b, 28 June) 'An Uphill Struggle'.

The Economist. (2004a, 27 March) 'Bravo Badawi'.

The Economist. (2004b, 5 June) 'No Criticism, Please'.

Eide, E. (2004) 'Warfare and Dual Vision in Media Discourse', in S.A. Nohrstedt and R. Ottosen (eds) *U. S. and the Others: Global Media Images on 'The War on Terror'*, Göteborg: Nordicom.

Eisman, A. (2003) 'The Media of Manipulation: Patriotism and Propaganda – Mainstream News in the United States in the Weeks Following September 11', *Critical Quarterly*, 45, nos 1–2: 55–72.

Ellis, R. (2003, 25 February) 'The Surrender of MSNBC'. *AllYourTV.com*. Online available: http://www.allyourtv.com/0203season/news/02252003donahue.html (accessed 10 March 2005).

el-Nawawy, M. and Gher, L.A. (2003) 'Al Jazeera: Bridging the East–West Gap Through Public Discourse and Media Diplomacy', *Transnational Broadcasting Studies* 10. Online available: http://www.tbsjournal.com (accessed 10 March 2005).

EXTRA!Update. (2004, February) 'Who are "We"?'.

FAIR: Fairness And Accuracy in Reporting. (2003a, 14 March) 'Do Media Know that War Kills?'.

FAIR: Fairness And Accuracy in Reporting. (2003b, 18 March). 'In Iraq Crisis, Networks are Megaphones for Official Views'.

FAIR: Fairness And Accuracy in Reporting. (2003c, 3 April) 'Some Critical Media Voices Face Censorship'.

FAIR: Fairness And Accuracy in Reporting. (2003d, 4 April) 'Media Should Follow up on Civilian Deaths'.

FAIR: Fairness And Accuracy in Reporting. (2003e, 4 April) 'Official Story vs. Eyewitness Accounts'.

FAIR: Fairness And Accuracy in Reporting. (2003f, 10 April) 'Is Killing Part of Pentagon Press Policy?'

FAIR: Fairness And Accuracy in Reporting. (2003g, 6 May) 'TV Not Concerned by Cluster Bombs, DU: "That's Just the Way Life is in Iraq"'.

FAIR: Fairness And Accuracy in Reporting. (2004, 15 April) 'CNN to Al Jazeera: Why Report Civilian Deaths?'

Far Eastern Economic Review. (2003, 9 August) 'Justice in Malaysia'.

Farhi, P. (2003, 6 April) 'Everybody Wins', *American Journalism Review*. Online available: http://www.ajr.org/Article.asp?id=2875 (accessed 10 March 2005).

Fatwa Council of Moro Youth Union. (2005) The Shariah Ruling On The Status of Jihad in the Bangasamoro Homeland. Online available: http://www.moroinfo.com/fatawa1.html (accessed 1 March 2005).

Fine, J. (2003) 'Al Jazeera Winning TV Credibility War', *Transnational Broadcasting Studies*, 10. Online available: http://www.tbsjournal.com (accessed 10 March 2005).

Fisk, R. (2002, 14 May) 'Why Does John Malkovich Want to Kill Me?', *Independent*.

Fisk, R. (2003a, 25 February) 'How the News will be Censored in the War', *Independent*.

Fisk, R. (2003b, 20 November) 'Under US Control, Press Freedom Falls Short in Iraq', *Madison Capital Times*.

Fisk, R., Goodman, A. and Cahill, J. (2003, 25 March) 'Live from Iraq, an Un-Embedded Journalist', *Democracy Now!* Online available: http://www.democracynow.org/transcripts/aaronbrown.shtml (accessed 10 March 2005).

Flanders, L. (2001, 9 November) 'Media Criticism in Mono', *Working For Change*. Online available: http//www.workingforchange.com (accessed 10 March 2005).

Flor, A. (2003) 'The Philippines', in M. Rao (ed.) *News Media and New Media*, Singapore: Select Books.

Folkenflik, D. (2003, 2 April) 'Fox News Defends its "Patriotic" Coverage', *Baltimore Sun.*

Friedman, J. (2003, 8 May) 'Editors See Success in Iraq Coverage', *CBS Market Watch*.

Getlin, J. and Jensen, E. (2003, 24 March) 'Images of POWs and the Dead Pose a Dilemma for the Media', *Los Angeles Times.*

Gilboa, E. (1998) 'Media Diplomacy: Conceptual Divergence and Applications', *Harvard Journal of Press/Politics*, 3, no. 3: 56–75.

Gloria, G. (2000, 6 June) 'Bearer of the Sword', *i Magazine*. Online available: http://www.pcij.org/mindanao/abusayyaf3.html (accessed 2 February 2005).

Golan, G. and Wayne, W. (2003) 'International Elections on US Network News', *Gazette: The International Journal for Communication Studies*, 65, no. 1: 25–39.

Goldstein, R. (2003, 26 March – 1 April) 'The Shock and Awe Show', *Village Voice*.

Goodman, A. (2000) 'Indonesian media suffer growing pains', *Thunderbird Online Magazine*, October. Online available: http://www.journalism.ubc.ca/thunderbird/2000–01/october/indonesia.html (accessed 8 March 2005).

Goodman, A., Brown, A., Rendall, S. and Scahill, J. (2003, 4 April) 'CNN's Aaron Brown on the Network's Coverage of the Anti-war Movement, the Media's Sanitization of the Invasion of Iraq and Why He Believes this is an Inappropriate Time for Reporters to Ask Questions About War', *Democracy Now!* Online available: http://www.democracynow.org/transcripts/aaronbrown.shtml (accessed 10 March 2005).

Gowing, N. (2003) 'Journalists and War: The Troubling New Tensions Post 9/11', in D.K. Thussu and D. Freedman (eds) *War and the Media: Reporting Conflict 24/7*, London: Sage Publications.

Greenslade, R. (2003, 17 February) 'Their Master's Voice', *Guardian*.

Grieve, T. (2003, 25 March) 'Shut your Mouth', *Salon.com*. Online available: http://www.salon.com/news/feature/2003/03/25/liberties/ (accessed 10 March 2005).

Guelke, A. (1998) 'Wars of Fear: Coming to Grips with Terrorism', *Harvard International Review*, Fall: 44–47.

Gunaratna, R. (2002) *Inside Al Qaeda: Global Network of Terror*, London: Hurst.

Gunaratna, R. (2003) *Inside Al Qaeda: Global Network of Terror*, London: Berkeley Publishing Group.

Gunaratne, S.A. (ed.) (2000), 'Indonesia', *Handbook of the Media in Asia*, London: Thousand Oaks and Delhi: Sage Nee.

Hafez, K. (2001) 'Al Jazeera Meets CNN', *Message*.

Hamilton, J.M. and Jenner, E. (2004) 'Redefining Foreign Correspondence', *Journalism: Theory, Practice and Criticism*, 5, no. 3: 301–321.

Hans, D. (2001, November 23) 'Bush's Definition of Terrorism fits Northern Alliance like a Glove', *CommonDreams.org*. Online available: http://www.commondreams.org/views01/1123–05.htm (accessed 10 March 2005).

Hansen, T.B. (2004) 'Politics as Permanent Performance: the Production of Political Authority in the Locality', in J. Zavos, A. Wyatt and V. Hewitt (eds) *The Politics of Cultural Mobilization in India*, Oxford: Oxford University Press.

Hantoro, J. and Nurhayati, N. (2003, 4–10 November) 'Insult Press Freedom Lies Bleeding', *Tempo*, No.09/IV. Online available: http://www.indonesia-house.org/focus/civ-society/2003/11/110403Press_freedom_lies_bleeding.htm (accessed 5 March 2005).

Harakah Daily. (2001, 15–30 November) 'Crusade v Jihad'. Online available: http://www.mggpillai.com/article.php3?sid=1255 (accessed 10 July 2004).

Harakah Daily. (2002, 16–31 January) 'Islam as the new enemy'. Online available: http://www.mggpillai.com/article.php3?sid=1290 (accessed 10 July 2004).

Harakah Daily. (2004a) 'Malaysian Police Detain 16 Indonesians for "Deviationist" Teachings'. Online available: http://www.harakahdaily.net/article.php?sid=516 (accessed 10 July 2004).

Harakah Daily. (2004b, 21 April) 'GMI lashed out Brendan Pereira Uncalled Statement on KMM'. Online, Available http://www.harakahdaily.net/article.php?sid=7661 (accessed 16 August 2004).

Harakah Daily. (2004c, 5 May) Nasharudin Mat Isa, 'PAS Concern at the Carnage in Southern Thailand, Wednesday'. Online available: http://www.harakahdaily.net/article.php?sid=7802 (accessed 16 August 2004).

Harsono, A. (2000) 'Indonesia: Dancing in the Dark', in L. Williams and R. Rich (eds) *Loosing Control: Freedom of the Press in Asia*, Australia: Asia Pacific Press.

Harvey, D. (2003) *The New Imperialism*, Oxford: Oxford University Press.

Hashim, S. (1998, April–May) 'Perhaps the Moro Struggle for Freedom and Self-determination is the Longest and Bloodiest in the Entire History of Mankind', *Nida'ul Islam magazine*. Online available: http://www.islam.org.au (accessed 1 March 2005).

Hastings, M. (2003, 26 February) 'Billboard Ban', *Newsweek*.

Herman, E. and Chomsky, N. (1998) *Manufacturing Consent: The Political Economy of the Mass Media*, New York: Pantheon.

Herman, E.S. (1999) *The Myth of the Liberal Media: An Edward Herman Reader*, New York: Peter Lang.

Herold, M.W. (2001) 'Who will Count the Dead?', *Media File*, 21, no. 1: 20–25.

Higham, N. (2001, 25 September) 'Media Confronts a New World'. *BBC News Online*. Online available: http://news.bbc.co.uk/1/hi/entertainment/tv_and_radio/1562594.stm (accessed 10 March 2005).

Hill, D.T. (2002, June) 'The Internet and Democracy in Indonesia', *Asiaview*.

Hill, H. (1996) *The Indonesia Economy Since 1966*, Australia: Cambridge University Press.

Höijer, B., Nohrstedt, S.A. and Ottosen, R. (2004) 'Introduction: Media and the "War on Terror"', in S.A. Nohrstedt and R. Ottosen (eds) *U. S. and the Others: Global Media Images on 'The War on Terror'*, Göteborg: Nordicom.

Hooker, V.M. (ed.) (1993) *Culture and Society in New Order Indonesia*, Kuala Lumpur: OUP.

Hudiono, U. (2004, September 17) ' "Tempo" Editor Gets a Year', *The Jakarta Post*. Online available: http://www.thejakartapost.com/Archives/ArchivesDet2.asp?FileID= 20040917.@01 (accessed 23 September 2004).

Hudson, M., Kalb, M., Al-Mirazi, H., Khouri, R.G. and Charmelot, J. (2002) 'Covering the War on Terrorism', *Transnational Broadcasting Studies* 8. Online available: http://www.tbsjournal.com (accessed 10 March 2005).

Huff, R. (2003, 24 March) 'Blitz of War Coverage on Nightly News', *Daily News*.

Human Rights Watch. (2003a, 24 March) 'Iraq Must not Parade POWs'.

Human Rights Watch. (2003b) *Muzzling the Messengers: Attacks and Restrictions on the Media*, 15, No. 9(C). Online available: http://www.hrw.org/reports/2003/indonesia1103 (accessed 8 March 2005).

Hussain, Z., Hookway, J., Yaroslav T. and Solomon, J. (2004, 6–8 August) 'Kin of 9/11 Terrorist Pose Threat to US', *Asian Wall Street Journal*.

Ibrahim, D. (2003) 'Individual Perceptions of International Correspondents in the Middle East', *Gazette: The International Journal for Communication Studies*, 65, no. 1: 87–101.

Idris, N. (2001) 'Indonesia', in A. Goonasekera and L.C. Wah (eds) *Asian Communication Handbook 2001*, Singapore: AMIC.

Ignatieff, M. (2003, 5 January) 'The American Empire (get used to it)', *New York Times Magazine*.

Independent. (2003) 'President Bush is Right to Condemn Iraq's Treatment of Captured Soldiers – but his Outrage Rings Hollow'.

International Federation of Journalists. (2001, 23 October) *Les Journalists du Monde entier Produisent un Rapport sur les Médias, la Guerre et le Terrorisme*.

Inq7.net. (2003a, 13 March) 'War is Stupid!', Online available: http://www.inq7.net/ globalnation/col_krm/2003/mar13.htm (accessed 5 February 2005).

Inq7.net. (2003b, 12 May) 'Palace to Decide on Proposal to Declare MILF Terror Group'. Online available: http://www.inq7.net/brk/2003/may/12/brkpol_9-1.htm (accessed 5 February 2005).

Inq7.net. (2003c, 22 May) 'MILF Terror Plan Uncovered'. Online available: http://www.inq7.net/reg/2003/may/22/reg_1-1.htm (accessed 5 February 2005).

Inq7.net. (2003d, 30 May) 'Pressure on the MILF'. Online available:http://www.inq7.net/ opi/2003/may/30/opi_editorial-1.htm (accessed 5 February 2005).

Inq7.net. (2003e, 28 June) 'Macapagal Calls on MILF Leders to stop Bomb Plots'. Online available: http://www.inq7.net/brk/2003/jun/28/brkpol_7-1.htm (accessed 5 February 2005).

Inq7.net. (2004, 29 December) 'MILF Sees Tough, Lengthy Peace Talks'. Online available: http://news.inq7.net/regions/index.php?index=1&story_id=22634 (accessed 5 February 2005).

Inq7.net. (2005a, 12 January) 'Army, Moro Commanders "Text Mates" '. Online available: http://news.inq7.net/nation/index.php?index=1&story_id=23918 (accessed 5 February 2005).

Inq7.net. (2005b, 13 January) 'MILF to probe Maguindanao raid'. Online available: http://news.inq7.net/nation/index.php?index=1&story_id=24053 (accessed 5 February 2005).

International Crisis Group. (2002) *Indonesia Backgrounder: How The Jemaah Islamiyah Terrorist Network Operates*, Asia Report N°43 11 December 2002. Online available: http://www.crisisgroup.org/home/index.cfm?id=1397&1=1 (accessed 30 March 2005).

Interview with Salamat Hashim. (1999, 16–31 March) 'Bangsamoro Muslims' Determination to Establish an Islamic State', *Crescent International*. Online available: http://www.moroinfo.com/interview2.html (accessed 1 March 2005).

Jackson, K.D. (1978) 'The Political Implication of Structure and Culture in Indonesia', in K.D. Jackson and L. Pye (eds) *Political Power and Communication in Indonesia*, Berkeley, CA: University of California Press.

Jakarta Post. (2004a, 23 September), 'More Condemnation of "Tempo" Verdict'. Online available: http://www.thejakartapost.com/Archives/ArchivesDet2.asp?FileID=20040920.B10 (accessed 23 September 2004).

Jakarta Post. (2004b, 9 November), 'World Bank Urges Quick Measures to Reinforce Indonesian Growth'. Online available: http://www.thejakartapost.com/detaillatestnews. asp?fileid=20041109145702&irec=0 (accessed 9 November 2004).

Jakarta Post.com. (2005, 10 January), 'Gunfire Breaks out near UN headquarters in Banda Aceh'. Online available: http://www.thejakartapost.com/detaillatestnews.asp?fileid=20050109122738&irec=6) (accessed 10 January 2005).

Jasperson, A.E. and El-Kikhia, M.O. (2003) 'CNN and Al Jazeera's Media Coverage of America's War in Afghanistan', in P. Norris, M. Kern and M. Just (eds) *Framing Terrorism: The News Media, the Government, and the Public*, New York: Routledge.

Jensen, E. (2003, 18 March) 'Network's War Strategy: Enlist Armies of Experts'. *Los Angeles Times*.

Job, B.L. (ed.) (1992) *The Insecurity Dilemma: National Security of Third World States*, Boulder, CO: Lynne Rienner.

Johnson, P. (2003, 24 February) 'Media Question Authority Over War Protests', *USA Today*.

Jones, C. (2003, 4 April) 'Peter Arnett: Under Fire'. *BBC News Online*. Online available: http://news.bbc.co.uk/1/hi/in_depth/uk/2000/newsmakers/2917635.stm (accessed 10 March 2005).

Kalb, M. (2003, 24 March) 'Journalists Torn between Purism and Patriotism', *Editor & Publisher*.

Kasper, B.M. (2001) 'The End of Secrecy, Military Competitiveness in an Age of Transparency', *USAF, Occasional Paper No. 23*, August, Center For Strategy and Technology, Air War College. Online available: http://www.fas.org/sgp/eprint/kaspar.pdf (accessed 8 March 2005).

Kazakh TV, Almaty. (2002, 18 January) BBC Monitoring, London.

Keeble, R. (2004) 'Information Warfare in an Age of Hyper-Militarism', in S. Allan and B. Zelizer (eds) *Reporting War: Journalism in Wartime*, London: Routledge.

Keeler, W. (1987) *Javanese Shadow Plays, Javanese Selves*, Princeton, NJ: Princeton University Press.

Kellner, D. (1990) *Television and The Crisis of Democracy*, Boulder CO: Westview Press.

Kellner, D. (2003) *From 9/11 to Terror War: The Dangers of the Bush Legacy*, Lanham, MD: Rowman & Littlefield.

Kern, M., Just, M. and Norris, P. (2003) 'The Lessons of Framing Terrorism', in P. Norris, M. Kern and M. Just (eds) *Framing Terrorism: The News Media, the Government, and the Public*, New York: Routledge.

Khouri, R.G. (2003) 'Shooting the Messenger', *Index on Censorship*, 32, no. 4: 170–172.

Kingsbury, D. (1997) *Culture and Politics: Issues in Australian Journalism in Indonesia 1975–1993*, Sydney: Centre for the Study of Australia–Asia Relations, Griffith University Australia.

Kingsbury, D. and Aveling, H. (2003) *Autonomy and Disintegration in Indonesia*, London: Routledge and Curzon.

Komsomolskaya Pravda v Kyrgyzstane, Bishkek. (2002, January 18) BBC Monitoring, London.

Kroll, T. and Champagne, E. (2002) '13 Months after the 9/11 Attacks – Terrorism, Patriotism and Media Coverage', *Transnational Broadcasting Studies* 9. Online available: http://www.tbsjournal.com/Archives/Fall02/Xchange.html (accessed 10 March 2005).

Krugman, P. (2003, 25 March) 'Channels of Influence', *New York Times*.

Kull, S., Ramsay, C. and Lewis, E. (2003–2004) 'Misperceptions, the Media, and the Iraq War', *Political Science Quarterly*, 118, no. 4: 569–598.

Kurniawan, H. (2004, 8 November) 'Legislators Slammed over Petition', *The Jakarta Post*, from *The Jakarta.post.com*. Online available: http://www.thejakartapost.com/detailheadlines.asp?fileid=20041108.A04&irec=7 (accessed 8 November 2004).

Langdale, J.V. (1997) 'Globalisation or Regionalisation: Telecommunications and Interactive Multimedia in East Asia', in P.J. Rimmer (ed.) *Pacific Rim Development: Integration and Globalisation in the Asia-Pacific Economies*, Sydney: Allen and Unwin.

Lieberman, D. (2003, 24 March) 'NBC Hopes Big Investment in News Coverage Pays Off', *USA Today*.

Lingao, E. (2000, July–September) 'A War Made for TV', *i Magazine*, VI, no. 3. Online available: http://www.pcij.org/imag/Media/wartv2.html (accessed 2 February 2005).

Lobe, J. (2003, 9 April) 'Press Watchdogs Protest U. S. Killings of Journalists in Baghdad', *OneWorld.net*. Online available: http://www.commondreams.org/headlines03/0409–02.htm (accessed 10 March 2005).

Love, M.C. (2003) 'Global Media and Foreign Policy', in M.J. Rozell (ed.) *Media Power, Media Politics*, Lanham: Rowman & Littlefield.

Lubis, M. (1983) *The Indonesian Dilemma*, Singapore: Graham Brash.

Lull, J. (1995) *Media, Communication, Culture: A Global Approach*, Cambridge, UK: Polity Press.

Ma, D. (2003) *Guojia liyi gaoyu yiqi (The interest of the state is greater than anything)*, Urumqi: Xinjiang Peoples Publishing House.

MacArthur, J. (2003, 6 June) 'All the News that's Fudged to Print', *Globe & Mail*.

McBeth, J. (2002a, 26 September) 'The Military Fans Out', *Far Eastern Economic Review*.

McBeth, J. (2002b, 7 November) 'The Army's Dirty Business', *Far Eastern Economic Review*.

McBeth, J. (2002c, 7 November) 'What if He Isn't Guilty?' *Far Eastern Economic Review*.

McBeth, J. and Lintner, B. (2004, 1 July) 'Swedish Surprise', *Far Eastern Economic Review*', 167, no. 26.

McCargo, D. (2003) *Media and Politics in Pacific Asia*, London: RoutledgeCurzon.

McChesney, R.W. (2003) 'The Problem of Journalism: A Political Economic Contribution to an Explanation of the Crisis in Contemporary US Journalism', *Journalism Studies*, 4, no. 3: 299–329.

MacFarquhar, N. (2003, 25 March) 'Arabic Stations Compete for Attention', *New York Times*.

Magder, T. (2003) 'Watching What We Say: Global Communication in a Time of Fear', in D.K. Thussu and D. Freedman (eds) *War and the Media: Reporting Conflict 24/7*, London: Sage Publications.

Mahathir, M. (2002) 'Islam, Terrorism and Malaysia's Response', Speech to the Asia Society, New York, 4 February 2002. Online available: http://asiasociety.org/speeches/mahathir.html (accessed 17 July 2004).

Majod, T. (1999) *Global Communications and World Politics: Domination, Development and Discourse*, Boulder, CO and London: Lynne Rienner.

Makarim, N.A. (1978) 'The Indonesian Press: an Editor's Perspective', in K.D. Jackson and L. Pye (eds) *Political Power and Communication in Indonesia*, Berkeley, CA: University of California Press.

Malay Mail. (2002a, 25 January) 'KL a Money Hub for KMM'.

Malay Mail. (2002b, 21 September) 'Terrorism Activities in Religious School'.

Malay Mail. (2002c, 5 October) 'Megawati on KMM Hit List'.

Malay Mail. (2002d, 12 November) 'Cops Seek More Details of KMM Members at JI Meetings'.

Malay Mail. (2002e, 27 November) 'Some Willing to Become Suicide bombers'.

Malay Mail. (2002f, 23 December) 'Thumbnail Sketches of Personalities Involved in JI as Reported by ICG'.

Malay Mail. (2003a, 11 February) 'On the Blood Money Trail'.

Malay Mail. (2003b, 11 February) 'Malaysia in List of JI Targets'.

Malay Mail. (2003c, 17 March) 'Atrocities in Bosnia Changed Military Man's View of Life'.

Malay Mail. (2003d, 22 March) 'Threat Still Exists'.

Malay Mail. (2003e, 20 April) 'Bashir: Bali Bombers Misguided'.

Malay Mail. (2003f, 13 May) 'Malaysian Professor Implicated in Indictment'.

Malay Mail. (2003g, 23 October) 'Terrorists Defiled Islamic Faith'.

Malay Mail. (2003h, 22 November) 'Terrorist-Linked School had Bigger Agenda'.

Malay Mail. (2003i, 26 November) 'Gift for Bali Bombers'.

Malaysiakini. (2003a, 11 July) 'Muslims to Lose Democracy in PAS Islamic State'. Online available: http://www.malaysiakini.com/letters/200307110034806 (accessed 5 July 2004).

Malaysiakini. (2003b, 7 August) 'Anger Rages over Bomb Attack'. Online available: http://malaysiakini.com/opinionsfeatures/200308070041294.php (accessed 5 July 2004).

Malaysiakini. (2003c, 23 August) 'Pan Islamic State More Fantasy than Fact'. Online available: http://www.malaysiakini.com/opinionsfeatures/200308230041316.php (accessed 5 July 2004).

Manila Bulletin. (2004a, 1 March) 'US Blackmailing Rebs—Ka Roger Tells MILF to Shun Washington's offers'. Online available: http://www.mb.com.ph/issues/2004/03/01/PROV200403013688.html (accessed 10 January 2005).

Manila Bulletin. (2004b, 9 March) 'Philippines Rebels must Support Anti-terror Drive: President'. Online available: http://www.mb.com.ph/issues/2004/03/09/MAIN200403094408.html (accessed 10 January 2005).

Manila Bulletin. (2004c, 18 April) 'Get Janjalani Alive, Military, Police Urged, P10-M Bounty Put up for Slippery Sayyaf head'. Online available: http://www.mb.com.ph/issues/2004/04/18/MTNN200404187512.html (accessed 10 January 2005).

Manila Bulletin. (2004d, 7 July) 'Militants here a Global Threat, says US Envoy'. Online available: http://www.mb.com.ph/issues/2004/07/07/MTNN2004070713564.html (accessed 10 January 2005).

Manila Bulletin. (2004e, 14 August) '17 Abu Sayyaf Members Sentenced to Death in South'. Online available: http://www.mb.com.ph/issues/2004/08/14/MAIN2004081416255.html (accessed 10 January 2005).

Manila Bulletin. (2004f, 21 August) 'Gov't Pursues Peace Talks with MILF and NDF'. Online available: http://www.mb.com.ph/issues/2004/08/21/MAIN2004082116782.html (accessed 10 January 2005).

Manila Bulletin. (2004g, 23 October) 'GMA Reiterates Promise to Pursue Peace Negotiations with NDF, MILF'. Online available: http://www.mb.com.ph/issues/2004/10/23/MTNN2004102321106.html (accessed 10 January 2005).

Manila Bulletin. (2004h, 26 October) 'AFP Urged to Disprove JI Bomb Plot'. Online available: http://www.mb.com.ph/issues/2004/10/26/MTNN2004102621314.html (accessed 10 January 2005).

Manila Bulletin. (2004i, 28 November) 'Army says 18 JI members Holed up Mindanao Jungle'. Online available: http://www.mb.com.ph/issues/2004/11/28/PROV2004112823447.html (accessed 10 January 2005).

Manila Bulletin. (2004j, 20 December) 'Did rebels Reject Unilateral Ceasefire? Palace Says no on Assurance made by NDF official'. Online available: http://www.mb.com.ph/issues/2004/12/20/MTNN2004122024793.html (accessed 10 January 2005).

Manila Bulletin. (2005a, 3 January) 'Concern Aired over 4,000 Dislocated by Abu Sayyaf Attacks'. Online available: http://www.mb.com.ph/issues/2004/03/09/MAIN 200403094408.html (accessed 10 January 2005).

Manila Bulletin. (2005b, 17 January) 'US Ambassador here Doubts MILF Sincerity on Peace Talks'. Online available: http://www.manilatimes.net/national/2003/oct/20/opinion/20031020opi1.html (accessed 10 January 2005).

Manila Times. (2003a, 19 February) 'New Rules for US Balikatan GIs in Sulu Sought'. Online available: http://www.manilatimes.net/national/2003/feb/19/top_stories/20030219top2.html (accessed 16 January 2005).

Manila Times. (2003b, 6 March) 'Abu: We bombed Davao, Extremist Group "Sorry" for Attack'. Online available: http://www.manilatimes.net/national/2003/mar/06/top_stories/20030306top1.html (accessed 16 January 2005).

Manila Times. (2003c, 12 March) 'Duterte on the Warpath'. Online available: http://www.manilatimes.net/national/2003/mar/12/opinion/20030312opi3.html (accessed 16 January 2005).

Manila Times. (2003d, 10 September) 'The Media Under Siege'. Online available: http://www.manilatimes.net/national/2003/sept/10/opinion/20030910opi1.html (accessed 16 January 2005).

Manila Times. (2003e, 10 September) 'AFP on High Alert for Anniversary of 9/11'. Online available: http://www.manilatimes.net/national/2003/sept/10/top_stories/20030910top4.html (accessed 16 January 2005).

Manila Times. (2003f, 20 October) 'But will Bush Deliver?'. Online available: http://www.manilatimes.net/national/2003/oct/20/opinion/20031020opi1.html (accessed 16 January 2005).

Manila Times. (2003g, 26 December) 'Struggle Continues for Rebels'. Online available: http://www.manilatimes.net/others/special/2003/dec/26/20031226spe1.html (accessed 16 January 2005).

Manila Times. (2004a, 8 April) 'AFP Plays Down Abu Suicide Bomb Threats'. Online available: http://www.manilatimes.net/national/2004/apr/08/yehey/metro/20040408met1.html (accessed 16 January 2005).

Manila Times. (2004b, 12 April) 'US Twits GMA on Abu'. Online available: http://www.manilatimes.net/national/2004/apr/12/yehey/top_stories/20040412top1.html (accessed 16 January 2005).

Manila Times. (2004c, 13 August) '80 Muslim Converts Trained under Janjalani'. Online available: http://www.manilatimes.net/national/2004/aug/13/yehey/top_stories/20040813top3.html (accessed 16 January 2005).

Manila Times. (2004d, 29 August) 'No Proof vs. Abu Sayyaf'. Online available: http://www.manilatimes.net/national/2004/aug/29/yehey/opinion/20040829opi4.html (accessed 16 January 2005).

Manila Times. (2004e, 14 November) 'Photojournalist Killed by Gunman in Jolo'. Online available: http://www.manilatimes.net/national/2004/nov/14/yehey/top_stories/20041114top5.html (accessed 16 January 2005).

Manila Times. (2004f, 16 December) 'Asian Islamic Militancy Rising After Year of Deadly Attacks'. Online available: http://www.manilatimes.net/national/2004/dec/16/yehey/opinion/20041216opi6.html (accessed 16 January 2005).

Mapes, T. (2004, 17–19 September) 'Democracy Takes Hold Ahead of Indonesia Poll', *Asian Wall Street Journal*, XXXIX, no. 13.

Mapes, T. and Hindryati, R. (2004, 17–19 September) 'Editor of Indonesian Magazine Gets 1-Year Prison Term for Libel', *Asian Wall Street Journal*, XXXIX, no. 13.

Massing, M. (2001, 15 October) 'Press Watch'. *The Nation*.

Menon, K. (2001) 'Attacks on the Press 2001', *CJP Online available*: http://www.cpj.org/attacks01/asia01/asia.html (accessed 8 March 2005).

Merriman, R. (2004, 11 March) 'Middle Eastern Studies Seen as Against American Interests', *Jordan Times*.

Miladi, N. (2003) 'Mapping the Al-Jazeera Phenomenon', in D.K. Thussu and D. Freedman (eds) *War and the Media: Reporting Conflict 24/7*, London: Sage Publications.

Milner, A. (1995) *Invention of Politics in Colonial Malaya: Contesting Nationalism and Expansion of the Public Sphere*, Cambridge: Cambridge University Press.

Mindanao Daily Mirror. (2005a, 1 February) 'AFP is Our Biggest Arms Supplier: NPA'. Online available: http://www.dailymirror.net.ph/ (accessed 1 February 2005).

Mindanao Daily Mirror. (2005b, 1 February) 'Abus Threaten Attacks During Bush's RP Visit'. Online available: http://www.dailymirror.net.ph/ (accessed 1 February 2005).

Mindanao Daily Mirror. (2005c, 1 February) ' "Unilateral Ceasefire": the MILF's Latest Moro-Moro'. Online available: http://www.dailymirror.net.ph/ (accessed 1 February 2005).

Mindanao Daily Mirror. (2005d, 1 February) 'Balikatan in Cotabato? Why Not?' Online. available http://www.dailymirror.net.ph/ (accessed 1 February 2005).

Mindanao Daily Mirror. (2005e, 1 February) 'Costly Mistake'. Online available: http://www.dailymirror.net.ph/ (accessed 1 February 2005).

Mindanao Daily Mirror. (2005f, 1 February) 'Bush Singles Out Abu Sayyaf', MILF. Online available: http://www.dailymirror.net.ph/ (accessed 1 February 2005).

Mindanao Daily Mirror. (2005g, 1 February) ' "Rogue Factions" in MILF, MNLF are "terror concerns" of US'. Online available: http://www.dailymirror.net.ph/ (accessed 1 February 2005).

Mindanao Daily Mirror. (2005h, 30 April) 'NPA Terrorists at their Worst'. Online available: http://www.dailymirror.net.ph/ (accessed 30 April 2005).

Mokhiber, R. and Weissman, R. (2003a, 26 February) 'Too Much', *CommonDreams.org*. Online available: http://www.commondreams.org/views03/0226-05.htm (accessed 10 March 2005).

Mokhiber, R. and Weissman, R. (2003b, 2 May) 'Christian Fundamentalists to Produce Iraqi News', *AlterNet.org*. Online available: http://www.alternet.org/story/15801 (accessed 10 March 2005).

MotherJones.com. (2003, 25 March) 'News'. Online available: http://www.motherjones.com (accessed 25 March 2003).

Nacos, B. (2002) *Mass Mediated Terrorism*, Oxford: Rowan and Littlefield.

Nader, R. (2003, 3 March) 'MSNBC Sabotages Donahue', *CommonDreams.org*. Online available: http://www.commondreams.org/views03/0303–06.htm (accessed 10 March 2005).

Nahdi, F. (2003, 3 April) 'Doublespeak: Islam and the Media', *openDemocracy.net*. Online available: http://www.opendemocracy.net/xml/xhtml/articles/1119.html (accessed 10 March 2005).

Nandy, A. (1970) 'The Culture of Indian Politics: a Stock Taking', *Journal of Asian Studies*, 30, no.1: 57–79.

Naurekas, J. (2004, February) 'POWs on TV a War Crime?', *EXTRA!Update*.

Navasky, V. (2002) 'Foreword', in B. Zelizer and S. Allan (eds) *Journalism after September 11*, London: Routledge.

New Straits Times. (2002a, 9 January) 'Is Malaysia Being Blamed for the Sept 11 Attacks?'. Online available: http://www.emedia.com.my/a/archive.htm (accessed 25 June 2004).

New Straits Times. (2002b, 25 January) 'KMM had Links with Al Qaeda'. Online available: http://www.emedia.com.my/a/archive.htm (accessed 25 June 2004).

New Straits Times. (2002c, 29 April) 'KMM Group Influenced by Foreign Gurus, Says DPM'. Online available: http://www.emedia.com.my/a/archive.htm (accessed 25 June 2004).

New Straits Times. (2002d, 19 June) 'We Underwent Afghan Military Training, KMM Duo Tell Suhakam Probe Team'. Online available: http://www.emedia.com.my/a/archive.htm (accessed 25 June 2004).

New Straits Times. (2003a, 17 February) 'Rais: Hadi's Trip Gives Impression Pas Backs militants'. Online available: http://www.emedia.com.my/a/archive.htm (accessed 25 June 2004).

New Straits Times. (2003b, 6 April) 'Full Interview with Dr Mahathir'.

New Straits Times. (2003c, 17 August) 'A Modern Return to Fundamentals'. Online available: http://www.emedia.com.my/Current_News/NST/Sunday/Columns/20030817085203/Article/ (accessed 25 June 2004).

New Straits Times. (2003d, 17 August) 'News Analysis: Price of Religious Zealotry'. Online available: http://www.emedia.com.my/Current_News/NST/Sunday/Columns/20030817085057/Article/ (accessed 25 June 2004).

New Straits Times. (2003e, 18 August) 'Venting Anger no Solution'. Online available: http://www.emedia.com.my/a/archive.htm (accessed 25 June 2004).

New Straits Times. (2003f, 19 August) 'Dr M Defines What an Act of Terror is'. Online available: http://www.emedia.com.my/a/archive.htm (accessed 25 June 2004).

New Straits Times. (2003g, 21 August) 'World Recognises only Might'. Online available: http://www.emedia.com.my/Current_News/NST/Thursday/Columns/20030821092104/Article/ (accessed 25 June 2004).

New Straits Times. (2003h, 26 September) 'Students Held in Pakistan Being Groomed to Lead JI'. Online available: http://www.emedia.com.my/a/archive.htm (accessed 25 June 2004).

New Straits Times. (2003i, 18 October) 'Case for Global Alternate Media'.

New Straits Times. (2004, 5 April) 'Keeping a Close Eye on Militants'. Online available: http://www.emedia.com.my/a/archive.htm (accessed 25 June 2004).

New Yorker. (2001, 10 December) 'Battle Stations'.

Ninan, S. (2002, 10 March) 'Media on the Rampage', *The Hindu*.

Oorjitham, S. (2000, 15 November) 'From Our Correspondent: Malaysia's Media', *Asiaweek.com*. Online available: www.asiaweek.com/asiaweek/foc/2000/11/15 (accessed 3 July 2004).

Ottosen, R. (2004) 'Mr. President: "The Enemy is Closer than You Might Think"', in S.A. Nohrstedt and R. Ottosen. (eds) *U. S. and the Others: Global Media Images on 'The War on Terror'*, Göteborg: Nordicom.

Pabico. A.P. (2000, October–December) 'Text Messaging and the Internet are now the Tools of Protest', *i Magazine*, IV, no. 4. Online available: www.pcij.org/imag/Online/hypertext3.html (accessed 30 March 2005).

Parenti, C. (2004, 18 March) 'Al Jazeera Goes to Jail', *The Nation*.

Patel, A., Padgaonkar, D. and Verghese, B.G. (2002) *Rights and Wrongs: Ordeal by Fire in the Killing Fields of Gujarat*, Editors Guild Fact Finding Report; released on 3 May.

Pe Benito, J. and Cagoco, J.T. (2004) 'Mindanao Coverage Revisited'. Centre for Media Freedom and Responsibility. Online available: http://www.cmfr.com.ph/pjr/2004/200401/0401benitocagoco.html (accessed 10 March 2005).

Pereira, D. (2004, 20 October) 'Yudhoyono's Top Priority: Fighting Terrorism', *Straits Times Online*. Online available: http://straitstimes.asia1.com.sg/sub/topstories/story/0,5562,280128,00.html? (accessed 20 October 2004).

Pesek, W. Jr. (2003, 19 March) 'An Image Problem in Asia', *International Herald Tribune*.

Pew Charitable Trusts. (2002, January) *Return to Normalcy? How the Media Have Covered the War on Terrorism*.

Pew Fellowships in International Journalism. (2002, 11 September) *International News and the Media: The Impact of September 11*.

Pew International Journalism Program. (2002) *America and the World: The Impact of September 11 on U. S. Coverage of International News*.

Pew Research Center for the People & the Press. (2002) *What the World Thinks in 2002: How Global Publics View: Their Lives, Their Countries, America*.

Pew Research Center for the People & the Press. (2003a) *Polls in Close Agreement on Public Views of War*.

Pew Research Center for the People & the Press. (2003b) *Views of a Changing World June 2003*.

Pew Research Center for the People & the Press. (2004a) *Mistrust of America in Europe Ever Higher, Muslim Anger Persists*.

Pew Research Center for the People & the Press. (2004b) *Trouble Behind, Trouble Ahead? A Year of Contention at Home and Abroad. 2003 Year-End Report*.

Phillip, A.J. (2002, 13 March) 'It Wasn't a Conventional Riot in Gujarat', *Indian Express*.

Philippine Revolution Web Central. (2005) '35 years of Being the Genuine Army of the Filipino People'. Online available: http://www.philippinerevolution.org/npa/index.shtml (accessed 1 March 2005).

Pilger, J. (2003, 6 April) 'We See Too Much. We Know Too Much. That's our Best Defense', *Independent*.

Pillai, M.G.G. (2001a, 12 October) 'Islam And The Christian Imperative'. Online available: http://www.mggpillai.com/article.php3?sid=1235 (accessed 10 July 2004).

Pillai, M.G.G. (2001b, 27 December) 'Osama Bin Laden outstares the US yet again'. Online available: http://www.mggpillai.com/article.php3?sid=1279 (accessed 10 July 2004).

Pillai, M.G.G. (2002a, 13 September) 'The Madness of 11 September'. Online available: http://www.mggpillai.com/article.php3?sid = 1500 (accessed 10 July 2004).

Pillai, M.G.G. (2002b, 17 October) 'The Bali Bombing: The World Held to Ransom'. Online available: http://www.mggpillai.com/article.php3?sid = 1519 (accessed 10 July 2004).

Pillai, M.G.G. (2002c, 2 December) 'The Global War on Ghosts'. Online available: http://www.mggpillai.com/article.php3?sid = 1554 (accessed 10 July 2004).

Pillai, M.G.G. (2002d, 27 December) 'The Bali Bombings: No One Knows Who did it, but Al Qaida it is!' Online available: http://www.mggpillai.com/article.php3?sid = 1572 (accessed 10 July 2004).

Pillai, M.G.G. (2003, 13 August) 'Orientalism, Jihad and the Amrozi Death Penalty'. Online available: http://www.mggpillai.com/article.php3?sid = 1741 (accessed 10 July 2004).

Porges, S. (2003, 19 September) 'Bush 9/11 Admission gets Little Play', *Editor & Publisher*.

Prerna, R. (2003, 1 July) 'Press Council Slams Gujarati Dailies for Role in Riots'. Online available: www.rediff.com/news/2003/jul/01guj4.htm?zcc = rl (accessed 1 July 2003).

Program on International Policy Attitudes and Knowledge Networks. (2003) *Misperceptions, the Media and the Iraq War*.

Program on International Policy Attitudes and Knowledge Networks. (2004) *US Public Beliefs on Iraq and the Presidential Elections*.

Project for Excellence in Journalism. (2002) *The War on Terrorism: The Not-So-New Television News Landscape*.

Public Education Radio TV, Bishkek. (2001, December 25) BBC Monitoring, London.

PUCL. (2002, May) *Violence in Vadodara: A Report*. Submitted to the Editors Guild of India by the People's Union of Civil Liberties, Vadodara and Vadodara Shanti Abhiyan.

Quintos de Jesus, M. (2003) 'Media Coverage of Terrorism: The Philippine Experience', *Journalism Asia*. Online available: http://www.cmfr.com.ph/ja/2003/media%20and%20terrorism/de%20Jesus.html (accessed 10 March 2005).

Raines, H. (2002) 'Foreword', in R. Bernstein and the Staff of *The New York Times, Out of the Blue: The Story of September 11, 2001 from Jihad to Ground Zero*, New York: Times Books.

Rajagopal, A. (2001) *Politics After Television: Hindu Nationalism and the Reshaping of the Public in India*. Cambridge: Cambridge University Press.

Ramakrishnan, P. (2001) 'Abuse of Power Under the ISA', *Aliran*. Online available: http://www.aliran.com/monthly/2001/11d.html (accessed 17 July 2004).

Rampton, S. and Stauber, J. (2003) *Weapons of Mass Deception: The Uses of Propaganda in Bush's War on Iraq*, New York: Jeremy P. Tarcher/Penguin.

Raymer, S. (2002, 21 November) 'Living Faith, Inside the Muslim World of Southeast Asia', *MSNBC*. Online available: http://www.msnbc.com/modules/ps/020220_LivingFaith/launch.asp (accessed 10 December 2002).

Rendall, S. (2003, May–June) 'Dissent, Disloyalty & Double Standards', *EXTRA!Update*.

Rendall, S. and Broughel, T. (2003, May/June) 'Amplifying Officials, Squelching Dissent', *EXTRA!Update*.

Rendall, S. and Butterworth, D. (2004, May/June) 'How Public is Public Radio?', *EXTRA!*

Reporters Without Borders. (2002), *Indonesia, Annual Report 2002*. Online available: http://www.rsf.fr/article.php3?id_article = 1464 (accessed 8 March 2005).

Reporters Without Borders. (2004a) 'The Philippines', *Annual Report 2004*. Online available: http://www.rsf.org/article.php3?id_article = 10089 (accessed 10 March 2005).

Reporters Without Borders. (2004b) *World Press Freedom Ranking 2004*. Online available: http://www.rsf.org/article.php3?id_article = 11715 (accessed 10 March 2005).

Reporters Without Borders. (2004c) *Indonesia, Annual Report 2004*. Online available: http://www.rsf.fr/article.php3?id_article = 10172 (accessed 8 March 2005).

Reuters. (2003, 25 March) 'Al Jazeera Banned from NYSE Floor'.

Rimban, L. (2003, January–March) 'The Many Lives of the Pentagon Gang', *i Magazine*, IX, no. 1. Online available: http://www.pcij.org/imag/PublicEye/pentagon2.html (accessed 2 February 2005).

Robbins, T. (2003, 15 April) 'A Chill Wind is Blowing in this Nation', Address to the National Press Club.

Robison, R. (2001) 'Indonesia: Crisis, Oligarchy and Reform', in G. Rodan, K. Hewison, and R. Robison (eds) *The Political Economy of South-East Asia: Conflict Crisis and Change*, 2nd Edition, Australia: OUP.

Rosen, J. (2002) 'September 11 in the Mind of American Journalism', in B. Zelizer and S. Allan (eds) *Journalism after September 11*, London: Routledge.

Roy, A. (2004, 24 January) 'Do Turkeys Enjoy Thanksgiving?', *OutlookIndia.com*. Online. Available http://www.outlookindia.com/full.asp?fodname = 20040124&fname = arundhati&sid = 1 (accessed 10 March 2005).

Rutenberg, J. (2003, 25 March) 'Newspapers: Words Reflect Changing Report', *New York Times*.

Said, E. (2003, 20–26 March) 'The other America', *Al-Ahram*.

Samudaranija, C.-A. and Paribata, S.S. (1987). 'Development for Security and Security for Development: Prospects for Durable Stability in Southeast Asia', in K. Snitwongse and S. Paribatra. (eds) *Durable Stability in Southeast Asia*, Singapore: Singapore Institute of Southeast Asian Studies.

Saraswati, M.S. (2004, 28 October) 'Press Freedom Eroding in RI: RSF', *The Jakarta Post. Online available*: http://www.thejakartapost.com/detailheadlines.asp?fileid = 20041028.A04&irec = 6 (accessed 28 October 2004).

Sardesai, R. (2002a, 7 March) 'The Media did not Ransack Shops, Take Lives, Mr Modi', *Indian Express*.

Sardesai, R. (2002b, 10 June) 'When the Mob Rules', *NDTV.com*. Online available: www.ndtv.com/columns/showcolumns.asp?id = 812 (accessed 10 June 2002).

Sardesai, R. (2004, January) 'Drawing the Ram-rekha', *Seminar*, no. 533.

Scarpello, F. (2002, 21 November) 'The Curtain Falls on Free Speech', *Index*. Online available: http://www.indexonline.org/news/20021121_indonesia.shtml (accessed 28 October 2004).

Schaefer, N. (2004, 28 January) 'Art as Diplomacy', *Wall Street Journal*.

Schaffert, R.W. (1992) *Media Coverage and Political Terrorists*, New York: Praeger.

Schatz, R. (2003) 'Foreword', in D. Schechter (ed.) *Media Wars: News at a Time of Terror*. Lanham: Rowman & Littlefield.

Schechter, D. (2003a, 1 May) 'The Media, the War and our Right to Know', *AlterNet.org*. Online available: http://www.alternet.org/story/15801 (accessed 10 March 2005).

Schechter, D. (ed.) (2003b) *Media Wars: News at a Time of Terror*, Lanham: Rowman & Littlefield.

Schechter, D. and Dichter, A. (2003) 'The Role of CNN', in D. Schechter (ed.) *Media Wars: News at a Time of Terror*. Lanham, MD: Rowman & Littlefield.

Schell, J. (2003, July 7) 'The New American Order', *The Nation*.

Schlesinger, A., Jr. (2003, 23 March) 'Today, it is we Americans who Live in Infamy', *Los Angeles Times*.

Schlesinger, P. (1991) *Media, State and Nation: Political Violence and Collective Identities*, London: Sage.

Schlesinger, P., Murdock, G. and Elliott, P. (1983) *Televising 'Terrorism': Political Violence in Popular Culture*, London: Comedia/Marion Boyars.

Schmid, A. and de Graaf, J. (1982) *Violence as Communication: Insurgent Terrorism and the Western News Media*, London: Sage.

Sehgal, R. (2003, May) 'State Secrets', *Television Asia*.

Sen, K. and Hill, D.T. (2000) *Media, Culture and Politics in Indonesia*, South Melbourne: Oxford University Press.

Shafer, J. (2003, 24 March) 'POW TV', *Slate*.

Shah, G. (1998) 'The BJP's Riddle in Gujarat: Caste, Factionalism and Hindutva', in C. Jaffrelot and T.B. Hansen (eds) *The BJP and Compulsions of Politics in India*, Oxford: Oxford University Press.

Sharkey, J.E. (2003, May) 'The Television War', *American Journalism Review*. Online available: http://www.ajr.org/Article.asp?id = 2988 (accessed 10 March 2005).

Sharma, K. (2002, 9 April) 'Gujarat and the Freedom of the Press', *The Hindu*.

Sinaga, E.J. (1989) 'Indonesia', in A. Menita (ed.) *Press Systems in Asean States*, Singapore: AMIC.

Smith, A. (1980) *The Geopolitics of Information: How Western Culture Dominates the World*, New York: Oxford University Press.

Smith, D. (2003, 6 May) 'TV News Networks better Cure their Myopia', *Newsday*.

Solomon, N. (2001, December) 'Media War without End', *Z Magazine*.

Solomon, N. and Erlich, R. (2003) *Target Iraq: What the News Media didn't Tell You*, New York: Context Books.

Sonwalkar, P. (2002) 'Murdochization of the Indian Press: From By-line to Bottom-line', *Media, Culture & Society*, Vol. 24, No. 6:821–834.

Steinberg, D.J. (ed.) (1987) *In Search of Southeast Asia: A Modern History*, Honolulu, HI: University of Hawaii Press.

The Strait Times Interactive. (2000, 19 March) Woon Wui Tek, 'Fairer Poll coverage in a calmer climate'. Oneline available: http://pgoh.free.fr/calmer_poll.html (accessed 16 August 2004).

Suanto, A. (1978) 'The Mass Communication System in Indonesia', in K.D. Jackson and L. Pye (eds) *Political Power and Communication in Indonesia*, Berkeley, CA: University of California Press.

Sued, A.I. (1989) 'Malaysia', In A. Mehra (ed.) *Press Systems in Asean States*, Singapore: Asian Mass Communications Research and Information Centre.

Suh, S. (2001, 21 September) 'An Islamic Fraternity?', *Asiaweek.com*. Online available: www.Asiaweek.com/asiaweek/magazine/Dateline/ 0,782,174692 (accessed 3 July 2004).

The Sun. (2004, 18 March) 'Send PAS right Message'.

Sun Star Davao. (2002, 11 December) Harley Palangchao, 'NPA Leader Seeks Stop to Gov't Offensive'. Online available: http://www.sunstar.com.ph/static/net/2002/12/11/npa. leader.seeks. stop.to.gov.t.offensive.html (accessed 7 February 2005).

Sun Star Davao. (2003, 9 July) Harley F. Palangchao, '500 NPA-influenced villages to get aid'. Online available:http://www.sunstar.com.ph/static/net/2003/07/09/500.npa.influ-enced.villages.to.get.aid.html (accessed 7 February 2005).

Sun Star Davao. (2004a, 10 February) Editorial 'Peace Talks and Terror Tags'. Online available: http://www.sunstar.com.ph/static/cag/2004/02/10/oped/editorial.html (accessed 7 February 2005).

Sun Star Davao. (2004b, 4 March) BOT 'NPA Denies Plot to Ambush Media'. Online available: http://www.sunstar.com.ph/static/dav/2004/03/04/news/npa.denies.plot.to. ambush.media.html (accessed 7 February 2005).

Sun Star Davao. (2004c, 11 October) Jeff M. Tupas, 'Murad Losing Control of MILF: Bangsamoro rep'. Online available: http://www.sunstar.com.ph/static/net/2004/10/11/ murad.losing.control.of.milf.bangsamoro.rep.html (accessed 7 February 2005).

Sun Star Davao. (2004d, 23 December) Lizanilla J. Amarga, 'NPA in N. Mindanao to Abide by 10-day Ceasefire'. Online available: http://www.sunstar.com.ph/static/cag/ 2004/12/23/news/npa.in.n..mindanao.to.abide.by.10.day.ceasefire.html (accessed 7 February 2005).

Taiara, C.T. (2003, 12 March) 'Spoon-Feeding the Press', *San Francisco Bay Guardian*.

Taylor, P.M. (2003, 30 March) 'Credibility: Can't Win Hearts and Minds Without it', *Washington Post*.

The Telegraph. (2002, 7 April) 'BJP Builds Bush Shield for Modi'.

Teodoro, L.V. (2003) 'Anti-terrorism and Human Rights in the Philippines', *Journalism Asia*. Online available: http://www.cmfr.com.ph/ja/2003/counter-terrorism%20and% 20human%20rights/teodoro.html (accessed 10 March 2005).

The Times of India. (2002a, 5 March) 'Media not Playing a Constructive Role: PM'.

The Times of India. (2002b, 2 March) 'Gag Orders Issued Against TV News Channels'.

The White House. (2002, 17 September) *The National Security Strategy of the United States*. Online available: http://www.whitehouse.gov/nsc/nss.html (accessed 2 October 2002).

Thussu, D.K. (2003) 'Live TV and Bloodless Deaths: War, Infotainment and 24/7 News', in D.K. Thussu and D. Freedman (eds) *War and the Media: Reporting Conflict 24/7*, London: Sage Publications.

Thussu, D.K and Freedman, D. (2003) 'Introduction', in D.K. Thussu and D. Freedman (eds) *War and the Media: Reporting Conflict 24/7*, London: Sage Publications.

Tiffin, R. (2000) 'New order Regime Style and the Australian Media in Kingsbury', D.E. Loo and P. Payne (eds) *Foreign Devils and Other Journalists*, Clayton: Monash Asia Institute.

Timberlake, I. (2002, 21 May) 'Press Feels Chill in Indonesia: Journalists See New Crackdown', *San Francisco Chronicle*. Online available: http://sfgate.com/cgi-bin/ article.cgi?f = /c/a/2002/05/21/MN209987.DTL (accessed 8 March 2005).

Timms, D. (2003, 24 April) 'Dyke Attacks "Unquestioning" US Media', *Guardian*.

Torres, J. (2003, April–June) 'Return of the Faithful', *i Magazine*, IX, No. 2. Online available: http://www.pcij.org/imag/SpecialReport/balik-islam3.html (accessed 2 February 2005).

Traugott, M.W. and Brader, T. (2003) 'Explaining 9/11', in P. Norris, M. Kern and M. Just (eds) *Framing Terrorism: The News Media, the Government, and the Public*, New York: Routledge.

Trillanes, A.F. (2001, October) 'The Trillanes Papers', *i Magazine*. Online available: http://www.pcij.org/HotSeat/trillanes.html (accessed 2 February 2005).

Tuman, J.S. (2003) *Communicating Terror: The Rhetorical Dimensions of Terrorism*, London: Sage.

Tyndall, (2003) A. *Tyndall Report. On Aftermath of September 11*. Online available: http://www.tyndallreport.com/0911.php3 (accessed 10 March 2005).

United States Embassy Stockholm. (2002) *Country Reports on Human Rights Practices for 2001: Malaysia*, Released by the Bureau of Democracy, Human Rights, and Labor, U.S. Department of State, March 2002. Online available: http://www.usemb.se/ human/2001/eastasia/malaysia.html (accessed 8 March 2005).

Varadarajan, S. (1999) 'The Ink Link: Communalism and the Evasion of Politics, in K.N. Panikker (ed.) *The Concerned Indian's Guide to Communalism*. New Delhi: Viking.

Varadarajan, S. (2002a) 'Chronicle of a Tragedy Foretold', in S. Varadarajan (ed.) *Gujarat: The Making of a Tragedy*, New Delhi: Penguin.

Varadarajan, S. (2002b) The Truth Hurts', in S. Varadarajan (ed.) *Gujarat: The Making of a Tragedy*, New Delhi: Penguin.

Varshney, A. (2002) *Ethnic Conflict and Civic Life: Hindus and Muslims in India*, Oxford: Oxford University Press.

Vecherny Bishkek. (2001, 14 December) BBC Monitoring, London.

Vecherny Bishkek. (2002, 15 January) BBC Monitoring, London.

Wade, R.H. (2003, 13 March) 'The Invisible Hand of the American Empire', *openDemocracy.net*. Online available: http://www.opendemocracy.net/debates/ article-3–77–1038.jsp (accessed 10 March 2005).

Wain, B. (2002, 26 September) 'Moving Target', *Far Eastern Economic Review*.

Washington File. (2003, 23 March) 'Time Frame Unknown but Regime's End Clear, Rumsfeld Says: Interview on CBS's *Face the Nation* with Bob Schieffer and David Martin'.

Weimann, G. and Winn, C. (1993) *The Theatre of Terror: Mass Media and International Terrorism*, London: Longman.

Wells, M. (2003, 8 May) 'ITC Tackles Fox News Bias Claims', *Guardian*.

Whitaker, B. (2002, 19 August) 'US Thinktanks Give Lessons in Foreign Policy', *Guardian*.

Wilkinson, M. (2003, 25 March). 'POWs Vanish Amid War on Nasty Images', *Sydney Morning Herald*.

Williams, B.A. (2003) 'The New Media Environment, Internet Chatrooms, and Public Discourse after 9/11', in D.K. Thussu and D. Freedman (eds) *War and the Media: Reporting Conflict 24/7*, London: Sage Publications.

Windmiller, M. (1954, December) 'Linguistic Regionalism in India', *Pacific Affairs*, 27, no. 4: 291–318.

Woodier, J. (2002, December) 'The Disenchantment of Southeast Asia: New Media and Social Change Post 9/11', *Asia Pacific Media Educator*, 12 no. 13: 82–104.

Xu, Y. (ed.) (1999) *Xinjiang fandui minzu fenliezhuyi douzheng shihua (History of the Struggle against Separatism in Xinjiang)*, Urumqi: Xinjiang Peoples Publishing House.

Zea, L. (2001) 'De la Guerra Fría a la Sucia', in F. Modak (ed.) *11 de septiembre de 2001*, Buenos Aires: Grupo Editorial Lumen.

Zerbisias, A. (2003, 16 September) 'The Press Self-Muzzled its Coverage of Iraq War', *Toronto Star*.

Zinn, H. (2003) 'Introduction', in N. Solomon and R. Erlich (eds) *Target Iraq: What the News Media didn't tell you*, New York: Context Books.

Index

Lightning Source UK Ltd.
Milton Keynes UK
20 January 2011

166080UK00003B/74/P